Successful Middle Leadership in Secondary Schools

With so much now expected of middle leaders in schools, this book aims to help those in middle leadership positions become more confident and effective in their roles. It systematically considers every aspect of the role, including team building, raising standards, holding others to account and managing change.

With a wealth of practical guidance, the book covers the essential skills needed by middle leaders such as managing meetings, conducting difficult conversations and development planning, while also offering insights into why some middle leaders are so much more effective than others. Covering all aspects of middle leadership, features include:

- insights into different leadership styles
- case studies written by current middle leaders in schools
- reflection and action points throughout
- practical tools to support evaluation and action.

This book is essential reading for secondary school teachers who are about to become middle leaders and need guidance on how to get to grips with the role. It will also be of value to existing middle leaders who want to improve their performance and effectiveness.

Peter Fleming is Lead Adviser for School Leadership and Workforce Development at North Yorkshire County Council. He has previously taught in both secondary schools and higher education and was Head of Teacher Training at York St John University.

Successful Middle Leadership in Secondary Schools

A practical guide to subject and team effectiveness

Peter Fleming

Routledge
Taylor & Francis Group

LONDON AND NEW YORK

First published 2014
by Routledge
2 Park Square, Milton Park, Abingdon, Oxon OX14 4RN

and by Routledge
711 Third Avenue, New York, NY 10017

Routledge is an imprint of the Taylor & Francis Group, an informa business

© 2014 Peter Fleming

British Library Cataloguing in Publication Data
A catalogue record for this book is available from the British Library

Library of Congress Cataloging in Publication Data
Fleming, Peter, 1957–
Successful middle leadership in secondary schools : a practical guide to subject and team effectiveness / Peter Fleming.
pages cm
Includes bibliographical references and index.
1. Middle school principals. 2. School management and organization. I. Title.
LB1623.F48 2014
373.12′011–dc23
2013040613

ISBN: 978-0-415-85791-8 (hbk)
ISBN: 978-0-415-85792-5 (pbk)
ISBN: 978-1-315-78009-2 (ebk)

Typeset in Palatino
by Cenveo Publisher Services

MIX
Paper from
responsible sources
FSC
www.fsc.org   FSC® C013056

Printed and bound in Great Britain by
TJ International Ltd, Padstow, Cornwall

Contents

Figures

Tables

Preface

Most people who become middle leaders have had little formal leadership training or development when they take up their posts and so tend to learn the skills needed on the job. As someone who has written and delivered leadership development programmes for teachers for fifteen years, I know what a difference exposure to basic leadership theory and practice can make to the confidence and effectiveness of middle leaders. Over the last decade I have witnessed ever increasing demands being placed on those in school who occupy middle leadership posts and the responsibility and accountability that goes with such posts is now considerable. This book is for those people who want to make a real difference through their work as middle leaders. Read the book and engage in the reflection and action activities included. If you can do this while following a middle leadership training programme, so much the better. Never underestimate the value of a trusted leader who is willing to act as a mentor and make a point of surrounding yourself with positive, like-minded people. As a middle leader you have the chance to have real impact. I hope this book will be of some value on your leadership journey.

Peter Fleming

Introduction

Effective leadership is critical to school effectiveness, with middle leaders playing a pivotal role in school improvement. The skills required to be an effective middle leader in a secondary school are many and varied but people management skills, sometimes called inter-personal skills, lie at the heart of getting the best out of both teachers and pupils. Motivating people and building a positive 'can do' culture is essential for success. This book is about how middle leaders can contribute to raising the quality of education in their schools through proficient team leadership.

Using evidence from a range of sources the book will provide practical advice on:

- What it means to be a leader and manager
- The importance of vision and ethos
- Getting the best out of people by using appropriate leadership styles
- How to develop your team
- How to make meetings and communication effective
- How to create a learning culture in your team
- Implementing change and development
- Evaluating the performance of teachers in your team
- How to challenge underperforming colleagues
- How to manage your time and avoid stress

The book includes two case study chapters written by highly effective middle leaders who have had real impact in their schools. In addition, throughout the book there are case study scenarios to prompt thinking, reflection opportunities and recommended action points intended to develop readers' skills and understanding. A number of evaluation tools and frameworks are provided covering many aspects of the work of a middle leader. While this book contains references to leadership theory and academic research that will illuminate themes and issues covered on middle leader development programmes, it is not primarily an academic text. It is intended to be a practical and accessible guide to being a successful middle leader. It draws on theory and research to deepen readers' understanding with the aim of supporting their effectiveness in role. It has a wealth of ideas, guidance and tips for success that have worked for many people in many different contexts. This is a 'self-help' book that will be of value to three distinct groups:

Newly appointed middle leaders

For you, the book aims to provide clear and practical advice to help you become effective and confident in your role. It will provide guidance on key aspects of middle leadership facing all team leaders, heads of department, coordinators, year heads, and others. Through the use of case studies it will highlight in a very practical way key aspects of your role with a view to helping you avoid making major mistakes as you settle into your new post.

Aspiring middle leaders

The book should also be of value if you are seeking a middle leadership post. By introducing you to a range of situations and issues that might form the basis of questions used in the selection process it will help you to prepare for interviews with confidence. It is important to remember that good leaders don't have all the answers but they do have a capacity for reflecting clearly on situations and they are able to make rational decisions on the basis of sound judgement. Reflection opportunities posted throughout the book will help you to think in a focused way about a range of middle leadership issues and how you might deal with them.

Existing middle leaders

Successful leaders never stop learning and they are continually reviewing their performance. More is expected of middle leaders than ever before and your leadership will be under scrutiny during school inspection. This book grounds comments on effective leadership in evidence drawn from a range of sources. You will be able to use this evidence to evaluate yourself as a leader and consider ways in which you might improve the performance of your team. The emphasis on vision, leadership, and creating effective teams will be of particular interest to those who may have underestimated the importance of people skills in the past.

Making use of the book

The book should initially be read from cover to cover to give a clear overview of the work of middle leaders. Some themes appear in more than one chapter as packaging leadership into neat boxes cannot easily be done. Reading the book and then returning to sections when you need them is the most beneficial way to use it. Of very practical use will be the many tools included to support you in your role as a middle leader (see appendices). No middle leader could possibly make use of all these tools in a single year, but over time you will be able to make productive use of what is there.

1

What is middle leadership?

Introduction

During the last thirty years the terms 'middle management' and now more commonly 'middle leadership' have become completely established in the language of secondary schools. Effective school leadership and management at all levels are now seen as essential to a school's success and the pivotal role of middle leaders vital to school improvement. Training and development for middle leaders appears regularly on school development plans, as middle leaders are in many respects 'the engine house of school improvement'.

Management and leadership have become, and will remain, of central importance in schools, and the current Ofsted inspection framework recognizes this by linking all elements of school effectiveness to the quality of leadership in school. While there are, rightly, some critics of an unquestioning application of certain aspects of management and leadership theory and practice to education, it is clear that a good understanding of management and leadership is important for those in 'the middle tier' in schools to be effective. More importantly, there is clear evidence to show that good school leadership is central to improving standards in schools and that well managed and motivated middle leaders contribute significantly to driving schools forward.

Defining middle leadership

The terms 'middle leadership' and 'middle management' are sometimes used interchangeably, though they do in fact refer to different things. Effective middle leaders need also to be effective managers and so it is important to clarify what these labels mean. Let's start with 'leadership'. In essence, leadership involves motivating people to act towards achieving a common goal. It follows therefore that leaders are people with a clear sense of where their team is heading. They have a vision of what excellence looks like and the ability to motivate others to join them on the journey towards excellence. By contrast, managers are people who can use available resources to accomplish tasks and reach targets; to move a team towards agreed goals; to plan the route. Middle leaders in schools constitute a layer of leadership between the senior leadership team and classroom practitioners and must be able to both lead and manage to be effective. They need to have a clear vision of excellence in their subject or team and be able to motivate colleagues. They must also ensure the smooth day-to-day operation of school business and monitor the progress of pupils and performance of staff. As most middle leaders are still actively teaching for much of their working week, middle leaders in schools must also serve as role models in the classroom. While these responsibilities are daunting middle leaders can take some comfort in knowing that many teachers and senior leaders alike see them as 'the voice of reason' in a school, displaying clear ambition for their students and their subjects but at the same time having their feet firmly on the ground in respect of what is really practical and possible.

The vast majority of middle leadership roles involve motivating and managing people in order to improve the quality of education and/or outcomes for students. Depending on the staffing structure, in a typical secondary school middle leadership and management jobs will include posts such as head of department, deputy head of department, head of year, head of faculty, curriculum coordinator, head of sixth form, head of learning resources, work experience coordinator, SENCo, key stage coordinator, inclusion manager, data manager and literacy across the curriculum coordinator. Most of these jobs will be undertaken by teachers but some, rightly, may be held by people without qualified teacher status (QTS) as the roles might not require a deep understanding of curriculum or pedagogy.

A quick look at the kind of questions asked at interviews for middle leadership posts (Table 1.1) helps to clarify the nature of middle leadership in schools.

These questions illustrate four major components of middle leadership:

- Having a clear vision of the importance of the subject or area you are responsible for and being able to enthuse others with this vision. This is leadership.
- Being clear about what constitutes good practice and using it. This is having specialist knowledge or know-how and being able to model good practice.
- Being an effective manager of people and resources. This involves being able to plan, motivate, monitor, encourage good practice, challenge bad practice, solve problems and see tasks through. This is management.
- Being able to put in place procedures to secure efficiency. This is administration. Although rarely asked about directly in interviews for middle leadership posts, efficient 'systems' support smooth management and effective leadership and their importance shouldn't be underestimated.

Successful middle leaders usually have, or very quickly develop, specialist knowledge relating to their roles. They then combine leadership, management and administration in the right proportions. Less effective middle leaders may be good in one area but less effective in others. We can all call to mind heads of department who are good administrators but fail to create any real vision for their team. This means people have no real goals to be aiming for (or don't understand the purpose of goals they have been given) and no real

TABLE 1.1 Interview questions for middle leadership posts

Head of department	Year head
What unique learning experiences can your subject bring to young people?	What should be achieved with pupils in time allocated to tutor groups?
What teaching and learning strategies would you expect your team to use and how would you ensure this happened?	What qualities does a good form tutor possess? What would you do about a tutor not showing these qualities?
How would you deal with a member of your team who was regularly experiencing difficulties meeting deadlines?	How would you deal with a tutor who failed to monitor his form's academic progress?
How would you ensure all pupils made acceptable progress in your subject?	How would you identify vulnerable children and what would you do to ensure their needs were met?
Tell us about any experience you have had of supporting the development of another teacher.	Tell us about any experience you have had of improving pastoral or PSHE provision.

sense of what a better future will look like. Equally, heads of department can be very charismatic and inspirational about their subjects but simply fail to put in place systems that result in good day-to-day organization. This can be frustrating and even demoralizing for their team. Some posts will require more of one skill than another. At certain times the proportion of each skill needed to achieve results may change. Effective middle leaders are sensitive to the need to develop their leadership, management and administration skills and are flexible in their application. Good leaders are also honest about their weaknesses and will often successfully compensate for them by using the strengths of others in their team. Done well, this use of distributed leadership can be very motivating for colleagues. It is reassuring to know that almost all the skills required to be an effective middle leader can be learnt, developed and improved. The art of middle leadership involves good judgement, the ability to assess a situation and the knack of combining leadership strategies and styles in just the right proportions. Really skilled middle leaders do this with considerable flair.

Over the last two decades there have been national agencies involved in investigating and disseminating effective practice in educational leadership and management. Although at the time of writing the coalition government is redefining the scope and reach of these agencies, we are left with some very worthwhile guidance which new middle leaders can learn a lot from. The Teacher Training Agency document *National Standards for Subject Leaders* (1998), though no longer in widespread use, remains a useful starting point for considering middle leader responsibilities, which it defines as:

- Strategic direction and development of the subject
- Teaching and learning

- Leading and managing staff
- Efficient and effective deployment of staff and resources

The National College for School Leadership (NCSL) document *The Heart of the Matter: A Practical Guide to What Middle Leaders can do to Improve Learning in Secondary Schools* (2003) provides some interesting ideas (still entirely relevant) about what middle leaders can do to improve learning and achievement:

- Focus on learning and teaching
- Generate positive relationships
- Provide clear vision and high expectations
- Improve the learning environment
- Provide opportunities for collaboration
- Distribute leadership
- Engage the community
- Evaluate and innovate

Action point

Use the self-evaluation schedule (Appendix A) to assess your skills as a middle leader. A trusted and experienced colleague who can act as a mentor should be well placed to guide you in areas you feel insecure in.

Leadership theory

Many of the underpinning leadership ideas advocated for schools can be traced to leadership theories from the industrial and commercial world. It is not my intention in this chapter to provide a comprehensive and detailed history of leadership theory, but to provide for middle leaders some insights into some of the key ideas that have come to have greatest influence in the world of education.

Total quality management

A look at typical secondary school staffing structures suggests, at least on paper, that most operate a hierarchical model of organization, based on the classical industrial model. This is best represented as a pyramid with the senior leadership team at the apex, a layer of middle leaders lower down and a broad base of main scale classroom teachers (see Figure 1.1).

In extreme cases the pyramid is a rigid structure. Roles within it are clearly defined and everyone 'knows their place'. Job descriptions, formal meetings and institutional procedures serve to reinforce the structure. It is now realized that this model holds back individual initiative with people straitjacketed in

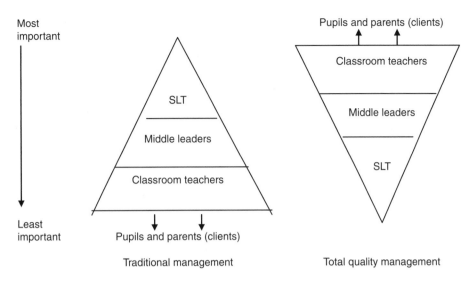

FIGURE 1.1 Traditional management and total quality management.

their roles and can lead to an 'us and them' mentality. At its worst it results in questions such as 'When is the SLT going to deal with....?' being asked and statements like 'That's for management to sort out – I'm paid to teach' being made. Most significantly of all, the views of the clients of the school (students and parents) are rarely listened to. Indeed, the clients may actually be blamed for deficiencies in the organization, exemplified through comments like, 'what do you expect, the kids here don't speak English' or 'we get no support from parents so what can we do to improve exam results?' Extreme cases of this culture are rare, but do still exist. In practice, the majority of schools are organized more flexibly and there is greater collaboration and empowerment than the pyramid would suggest. Schools now try and meet individual pupil needs effectively and are significantly more client focused than thirty years ago. This shift in outlook and organization echoes what has been happening in industry also.

Management gurus, writing about management in industry and commerce, have argued for almost half a century for a less hierarchical approach. Peter Drucker advocated the empowerment of workers and Tom Peters highlighted the importance of companies creating learning cultures in which innovation is the norm and employees are focused on client satisfaction. In the 1990s these ideas were refined into an approach known as *total quality management* (TQM), 'a philosophy with tools and processes aimed at achieving a culture of continuous improvement driven by all members of an organization in order to satisfy and delight customers.' (Marsh 1992: 12).

Total quality management is underpinned by the belief that an organization (in our case the school) should be focused on client satisfaction and that there is always scope for improvement in the service being provided. A second element of TQM is the idea that every organization has internal customers who also deserve a high quality service. Thus, in school, subject teams provide a service to pastoral teams and vice-versa. If a subject teacher fails to complete a report for a form tutor on time the service has fallen below an acceptable level and action is taken to address the problem. Finally, TQM involves the effective use of data to measure performance and establish targets for improvement.

In most schools you will now find elements of the TQM approach, with a clear focus on meeting the needs of all pupils (clients) and every effort to engage parents and make use of 'student voice'. The SLT and middle leaders should see their roles, at least in part, as serving colleagues in the classroom as effectively as possible by creating the climate and systems that enable them to provide a high quality learning experience for their students.

The interest shown by schools in 'Investors in People' represents a realization that systematically developing and empowering teachers and others in school can dramatically improve their performance, which results in better outcomes for students.

Talk of 'distributed leadership', 'empowerment' and 'continuous improvement' is commonplace. Teams are more fluid. Leadership roles are encouraged on the basis of knowledge and skill rather than position in the hierarchy. For example, a young teacher with good ICT skills could quite legitimately be encouraged to lead a working party investigating the use of ICT across the curriculum. They would be supported and assisted by more senior colleagues who would encourage a culture of collaboration. Schools now systematically use data to provide evidence of how they are performing and are not frightened of asking probing questions about differences in performance between schools and teams within schools. At team level, similar questions are asked about differences in performance between teachers. This should not be done to 'blame' particular teachers for poor performance but to establish reasons for under-performance and to address them.

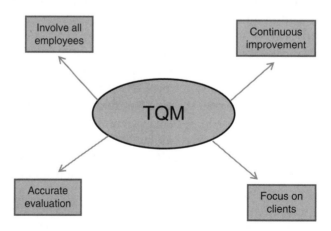

FIGURE 1.2 Components of total quality management.

Of course, this approach can cause anxiety for any teachers who prefer to work in the rigid pyramid. Knowing 'where you stand' can provide a sense of security, but rarely enables people to grow and excel. There is a wealth of evidence to suggest that rigid pyramid schools are ill equipped to cope smoothly with change and that, by contrast, a collaborative approach produces dynamic and adaptable institutions (see chapter 2). This approach does not remove the need for middle leaders but it does require of them a particular frame of mind. They must be capable of:

- Monitoring levels of client satisfaction and responding to client needs
- Using data to analyse performance and plan for improvement
- Motivating and empowering colleagues in their teams to perform to their maximum potential
- Holding to account those who under-perform
- Thinking clearly and creatively in order to solve problems

Good middle leaders are not trapped in rigid straitjackets but are flexible and adaptable, always on the lookout for ways to improve the education provided by their teams. They are able to move easily between roles – teacher, team leader and team member – as required. They gain satisfaction from empowering colleagues and seeing them succeed and constantly reflect on their own practice in the belief that better performance is always possible.

A caveat is needed at this point. For seriously under-performing schools there is usually a need to impose rigid systems and tight line-management in order to bring the practice of all teachers up to an acceptable standard. Only when this is secure is it safe to move to the more flexible and empowering approach advocated above. Even then, empowerment and innovation occur as a means of maintaining and improving already excellent provision and performance. The ends are clear, but there is freedom over the means.

Authentic leadership

There is currently a great deal of interest in what has become known as *authentic leadership*. This model of leadership sits comfortably with educational professionals as it has at its heart moral integrity: doing things for the right reasons not just because clients (be they pupils, parents or governments) demand it. Using definitions provided by Walumbwa et al. (2008) authentic leaders have four components that combine to make them massively influential:

- *Self-awareness* – authentic leaders know who they are and what they stand for; there is no mismatch between their stated values and their actions. They walk the talk.
- *Relational transparency* – authentic leaders develop open relationships with others. They are genuinely interested in the development and success of

their colleagues. They develop team members and empower them to lead. They are consultative and open about why and how decisions are made.

■ *Balanced processing* – in decision making and strategic planning authentic leaders rely on evidence (data). They listen to a range of views and arguments. They can live with diverse views and ambiguity. They realize the world is complex and appreciate shades of grey.

■ *Moral integrity* – authentic leaders do the right things for the right reasons. The vision they work to is a shared vision. They operate consistently to a set of principles that reflect what their team or school stands for.

Authentic leaders are active not passive; they balance the need to achieve goals with a commitment to developing others; they are able to read and empathize with people and they build on strengths rather than trying to correct weaknesses. Their mindset is positive. Evidence from studies of leadership are beginning to suggest that teachers trust and engage more willingly with leaders they see as authentic (Branson 2007, Bird et al. 2009).

The context of middle leadership

Schools are subject to national legislation and must always be mindful of centralized accountability mechanisms such as Ofsted, which can influence how they operate. Nevertheless, each school exists within a particular locality and this helps shape the unique identity of the school. National data shows that schools serving pupils from similar socio-economic backgrounds can have very different performance profiles. Likewise, within the same school,

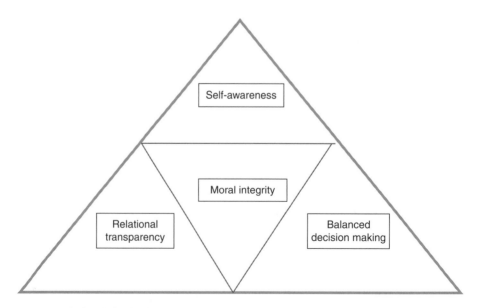

FIGURE 1.3 Authentic leadership.

departments and teams can be differentially effective, with pupils of similar abilities performing far better in some subjects than others. Middle leaders make a significant difference to the life chances of pupils. At the time of writing, the coalition government's approach to education under Michael Gove is to offer greater freedom to schools to shape their own future but within a tighter framework of accountability through ever more demanding Ofsted inspection. In these circumstances the skills of school leaders to engage their teams will be even more critical. Schools that embrace a leadership style that encourages excellence, initiative and flexibility are likely to be well equipped to face the future. For now, most secondary schools, on paper at least, remain hierarchical in structure if not in culture. There are several reasons for this, one obvious one being that at present conditions of service and pay frameworks demand it. A typical secondary school might have the layers identified in Figure 1.4.

It has been argued that head teachers of large secondary schools are forced to operate like managing directors, with education as the product and pupils and parents as clients or customers. Increased parental choice of school and greater accountability through performance data and Ofsted, have forced greater market awareness on schools. Within schools, departments are conscious of market forces resulting in competition for pupils when GCSE and 'A' level options

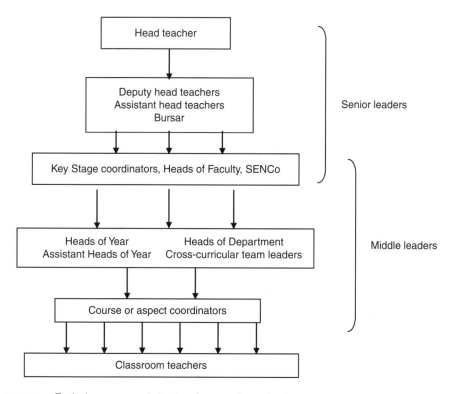

FIGURE 1.4 Typical management structure in secondary schools.

come round. Heads of department are aware of the (often unspoken) competition for 'bums on seats'. They have to tread a careful line between defending and promoting their own subject and cooperating with fellow heads of department, with whole school aims in mind. Tact, diplomacy and good judgement are vital qualities needed under these circumstances.

Middle leaders should have knowledge and understanding of whole school issues. Though they will 'fight their corner', good team leaders are able to take a wider perspective and should be supportive of the agreed school aims, especially those emphasized in the school's mission statement. In turn, good senior leaders will, of course, involve middle leaders and other colleagues in defining the mission and aims of the school so that there is a sense of ownership and clear direction. Some schools now invite middle leaders to become associate members of the SLT for a fixed time so as to ensure there is no divide between middle and senior leaders.

Middle leaders work in schools that have contact with many outside agencies and they may be expected to liaise with a wide range of professionals, including local authority advisers and other representatives, Ofsted inspectors, educational welfare officers, social workers, educational psychologists, specialist leaders, educational consultants, university researchers, examination board personnel and teaching school representatives.

The ability to move easily into a range of situations and communicate in a style that is fit for purpose is required. Dealing with fellow professionals involves the ability to adapt style and approach to suit the context. Written and spoken communication skills are important, with the ability to match language to audience. As well as meeting other education professionals, middle leaders are likely to have dealings with a range of client groups – parents, local employers, further and higher education colleagues, journalists, etc., and again effective communication skills are vital.

Middle leadership in practice

Being a middle leader does involve a variety of roles and wide ranging tasks, but it does not mean 'being all things to all people' or never refusing to take on a commitment. To retain their sanity, teachers holding posts of responsibility must be clear about what is reasonable and what is not. This does not mean being petty about job descriptions, but it does mean being confident and assertive enough to draw the line when unreasonable requests are made. Ultimately, a stressed and over-worked middle leader will be ineffective and this is not what being a dedicated professional is about.

Most middle leaders in schools are also teachers. Indeed, the bulk of their work is classroom based. Middle leaders must consider their teaching role in the context of their leadership role. The values they hold as leaders should be in harmony with the values they hold as teachers. Likewise, they should be able to model the good practice they expect their teachers to employ. For example, heads of department and curriculum leaders who promote differentiation at team meetings but don't apply differentiation in their own classroom will soon lose respect and credibility. This doesn't mean that middle leaders must always be the best and most skilled teachers and good middle leaders will acknowledge this and celebrate the skills of their team. It does mean, however, that team leaders should set a good example in their practice and should not expect of colleagues what they cannot achieve themselves.

Two major areas of responsibility assigned to middle leaders are subject and pastoral leadership. Job descriptions provide a somewhat clinical statement of what a given middle leadership job entails. Knowing what is required in practice is the key to interpreting a job description successfully. It is essential for middle leaders to identify their roles in terms of

- Tasks
- Responsibilities
- Relationships (internal and external)

In order to do this they must be clear about the management and communication structures in operation in their school and familiar with all school policies.

In practice, being an effective middle leader involves:

- *Leading*, by having a clear vision and being a role model for other staff
- *Serving* pupils, teachers and senior managers
- *Managing* the implementation of school and team aims and policies
- *Monitoring* the effectiveness of teaching and provision
- *Challenging* ineffective practice
- *Supporting* continuous improvement

The art of getting the right balance can be elusive. Newly appointed middle leaders often try so hard to serve that they neglect the managing, monitoring and challenging dimensions of the role. In order to get things right *critical reflection* is essential and the ability to reflect also equips middle leaders to solve effectively the many problems and dilemmas they will face.

Middle leadership is not easy. In some schools responsibility allowance holders can feel trapped between members of their team and the SLT as a result of conflicting expectations from these two groups of people. When teachers gain promotion internally to a middle leadership post, they take with them 'baggage' from their earlier roles and can sometimes find it quite stressful to settle into new relationships with colleagues, especially holding people to account. Middle leaders must be consistent in their behaviour and professional at all times. Sitting in any staff room and listening to conversations soon exposes team leaders who have not learnt the art of discretion. Professional integrity

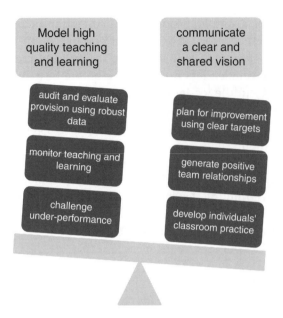

FIGURE 1.5 Priorities effective middle leaders manage to balance.

is very important for middle leaders, as colleagues will only trust and respect them if they are certain that they can be approached in confidence.

Middle leaders continually face role ambiguity and role conflict, with difficult choices to be made and, on occasions, difficult people to be confronted. How they approach such situations reflects on their integrity and often requires courage. Listening skills, sensitivity, reflection and persistence are all vital. The rewards of good middle leadership are visible in staff performance and pupil progress. It is also the case, in most schools, that good middle leaders are respected and appreciated by junior and senior colleagues alike.

Middle leaders are vital for the smooth running of a school. Posts of responsibility can be exciting, rewarding and fulfilling. Hard working and professional team leaders can make a real difference in a school. They can bring a unique ethos to a team, transform a lacklustre department and make a significant difference to pupil performance. Newly appointed and enthusiastic heads of year and heads of department often find that they serve as a catalyst for change, allowing a team to shape provision or rediscover its commitment and enthusiasm. Most teachers are reasonable people who respond positively to good leadership and want the best for their pupils. Effective middle leaders should be clear that they are a vital part of the drive to improve standards in schools, and their motivation, at least in part, comes from a desire to do the best they can for their pupils. 'Throughout their work (a middle leader) ensures that practices improve the quality of education provided, meet the needs and aspirations of all pupils and raise standards of achievement in school' (Teacher Training Agency 1998: 4).

Head teachers of successful schools understand the vital role of middle leaders. Peter Clarke, one of the first high-profile head teachers instrumental in 'turning round' troubled schools, accepts this view and acknowledges the vital role middle leaders play in effective schools. 'Successful management of schools requires effective middle managers who take responsibility for managing their teams and achieving objectives..... strong middle managers become the *engine room* of the school, taking initiatives and making decisions' (Clarke 1998: 41). Twenty years on this still holds true, supported in the literature on school leadership and in the everyday experience of successful middle leaders. Jamie Portman's blog (2012) contains many comments to this effect. 'They (middle leaders) have direct roles in improving the quality of teaching and learning and are often the driving force at the chalk face. They act as lynchpin between the talk of a senior leadership team and enacting actions on the ground – ultimately making things happen and work' (Portman 2012).

Case studies

Below are two imaginary situations. Read each one and reflect on it from a leadership perspective. Think about the failures of middle (and senior) leaders in these cases. How would you have dealt with each case? When you are clear about what you think read the reflections on the case studies.

Case 1

John Smith is a thirty-year-old History teacher with eight years' teaching experience, all in his present school. He is a knowledgeable teacher who gained a good first degree but ever since his none-too-successful first year in the school, his head of department and year head have carefully selected only the most amenable groups for him to teach. He seems unaware of the poor reputation for discipline he has acquired. When he is 'on duty' or 'covering' for absent colleagues, John faces behaviour problems. His head of department has employed a strategy of 'working round' John and playing to his strength, which is academic 'A' level teaching.

John is a caring tutor, though he is disorganized in matters of administration and his pupils sometimes 'take him for a ride'. Generally, though, his relationships with them are good. He takes an active part in school social activities and is usually very cooperative. He has undertaken little sustained professional development since he joined the school and has never volunteered to lead any new initiatives.

John's head of department has indicated his intention to retire. John has approached the head teacher with a request to be considered for the job. He feels he is the natural successor and he cites his excellent subject knowledge and first degree as evidence of his suitability for the job.

Reflection

Where have school leaders gone wrong with John?
What would you have done if John was in your team?

It is possible to identify failures on the part of both middle and senior leaders in this situation, which tells us something about the culture of the school. The following points should have been noted:

- Poor use of the first year of teaching to identify weaknesses and implement a programme of development suggests inadequate induction, monitoring and mentoring.
- Leaders preferring to 'work round' John's weaknesses rather than helping him to address them suggests lack of courage and determination on the part of middle leaders and senior colleagues.
- John's failure to realize his own weaknesses and to be aware that running a department takes more than subject knowledge suggests that both appraisal and professional development have been ineffective in this school.

John might be a very different teacher at thirty if:

- His head of department had worked closely with him as a new teacher to improve approaches to discipline and develop his teaching skills with less academic children.
- His year leader had insisted on and supported him in efficient administration.
- Senior staff had not ignored problems facing John when on duty and on cover.
- The school had in place effective appraisal reviews so that John's career plans were known and training towards subject headship had been provided.
- Professional development in the school was differentiated and linked to identified needs of teachers.

Clearly, there has been failure of leadership at many levels. John did not reflect critically on his performance but it would be wrong to blame him entirely for his failings. He is clearly a willing and cooperative teacher with strengths in some areas. Through their failure to address his weaknesses, John has been let down by leaders, who have created problems for themselves by 'working round' him. If he is now interviewed for the post as Head of History, he is unlikely to do the job effectively. If he is not appointed, he may well become disgruntled and withdraw his goodwill. Taking what seemed like the easy way out may prove costly for this school and for John.

Case 2

A GCSE pupil approaches the Head of Business Studies, Mrs Brown, with a complaint. Miss Smith (his Business Studies teacher) has lost his GCSE assignment, he claims. He gave it to her in her form room but she says he has not handed it in. He is annoyed and says that it is not the first time she has lost work belonging to students in the class. Also, he says, Miss Smith doesn't explain things clearly when he asks for help and never bothers to mark their books. He produces his exercise book to substantiate his claim.

The head of department goes to Miss Smith, who teaches part-time and is rarely in school. She mentions the missing assignment but not the unmarked book and Miss Smith responds aggressively. She says the boy never handed the work in and accuses him of being arrogant, always expecting special attention in class. She also says the class concerned is disruptive and uncooperative. She says she is simply not prepared to work herself into an early grave for students who 'know their rights but not their responsibilities'. She blames the head of department for giving her such a bad group and says she is suffering stress because of it.

Mrs Brown talks to the boy's year head. Apparently, he is a bright and confident youngster who will do well in his GCSEs. It is true that the group he is in needs careful handling because it contains several difficult pupils, but they are certainly not the worst group in the year as far as behaviour goes.

Mrs Brown tells the boy he must do his assignment again. She says she believes Miss Smith's version of events. She discusses with Miss Smith the possibility of moving some disruptive pupils out of her GCSE class into her own group.

Reflection

Where has the head of department gone wrong?
What would you have done?

It is possible to identify many mistakes made by the Head of Business Studies. The fact that a pupil was able to come to her with accusations of lost work, books not marked and problems with teaching suggests she does not know what is going on in her department. The best of teachers can, of course, lose work occasionally, but this situation is more serious as Miss Smith is clearly stressed, shows unacceptable aggression to her immediate manager and appears to be failing her students in several respects.

We might well ask:

- Is there a system in place for monitoring the performance of pupils in GCSE Business Studies so that underachievement is quickly identified?
- Does the Head of Business Studies have a way of monitoring assessment and the marking of books?
- Why has Miss Smith not felt able to approach Mrs Brown about the difficulties she has encountered?

- Has Mrs Brown tried to set up a regular meeting time with Miss Smith to ensure she feels valued as part of the team, even though she is part-time?
- Does Mrs Brown observe members of her team in the classroom so that she is aware of their strengths and weaknesses?
- What channels are there in school to address pupil concerns and who monitors actions taken in response?

Of course, the culture of the school will, to an extent, determine the way the heads of department operate. In this example, as in the last, a 'hands-off' or 'working round' approach has been adopted. Unacceptable behaviour has deliberately gone unnoticed and unquestioned. There has been a failure of leadership as well as a failure to put students at the heart of what the school should be about. It is always worth understanding the point of view of the clients:

- This student has been treated badly. He will feel resentful towards the school. He may fail to repeat the assignment and this will affect his GCSE result. He may involve his parents. This may create the need to involve a senior member of staff. If the parents feel badly treated they will speak ill of the school to their friends and neighbours. This may influence whether or not they send their children to the school. The boy concerned may decide to attend a different school to study 'A' levels.
- Miss Smith has not been served well. Removing a few difficult children from her class is a 'quick-fix' but it does not address her failure to mark books and the problems she is experiencing in the classroom. She is stressed and feels angry. Her head of department has not explored these issues. If Miss Smith is not supported she could end up taking time off work due to ill health and more serious problems could then follow.

Mrs Brown has behaved in a way that is incompatible with authentic leadership. Her decisions are not based on ethical considerations and are not even acceptable from a pragmatic point of view. They are likely to result in bigger problems in the future. Mrs Brown's credibility with students and staff is potentially at risk. In this case, ineffective middle leadership could result in the school losing students and the revenue they bring with them. It should have been possible to treat the student concerned more sensitively and support him in repeating his assignment. Miss Smith's weaknesses should not have gone unnoticed for so long. She now needs support but must also be challenged about her unacceptable behaviour.

Summary

Over the past two or three decades management and leadership theory and practice has been adapted and applied to the education system, with the aim of improving outcomes for students. There is clear evidence that effective leadership makes a difference to standards in schools and for this reason Ofsted looks closely at leadership and the impact it has when inspecting schools.

Schools taking a collaborative approach to leadership empower teachers to be creative and use their skills and talents to improve the education of the young people they serve. However, this is within a context of a clearly understood vision and with clear and high expectations of student outcomes. These schools have a clear client focus and encourage collective responsibility. When things go wrong blame is shared and people work together to find solutions. They cope effectively with change through ensuring people feel ownership of new developments.

Middle leaders in any secondary school should be concerned with creating a clear sense of purpose for their department or year group; managing teams of people, individuals and other resources effectively to achieve agreed targets; and ensuring that routine administration is efficient and effective. In many schools ideas taken from total quality management are well established and middle leaders are engaged in supporting a clear client focus and in ensuring that internal customers, as well as students, parents and other client groups, are provided with a good quality of service.

Middle leaders play many roles and need to be able to adapt comfortably to each situation they face. As teachers, team leaders and team members they need to behave appropriately and display a level of commitment and integrity deserving of respect. Middle leaders lead by example; they are active in helping to shape the school's mission while at the same time sensitive to the pressures faced by classroom teachers. Good middle leaders develop clear reflective thinking as a means of solving problems they encounter and to help them to be more proactive in the shaping of events.

All middle leaders face challenges, demands, dilemmas, and obstacles. At times they can feel frustrated and even demoralized but it is also the case that middle leadership can be exciting, challenging, rewarding and fulfilling. Middle leaders who help a team or department create a clear identity and group loyalty, develop a sense of purpose and begin to make a real difference in the quality of education provided feel rightly proud.

The satisfaction middle leaders get out of their roles is usually proportionate to the effort they put in.

2

The importance of culture

Introduction

Reference was made in the first chapter of this book to a collaborative approach to leadership. Collaboration will be encouraged throughout this book but as you read on you will, hopefully, become more nuanced in your thinking and understanding of the concept and what collaboration might mean in practice. At the outset it is important to understand how the culture in your school will influence, shape and even limit the way you work as a middle leader. If you are new to the role, you will inherit a team with an established way of doing things. Reshaping the team culture will become your key aim if you believe your team's current outlook and practices inhibit what can be achieved for students.

When you enter a school (or visit a department) and feel a positive ethos and culture of cooperation, high expectations and achievement you can be sure that this doesn't exist by accident. It is likely to be the result of a vision shared by all staff, good selection and training procedures and effective policies, which give staff and students a clear sense of direction, together with considerable autonomy and responsibility. It is likely that in these schools members of staff have high expectations of each other as well as their students and that there is a strong belief in involving students in decisions about their learning. It is possible to be fairly confident about these claims, as there is now a wealth of research evidence to support the notion that some school cultures are more effective than others.

Some thoughts on culture

As school culture or ethos seems to be so important it is worth being clear about its meaning. *Culture* in its broadest sense can be defined as the 'way of life' of an entire society. This includes the codes of manners, dress, language, rituals, norms and beliefs held by people in the society in question. Within societies there are also *sub-cultures*; a system of beliefs, values and norms shared by an appreciable minority of people within a particular culture.

Just as societies can be analysed and explained in terms of cultures and sub-cultures so can organizations, where, according to Ainscow (1994: 9) culture can be seen as 'an amalgam of the values, norms and beliefs that characterize the way in which a group of people behave within a specific organizational setting'. Ravasi and Schultz (2006) go on to point out that in larger organizations diverse and conflicting cultures often coexist.

Middle leaders in all walks of life, including schools, operate in the context of wider organizational cultures, which influence and restrain their actions; encouraging some forms of behaviour and making others more difficult. Just as in wider society, organizations can contain sub-cultural groups, operating in ways that are at odds with the dominant culture. It is important for team leaders in secondary schools to be aware of this basic organizational sociology, as many of the challenges they face and frustrations they feel will be able to be explained through a consideration of organizational cultures and sub-cultures.

Considerable research was undertaken into organizational cultures during the 1980s and 1990s and much has now been written about school cultures and incorporated into school improvement literature. It is important to bear two things in mind before considering some key ideas about school cultures.

- Firstly, most teachers accept they have a duty to do the best they can for every child both in terms of exam results and in helping them to develop an outlook that will enable them to become responsible and active citizens in a democratic country. The culture of a school has a direct bearing on both of these aims and that is why getting the culture right is so important. 'The challenge is to move schools to develop responsive cultures for the moral purpose of more effectively working with students and parents to enhance the level of student learning' (Davies and West-Burnham 1997: 224).
- Secondly, there is now much evidence from Ofsted reports and other sources to show that even in schools where the dominant culture leaves much to be desired, sub-cultures and even individual teachers can thrive, working in ways that are more effective and result in higher achievement levels for their students. Team leaders who find themselves in badly led schools can take heart from this. While it is difficult to swim against the tide real progress is possible and effective team leaders can become real *change agents* in a school. With regular inspections now a feature of the education system, all schools are rising to the challenge of developing cultures that match those of the most successful schools. Outdated and ineffective school cultures, like the dinosaurs, will simply not survive this process of evolution.

Organisational cultures

Handy and Aitken (1986) and Fullan and Hargreaves (1992) have identified a number of cultures relating to schools as organizations. Aspects of these cultures can still be found in many schools and they provide a useful starting point for middle leaders wanting to reflect on the functioning of the organization in which they work. When considering these cultures bear in mind that, as with leadership styles, the pure form may not exist in practice. However, organizations and teams may display distinct traits from one or more of these cultures and there is likely to be a dominant culture or ethos, best summed up as 'the way we do things around here'. Consider also that the true culture cannot always be identified by what is displayed on the surface. For example, a school may have a meeting structure and professional development sessions in place that suggest a great deal of collaboration and shared learning is taking place. However, it would only be through a careful analysis of what actually went on in these meetings and sessions and the way people related to each other that we would know for sure that a collaborative culture was embedded in the organization.

The role culture

Here the organization is traditional and hierarchical. There are clear job descriptions and role boundaries, formalized communication and procedures and an emphasis on individuals keeping to their area of expertise. Schools that fit this model are usually well managed but not dynamic. Vision can be lacking and the full potential of employees not realized. They are efficient and well suited to a stable world, but schools of this type are not well equipped for coping with the rapid changes that are now a permanent feature of education.

The club culture

Here the organization has a head teacher who cultivates the support of like-minded colleagues. Circles of intimates develop and can have greater influence than formal post holders who fall outside the 'club'. The head in such schools often uses power in an arbitrary way, rather than following agreed procedures; decisions are often made informally through discussions with the 'in-crowd' and few things are written down and communicated to all staff. Such organizations can be exciting places to work for people who have the head's patronage but other colleagues can feel marginalized and unimportant. The nepotism that exists in these schools is certainly unfair and works against principles of equal opportunities and the reliance placed on the head teacher is very unhealthy. While the club culture is more common in primary schools many secondary teachers would argue that aspects of the club culture are evident in their schools also. It is easy to see how this culture could take hold unintentionally at department or team level, if the middle leader became too close to 'favourites' in the team. A real challenge for a middle leader is to be able to use the dynamism and commitment of really motivated colleagues while not creating a clique that alienates others in the team.

The task culture

Warmth, friendliness and cooperation with little evidence of hierarchy are features of the task culture. People work as teams and groups can be changed or disbanded as the task changes. Such cultures aid problem solving and enable all individuals to contribute to moving the organization forward. There is open questioning of past procedures and a commitment to improving the services provided. Young, energetic and self-confident people thrive in such communities. Some schools make use of the positive aspects of the task culture by having working parties or learning groups drawn from across the school and formed with a specific aim in mind. The task culture is not liked by people who cling to job titles for security or by people who feel threatened by 'young blood' and/or constant change.

The person culture

In organizations where a person culture exists individual autonomy is seen as important. The organization allows individuals to display their talents and leaders interfere as little as possible, leaving the 'experts' to get on with the job. Professionals are persuaded, influenced, cajoled and bargained with but not commanded or instructed. The achievement of the team is really the result of dynamic individuals 'doing their own thing' rather than strategic leadership. The creative industries where innovation is so important often display a person culture. Teachers working in schools thirty years ago had much autonomy and procedures and monitoring that are now commonplace would have been anathema. In these circumstances the person culture was able to thrive. While the person culture in its pure form is now very rare in schools there are still echoes of it which, in part, explains why some leaders are still very reluctant to challenge the behaviour of colleagues, even when their performance is of an unacceptable level.

The individualistic culture

Here people work in isolation. There is little collaboration and sharing of ideas and people rarely receive feedback on performance. People avoid innovation and risk taking and new ideas are not embraced. Individuals do not seek or welcome help and there is little incentive to improve performance (even though they may be very capable) and learn from each other. When meetings do take place few people contribute and even interaction at a social level is rare. There is a real danger that in very large schools, where departments do not have base areas and staff meetings are unproductive, individualized cultures can develop. In these schools and teams, teachers focus on 'getting the job done' and are resistant to change.

The balkanized culture

In balkanized schools teachers develop loyalty to separate groups and there is competition between groups. Departments behave like nation states and distinct sub-cultures exist that make working with a common purpose and ethos difficult. There is a lack of communication between groups and a tendency to assume negative stereotypes about members of other groups. Conflict over time, rooms, resources and exam option systems are common. In balkanized schools making a success of whole school initiatives is very difficult. At its worst, there can be balkanization within faculties, with no common vision and different subject teams unhealthily competing and being in conflict.

The collaborative culture

In schools, departments or teams where a collaborative culture exists there is a clear and shared vision about the values and purposes of the school or team and this vision is regularly reviewed and examined. Teachers and others supporting learning have strong voices, disagreements are visible and teachers are both empowered and accountable. Team teaching and joint planning are common, teachers are willing to be learners and there is a commitment to ongoing professional development. Teams work effectively and there is a high level of trust and openness. Hierarchies are not so obvious and banter, jokes and celebrations reflect mutual understanding and respect.

Reflection

- *Which culture or cultures do you associate with the school you work in?*
- *Does the culture in your team reflect the wider school culture?*
- *In which culture would change occur most easily?*
- *What effect would each of these cultures have on students?*
- *Which culture would generate the most positive ethos?*
- *How can middle leaders help to change the culture in their team and the school culture?*

Clearly, schools that are successful in today's educational world are those that can respond to change effectively and successfully focus on raising achievement. The collaborative culture is promoted in much literature on school effectiveness and through management training, though it is important to remember that this culture will only deliver high standards when it is linked to a clear vision, high expectations and lines of accountability. Middle leaders mustn't assume they have a collaborative culture just because a friendly and cooperative ethos exists. Critical analysis of performance is a key feature of dynamic collaborative teams.

At the heart of the collaborative culture is the idea that schools develop and improve best through the creative involvement of all those who work in them. While a leadership hierarchy or structure is in place, efforts are made to avoid the divide which exists in some schools between 'leaders' and 'teachers', allowing all members of staff to contribute fully to achieving an agreed vision. It is now recognized that *empowerment* helps to generate commitment and means all teachers, regardless of their job title, can contribute their skills and enthusiasm to moving a school forward.

> An important aspect of the character of effective schools is that management is not the unique task of those at the apex of a hierarchy but a shared responsibility of all who are involved in the school. A culture which proclaims that heads (and deputies) manage but teachers teach is not conducive to effective development.
>
> (Hargreaves and Hopkins 1991: 30)

This helps to explain why there is now an emphasis on *distributed leadership* in schools, with all teachers encouraged to be *leaders of learning* (i.e. to take responsibility as leaders for the learning in their classroom), and accept *collective responsibility*. While staff are valued, recognized as professionals and assumed to want to do their best for their students, this does not mean they are simply left to their own devices. Schools serious about quality have in place mechanisms for monitoring staff performance and student progress. Schools in which a positive ethos is instantly recognizable are likely to have in place sensible structures, procedures and monitoring, balanced with a good deal of individual autonomy for both staff and students.

School culture and effectiveness

In 1993 a report was produced for the Department for Education on effective school management. Twenty-four secondary schools were involved in the survey and the staff in those schools recognized the following as contributing to effective management practice which helped to generate a positive school ethos:

- Students play an active part in the life of the school and there are high expectations of them in terms of behaviour and achievement
- Complacency among staff is actively discouraged in favour of a questioning, critical attitude
- There is an open atmosphere; staff respect one another and talk freely about professional matters
- Staff are involved in developing the school's aims and policies
- All staff have a clear understanding of the school's vision
- The head is accessible to staff and has a consultative 'listening' style
- The head praises staff and celebrates their achievements

- Senior leaders delegate tasks to develop and empower staff but also monitor performance
- Working parties operate to reach decisions and write policies
- Struggling staff are supported
- Staff feel valued and their views are taken seriously
- Professional development for all staff is encouraged
- Many decisions are made collaboratively

This is not the complete list, but the points above are useful in guiding us to a conclusion regarding effective school cultures. A good summary is provided by Ainscow et al. (1994: 9) who suggest, 'the type of school cultures most supportive of school improvement efforts are those that are collaborative, have high expectations for both students and staff, exhibit a consensus of values, and support an orderly and secure environment'. While the existence of these features will not be a guarantee that *all* staff in schools displaying them will be motivated, involved and productive, it is more likely that a *critical mass* of the staff will be.

Further evidence of effective school cultures was provided by Sammons et al. (1995). They were commissioned by Ofsted to undertake a review of international school effectiveness literature, particularly from the United Kingdom, North America and the Netherlands. They were asked to assess whether or not, despite very different approaches to education in different countries, successful schools had common distinctive features. They came up with eleven key characteristics found in effective schools in all the countries studied:

- Professional leadership that encourages participation
- Shared vision and goals generated by collaboration
- An orderly learning environment
- A focus on achievement
- Purposeful teaching
- High expectations
- Positive reinforcement
- Effective monitoring of progress
- Active involvement of pupils
- Parental involvement
- A strong emphasis on staff development

Over time, the emphasis on collaboration has not waned. Harris and Spillane (2008) suggest the concept is growing ever more popular. It is also increasingly linked to school improvement, a trend accounted for by Hammersley-Fletcher and Brundrett (2008) who contend distributed leadership and collaboration allow a pooling of ability and produce outcomes that are greater than those that individuals working alone could achieve and allow teachers who do not aspire to leadership an opportunity to unlock their creativity.

It is important, however, to distinguish between collaboration and collegiality.

> Collegial models assume that organizations determine policy and make decisions through a process of discussion leading to consensus. Power is shared among some or all members of the organization who are thought to have a mutual understanding about the objectives of the institution.
>
> (Bush 1995: 39)

It is simply not possible to run a school or department on the basis of consultation and consensus about everything. Of course, it is right that people are consulted and contribute to the development of policy (this is the essence of a collaborative culture) and that leaders try hard to release the full potential of all staff members, but there are some occasions when there is no consensus and difficult decisions have to be made in order to move a school or team forward. It is possible, of course, that a senior leadership team uses a form of collegiality in making key decisions. Similarly, a middle leader will use elements of collegiality with their team, especially when it comes to decisions about *how* things will be done. Whatever your inclinations as a leader, you need to be pragmatic about collegiality because consensus building is a way of getting things done. 'Power is not something subject leaders need for its own sake, but as the vehicle by which to engender school effectiveness and improvement. When it works, collegiality is a much vouched way to ensure this' (Jarvis 2012: 490).

However, consensus on key aspects of development might not always be possible and a compromise that 'keeps everyone happy' might fail to please anyone and could be selling students short. While understanding that colleagues need to be consulted and listened to, an effective leader is able to make key decisions based on sound reasoning and evidence coupled to a clear vision of what they want to achieve. Doing the right things for the right reasons (and providing team members with a clear and rational explanation for decisions made) is a feature of authentic leadership.

Collaboration and learning

What might seem an obvious point to make is that schools should be *learning organizations*. That is, their core purpose should be learning and therefore the learning of all – students and staff – should be central. The head should model expectations by being the lead learner and middle leaders should be committed to continuing to learn themselves and creating the conditions in which their teams can continue to learn. Collaboration is the vehicle by which much effective learning takes place. Pulling together international research into the relationship between leadership and organisational learning Cibulka et al. (2000) identified some essential elements for developing collective and individual learning, including:

- Collaborative goal development
- Anticipation of constraints
- Seeing obstacles as minor impediments
- A capacity to learn and build on teachers' perceptions
- Openness to new information
- A strongly reflective disposition to learn from experience

They concluded that these features suggest the development of a viable learning community requires educational leaders to engage in an on-going and reflective learning process to recast themselves as leaders as learners. In recent times, a harder edge has been brought to the notion of 'on-going reflection' by the sharper use of ever more detailed student performance data to inform discussion and analysis and the increasing use of monitoring of teaching as a means of enforcing expectations and focusing practitioners on the aspects of pedagogy they should be developing. The challenge for middle leaders is to balance monitoring and clarity for individuals and the team about what improvements are needed with a culture that encourages risk taking in the classroom, learning from peer observation, coaching and collective problem solving. If colleagues feel threatened by the monitoring and accountability elements of your leadership they can become defensive and defensiveness is incompatible with improvement and change. Using different leadership styles with different individuals within an overall collaborative culture is one way this balance can be achieved (see chapter 4).

The power of culture

Leaders at all levels who underestimate the importance of culture will be limiting the impact they can have. It is increasingly clear that changing the culture of an underperforming school or team is absolutely fundamental to success. Of course it is possible to bring about some improvements through changes in practice, policies and procedures but very often these improvements will be superficial and unlikely to last because the core values – and culture – haven't changed. As a new middle leader it is important to understand that cultural change takes time. You will need to gain the confidence of your team. If they have not previously been actively involved in ownership of decisions and/or if they have not been expected to focus on improving teaching and learning they will need to be encouraged into this.

Ideas about how this can be done can be found in chapter 9, but for now here are a number of suggestions, modified from an article on the National College for Teaching and Leadership website (http://www.nationalcollege.org.uk/index/interactiveinfo.htm?id=186183). Don't be daunted by the list, you can introduce these ideas (and many more besides) gradually. The important thing is to begin working collaboratively, with a focus on high quality teaching and learning.

Be a sales person

You are in a sales role for getting people interested in their own and others' professional development around issues of teaching and pupil learning. Encourage and enthuse your colleagues for professional learning and its ongoing development. Highlight its importance by modelling your commitment to your own professional learning. Acknowledge and value the professional learning of colleagues.

Show an interest

Encourage professional learning by showing an interest and regularly talking to people about their own development. If a member of your team attends a course make sure they are allowed to cascade what they have learnt to the rest of the team. This will show you value the teacher's professional development and create opportunities for reflection for the colleague and the team. This interest you show and the conversations you have around colleagues' professional learning encourages further development. A leader's interest in, enthusiasm for, and valuing of individuals' engagement in professional learning is often reciprocated by colleagues. They respond by taking a greater interest in their own development and engaging in conversations with the leader on this.

Keep yourself close to pupil learning and classroom teaching

As a grounded leader you need to understand:

- What effective practice looks like
- Or the concerns of teachers about pedagogy
- Or why some things can be hard to do or implement
- Why learning can be so problematical for some children in some situations

This will then enable you to have impact around supporting the learning of your colleagues in the business of effective pupil learning and classroom teaching. As a middle leader you do not have to be the 'expert' but you do need to be able to teach well and model what you expect of others.

Create connections and networks

Your role is to help connect people. Rich connections improve the capacity of individuals both to cope with and manage the process of change and generate different ways of doing things. Help nurture links for yourself and your colleagues both within the immediate team, through the school and beyond. Some schools will already have established internal teaching and learning groups or 'communities' and may be collaborating actively with other schools. If so, engage your team in discussions about the difference this is making in their classrooms. If these initiatives do not exist, talk to other middle leaders about establishing them.

Highlight to colleagues their personal responsibility for their professional learning

Professional learning is not a top down process but rather relies on individuals committing to and actively engaging in their own on-going learning and development. The leader's role is to help make this clear to colleagues, helping unblock any difficulties and providing appropriate support to make the process sustainable.

Support non-formal learning opportunities

Frequently a dependency culture can develop in a school with the view that effective professional learning must be formally devised, cost money and be externally delivered. Your role as a leader is to help colleagues identify and exploit the myriad of non-formal professional learning opportunities open to them within the school. This can be as simple as two teachers in the staffroom talking about improving a lesson over a cup of coffee to someone taking a lead role on the development of a new piece of the curriculum. In terms of quick things that the middle leader can do, a key one is to ensure team meetings always focus on teaching and learning rather than administration. Routine matters can be dealt with in a weekly bulletin and should not be allowed to dominate meetings which could become rich learning opportunities.

Get everyone reading

There is a wealth of easily accessible texts, research, on-line journals and magazines for teachers to read. An easy leadership role is to start passing on snippets of relevant research readings, informative articles and on line references to colleagues. This can stimulate discussion in meetings (see Support non-formal learning opportunities). On a similar note the leader should be a magnet for references and readings from colleagues. The importance of this cannot be overestimated. Professional reading supports a process of deep reflection, can generate new approaches and helps stimulate colleagues thinking.

Help colleagues realize their potential

You need to believe that all your colleagues are capable of more, however good they are. The former Milk Marketing Board ran a series of advertising campaigns many years ago with the catchphrase, 'Be All You Can Be'. Hold this true for your colleagues (as well as your students). Help them develop and extend their potential. Don't give up on them. Don't give up on yourself.

(Further suggestions for developing professional learning are given in chapter 9.)

Action point

Select at least two things you are not already doing from this list and put them into practice over the next few months.

Summary

Institutions of all kinds display different cultures or 'ways of doing things' and schools are no exception. Over the past twenty-five years, a range of school cultures has been identified by researchers and there is now a considerable body of evidence indicating that secondary schools that adopt a collaborative approach can be very effective.

To have maximum impact a collaborative culture needs to be linked to high expectations and a clear vision, staff involvement in collective problem solving and a culture of critical reflection, learning from peers and on-going professional development. Teachers working in a collaborative culture are likely to have considerable autonomy, flexibility and responsibility, within a framework of clear expectations, monitoring and evaluation of their performance. There is also likely to be much discussion about how to improve teaching and learning and the students themselves will probably be involved in this.

To be effective in such cultures middle leaders need to be good team players, supportive, self-critical, reflective and not frightened by the prospect of empowering colleagues in their teams to achieve agreed and ambitious goals. They will not be concerned by status, hierarchy and the kind of power that comes from rigid job descriptions. They will be good at delegating and will take pride in allowing others in their team to flower and grow. Middle leaders need to be role models, reflecting critically on their own teaching and being open to innovation and new learning themselves. Middle leaders not working in schools characterized by collaborative features can still achieve a great deal of cooperation and collaboration within their own teams. However, while some staff not used to working collaboratively will rise to the challenge, others may be reluctant and fearful and will need careful nurturing away from the state of dependency they have been allowed to exist in.

3

Leadership basics

How your behaviour impacts on other people

Introduction

While it is true that all human beings are unique individuals it is also obvious that certain traits common to large numbers of people make it possible to group similar individuals together and predict their behaviour. Social scientists have studied common traits and the predictability of behaviour in order to classify people according to personality, social class, culture and so on. It is now generally felt that the behaviour we observe in individuals is a product of genetic make-up, social learning, and the contexts in which individuals operate. This is as true for leaders as it is for any other social group.

As a middle leader some understanding of basic leadership styles and models identified by theorists over time can be helpful in understanding your own behaviour and people's reactions to it. Before doing this, however, it is important to consider the following points:

- Leadership style is not fixed. While certain personalities are more likely to approach the leadership and management of others in a particular way, everyone can learn new ways of leading and managing people and are capable of moderating their 'natural' style. The important thing is to be open-minded and self-critical. If you are predisposed to a particular style, but there is clear evidence that other styles seem to be more effective, then the good leader will learn to use the features of the style that is known to work.
- Different situations require different leadership styles. This will be discussed in more detail in chapter 4 but for now it is important to understand that effective leaders are able to adjust their approach to suit the task, the context and the individuals with whom they are working. Even when there

is evidence that a particular style of leadership is *usually* effective there may well be specific circumstances in which other styles are needed to produce the required results. Being able to assess which situation requires which style is critical.

■ Middle leaders work in teams. By knowing the personalities of your team you will be able to use the skills of others to complement your style of leadership. Again, this requires honesty and critical reflection. Don't be afraid to use the strengths of others; knowing more about leadership styles will help you to assess yourself and see how others in your team can be used to complement your particular strengths. Skilled leaders make this look easy, but it is something those new to leadership often struggle with, believing, wrongly, that they should be capable of being all things to all people.

Models of leadership

Research on management and leadership styles has identified clear traits and theorists have assembled these traits into typologies of leadership style and leadership models. Some of the models, naturally, have similarities, and a synthesis of the models can help in reaching a clear understanding of the key characteristics of leaders you know and of yourself as a leader.

The authoritarian/laissez-faire axis

One simple model of leadership places all leaders somewhere on a continuum from *authoritarian* to *laissez-faire*, with most leaders showing traits that place them in one of the following groups:

Authoritarian _____	Democratic _____	Laissez-faire

The groups are based on an analysis of how leaders behave towards the people who work in their teams. At one end of the scale are authoritarian leaders; dictators who need to control all aspects of a team's work. At the other end of the scale are laissez-faire leaders; those who are happy to allow colleagues to do just as they please. You might, of course, argue that the latter group can hardly be called leaders (or managers) if they allow colleagues to do just as they please! In the middle are democratic leaders who share a clear sense of purpose with team members and involve colleagues in deciding the most appropriate ways of achieving agreed goals.

Table 3.1 provides a few more characteristics associated with these three leadership groups.

TABLE 3.1 Authoritarian, democratic and laissez-faire leaders

Authoritarian	Democratic	Laissez-faire
• Tells people what to do • Keeps information from team members • Stifles debate • Tightly controls meetings • Gives the impressions that decisions are made before they are discussed • Employs rigid procedures • Seems to have 'tunnel vision' • Fails to develop colleagues by refusing to delegate	• Directs or supports people as necessary • Shares information of relevance to the team • Plans well-structured meetings, which allow for debate but reach decisions • Agrees clear procedures with the team • Has a clear philosophy but listens to other views • Develops colleagues by negotiating the delegation of some tasks	• Doesn't like directing people • Shares information unnecessarily • Allows so much debate clear decisions are rarely made • Allows meetings to drag on • Lacks procedures • Gives the impression of having no clear vision for the team • Fails to develop colleagues by not planning delegation

The McGregor X–Y axis

While the laissez-faire approach amounts to a failure to manage or lead, the authoritarian and democratic typologies seem to reflect conflicting underlying assumption about human nature and how people should be treated in order to get the most out of them in a work situation. The American management consultant Douglas McGregor first identified two extreme and opposing sets of beliefs held by managers in his book *The Human Side of Management* (1960). McGregor's categories are given in Table 3.2.

Newtonian and Whiteheadian managers

There are echoes of the McGregor X–Y axis in the materials developed by the *Pacific Institute* for their 'Investment in Excellence' programme, which became popular in the 1990s. According to The Pacific Institute (1997), people can be classed as either Newtonian or Whiteheadian, depending on how they see the world. These views of the world can have a profound influence on the way they manage and lead others.

TABLE 3.2 McGregor X and Y thinking

McGregor X thinking	McGregor Y thinking
• People are naturally lazy • People are not interested in improving their performance • People need to be closely monitored and supervised • People can't be trusted with making decisions	• People are naturally motivated • People want to do well and improve their performance • People want to take responsibility • People thrive on being involved in decision making

Isaac Newton, in the seventeenth century, was deeply interested in religion. Through his scientific work he wanted to show the order that existed in God's universe. He believed the world was entirely predictable except for human beings, who represented a threat to God's creation. Therefore, according to Newtonian logic, human beings must be controlled. In organizational terms this means people must know their place, must have rigid procedures to follow and must not be given the autonomy to take risks. Managers and leaders are there to keep people on task and prevent them working against their employers and disrupting the smooth running of the organization.

Alfred North Whitehead (1861–1947) was a mathematician physicist and a philosopher whose world-view was very different. In contrast to Newton, he believed that God was working to make a better world. Far from being a threat to God's ordered world human beings were, in fact, capable of inventing better ways of doing things; they were helping to move the world towards perfection. Applied to organizations a Whiteheadian approach results in people having more autonomy and accountability being spread throughout the organization. The job of management and leadership is to empower people and release their creativity to achieve the goals of the organization. Far from being seen as a threat the workers are seen as the key resource of an organization.

During the last thirty years, accelerated by the decline of heavy industry and the manufacturing sector in the U.K., more and more organizations have embraced the Whiteheadian perspective. Through initiatives such as *Investors in People* the importance of developing individual potential so that people can contribute fully to the organization has been acknowledged. In schools there is now a general assumption that involving all staff in planning and decision making and encouraging both greater autonomy and accountability is a good thing, providing it is done in the context of a clear and shared vision and high expectations.

TABLE 3.3 Newtonian and Whiteheadian leaders

Newtonian leaders	Whiteheadian leaders
• Assume a basically stable environment	• Assume constant change
• Assume people are basically lazy and incompetent	• Believe people can be creative and inventive
• Think control must come from above	• Think control should be shared
• Think only managers are accountable	• Think accountability should be shared
• Get self-esteem from power and position	• Get self-esteem from supporting and nurturing others
• Think people work best when given set tasks	• Think flexible people are more useful

Task-orientated leaders and people-orientated leaders

Another way of classifying leaders is to place them on a continuum somewhere between the extremes of *people-orientated* and *task-orientated*.

People-orientated _____ Task-orientated

Leaders who are strongly task-orientated tend to be good at planning and administration. They are often efficient and can be relied on to 'get the job done' (you might argue they are actually managers and not leaders in the full sense of the term). However, the downside of being strongly task-orientated is a tendency to lack tolerance for those who are unable to work as efficiently as the team leader and a frustration with those who challenge plans being put into action. Task-orientated leaders are often seen as aloof and can sometimes fail to consult colleagues, being over-zealous about 'getting on with it'.

In contrast, people-orientated leaders tend to be much less bothered about planning and administrative efficiency and much more concerned with keeping up the morale of people in their team. They are usually prepared to devote a great deal of time to listening and feel that consulting colleagues is an essential aspect of leadership. Strongly people-orientated leaders can sometimes spend so much time on 'keeping people happy' that they neglect to move their team forward towards achieving agreed goals and/or are reluctant to address underperformance in their team.

Of course, a successful leader is someone who can combine a concern for people with administrative efficiency and task completion. In reality, most middle leaders fall somewhere between the two extremes mentioned, and it is certainly possible for leaders with a tendency to one extreme or the other to compensate for this by conscious effort based on critical reflection and the learning of new skills.

There are, in fact, similarities between the 'people-task' model of leadership and the 'authoritarian–laissez-faire' model. Leaders who fail to consult and are obsessed with administrative systems are sure to be seen as authoritarian by colleagues. Likewise, those who are so concerned about the different views and feelings of colleagues that they are never able to lead a team to a consensus or a clear decision end up, even if unintentionally, being laissez-faire leaders. Figure 3.1 illustrates the links between some of the leadership characteristics mentioned earlier in the chapter and the people-task classification.

Position A leaders are strong on people but weak on task. They are fair and considerate to team members, trusting them to be professional and get on with their jobs. Such leaders may, however, fail to give a clear sense of direction and may also fail to develop the skills and potential of those in their team. With a highly motivated and highly skilled team, in a fairly stable organization, it is possible for *people leaders* as described to be successful. However, they are ineffective when rapid change is needed and/or where performance needs to improve quickly.

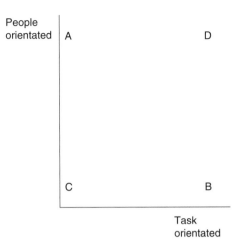

People orientated | A   D

C   B

Task orientated

FIGURE 3.1 People-orientated and task-orientated combinations.

Position B leaders are very efficient and well organized, with a clear sense of what needs doing to move their team or department forward. However, it is likely that such leaders do not adequately involve colleagues in deciding on goals or ways of achieving goals. B leaders may be irritated by people in the team who do not share or understand the goals and are unlikely to be sympathetic to people slowing down the process of change. In rigid, hierarchical organizations there are plenty of these *authoritarian leaders*. Arguably, such people can be useful as middle leaders in schools, when particular tasks need accomplishing quickly and efficiently. Schools in 'special measures' often require a strong degree of authoritarianism initially in order to set clear expectations and get a school moving on the road to improvement. However, schools are people-orientated organizations that depend on teams working together and individuals being nurtured to perform to the best of their ability. For this reason B leadership alone is of only limited value for sustained school improvement.

Position C leaders are weak on both task and people skills and as such fail to manage or lead at all. C managers are *laissez-faire managers* of the worst kind, being unable to get tasks done but also leaving colleagues to their own devices with no concern or support being offered. In most schools, thankfully, laissez-faire leaders are becoming extinct, as the pressure of constant change, greater accountability and regular inspection makes it impossible for such individuals to survive.

Position D leaders are able to combine the ability to accomplish tasks with a genuine concern for colleagues. Such leaders have clear goals and clear ideas about how to move towards those goals. In addition, D leaders are capable of engaging other team members in deciding on how goals can be achieved and are supportive of colleagues who encounter difficulties with change. D leaders are good listeners, make effective use of the skills of people in their team and are flexible. Above all else D leaders are able to keep the morale of the team high and, by so doing, enable the team to reach agreed goals. They have what it takes to be successful over time.

Leadership styles and fitness for purpose

The problem with looking at models of management and leadership styles is that they distort reality. While most people display traits that make it easy to place them in a particular category, it is likely that most authoritarian leaders have some people skills and most people-orientated leaders have some planning ability and an awareness of tasks to be done. The important thing is that leaders are realistic and honest about their strengths and weaknesses as a starting point for improving their performance.

It is important that leaders are genuinely self-critical and aware of how they are seen by others. Armed with this knowledge it is possible to begin working on areas of weakness in order to become a better and more rounded leader. Adair (1997: 35) sums up the importance of understanding how others perceive you rather amusingly as follows:

> If one person says that you are a horse,
> Smile at them.
> If two people say that you are a horse,
> Give it some thought.
> If three people say that you are a horse,
> Go out and buy a saddle.

Further consideration will be given to the need to be self-aware and flexible in applying leadership styles when we consider *situational leadership* in chapter 4.

Reflection

- *Think about leaders you have met and worked for. Do you recognize any of their leadership traits in the models outlined above?*
- *Consider your own approach to leadership and management. Do you feel you veer towards task accomplishment or concern for people's feelings as a natural way of working? What strategies do you (or could you) use to ensure your preference does not impact negatively on people in your team?*
- *How do you know your assessment of yourself is accurate? How could you learn more about how others see your leadership? Why is it important to understand how others see you?*

In thinking about how the behaviour of leaders impacts on others it is important to consider what has been written over time about motivation in the workplace.

What motivates people?

Psychologists and sociologists have produced many theories that attempt to explain what motivates people in work. Over the years various companies have experimented with altering the working environment, providing financial rewards for increases in productivity and using a range of sticks and carrots in order to get the best out of their employees. In education, the production of performance tables based on national tests and exam results has made target setting a standard feature of school life and in 2013 performance related pay for teachers was introduced, making the target culture even more significant. Of course, regular appraisal of teachers and target setting can improve results in areas that are easily measured, but not everything that is valuable in schools can be measured. If teachers cease to give time to areas of school life that are not so easily measured target setting becomes counter-productive. Middle leaders need to make use of appraisal and targets but there is much else that can be done to motivate colleagues.

In the commercial world companies have come to appreciate the importance of developing loyalty in their workers. Through initiatives such as *Investors in People* they have attempted to organize themselves in ways that show that their human resources are valued. Most companies have a *mission statement* and employees are encouraged to share the company's *vision* and help the organization move towards achieving its goals. Schools, also, are using these techniques as a way of helping to create a clear set of values and shared sense of purpose (often expressed as *moral purpose*). It is obvious that teachers are the most important and expensive resource in schools and their commitment is vital to the success of any improvement initiatives.

> Of all the resources at the disposal of an organization it is only people who can grow and develop and be motivated to achieve certain desired ends. The attaining of targets is in their hands and it is the way people are led and managed...which is at the heart of human resource management... and optimum management.
>
> (Riches and Morgan 1989: 1)

It is essential, therefore, actively to engage teachers in the shaping of the school and ensure that they feel valued and in possession of high levels of skill. As already suggested, democratic leadership styles and collaborative school cultures are more likely to generate success and commitment from most teachers than other approaches. This can partly be explained by the ideas of Abraham Maslow.

Maslow (1943) produced a theory of motivation that sought to go beyond financial and environmental considerations when explaining employee behaviour. This theory, conceived in the 1950s, still has much to commend it and certainly seems to explain why so many teachers work as hard as they do with seemingly little financial reward. According to Maslow there are various needs that humans have to satisfy and these should be seen as a hierarchy. More basic or low-level needs, he argued, must be satisfied before a higher need becomes important (see Figure 3.2). The lowest order needs are physiological ones: hunger, thirst and warmth. In most cases, people at work have already satisfied these needs through having money to pay for them. Regarding safety needs, Maslow argues that, in today's society, these only act as motivators at times of crisis that threaten safety or life, such as fire, natural catastrophes, crime waves and other emergency situations. Social needs, however, do act as motivators in the workplace as most people need to feel they *belong*. Most people don't just go to work to put in the hours so that they can earn enough money to enjoy the time they are not at work. If the work satisfies social needs, the next stage in the hierarchy is that of esteem needs. To have self-esteem you need to feel a sense of achievement in what you do and to gain the respect of those you work with; from self-esteem stem feelings of self-confidence and self-worth. According to Maslow *self-actualization* is the most developed level, and not all humans will manage to reach it. Self-actualization, the need for self-development and realizing one's potential, is certainly what drives many teachers. It is not possible to generalize, of course, but many teachers do not present as overly materialistic and often seem more motivated by a genuine desire to achieve their full potential and that of their students than by financial rewards.

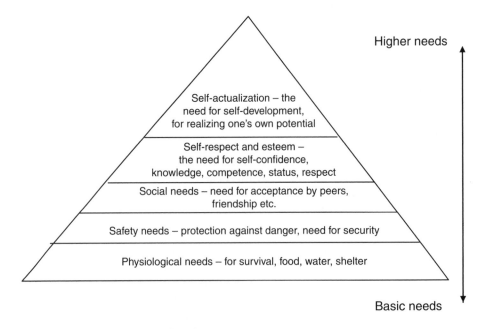

FIGURE 3.2 Maslow's hierarchy of needs.

Case studies

The following comments illustrate just how motivational Maslow's notion of 'higher needs' can be.

Case 1

'I am absolutely determined to get this class through with brilliant grades. Bob trusted me with "A" level work and I will give extra lessons every lunch hour if necessary to prove that I am up to it.' (English teacher in her second year of teaching)

Case 2

'I know it's a lot of money, but I'm doing this for myself. If school can't pay the fees I will pay them. I've told myself for years that once my children are old enough I'll study for a Masters and that's what I'm determined to do.' (Middle-aged applicant for M.Ed degree)

Case 3

'I am more interested in gaining this post for the challenge than the money. A few hundred pounds won't make much difference to my lifestyle; I just feel ready for a change, a new challenge, a different role. I'm very happy at this school and I know I'm respected but I feel as if I've not yet achieved my full potential – and I don't want to regret that later in life.' (Colleague discussing applying for a senior teacher post in a new school)

Case 4

'I felt really deflated, as if he didn't trust me. I know I'm capable of producing a brilliant magazine and the kids are so keen. He kept saying I needed more experience before starting something so major and he kept going on about the time and effort needed. Surely I'm the best judge of how much time I can give and I really wanted to prove I could handle a whole school initiative.' (Teacher with two years' experience, after speaking to her head of department about taking on responsibility for the school magazine)

Reflection

There is much to be learnt from these examples. Many colleagues work very hard indeed in response to being given a responsibility that boosts their self-confidence and sense of worth. Making people feel trusted, skilled and valued are strong motivators. Many teachers undertaking part-time study towards a higher degree pay their own fees. Of course, many of them feel that gaining such a qualification will improve their chances of promotion but for others the desire for self-actualization is what drives them. Likewise, many teachers who take on promoted posts do so as much for fulfilment as for the small financial reward that is so often involved. Many people enter teaching from a genuine desire, a calling, to work with young people. These teachers represent a significant proportion of the profession and, when led and managed effectively, can achieve remarkable things.

Middle leaders must help members of their team to develop. It is very demotivating and deskilling (as in Case 4) to reject the suggestions of team members without discussion and to undermine their hopes and plans. If their desires are unreasonable or genuinely incompatible with the vision of the school or the needs of your area then careful handling is required so that they can be let down gently. Likewise, if you have good reason to think a team member is being over ambitious then think of ways in which they can be supported or their plans can be modified, rather than simply rejecting them. Always try and support team members in what they want to do. Take pride in their achievements and be grateful that they are so highly motivated. Dealing with disillusioned and disgruntled colleagues is far more challenging than supporting and empowering the enthusiastic.

Basic rules for motivating others

Maslow's hierarchy shows us that people are motivated by a range of needs and may be motivated in different ways at different stages of their life. However, the importance Maslow places on higher level needs provides valuable insights into people's motivation and gives us a useful starting point for some general rules on good practice for middle leaders. If Maslow's contention that people are driven by the desire for acceptance by peers, self-respect, and self-actualization is correct then leaders would be wise to reflect on their behaviour towards colleagues in terms of how it affects their feelings of acceptance, their self-respect and their opportunity for self-actualization. Listening to teachers complaining about the way they have been treated by leaders adds weight to Maslow's theory and also to the importance of creating collaborative school cultures.

The following statements apply to most, though not all, teachers.

- Teachers like to be consulted about what they have to do – just being told what to do does not generate feelings of *ownership* for a particular policy.
- Teachers appreciate leaders who are willing to listen – feeling that your views are of no significance is demotivating.

- Teachers appreciate being valued for their specialist knowledge and skills – being seen as a mere cog in the machine, easily replaced by other cogs, does not build self-esteem.
- Teachers respond to sensitive leadership – heavy handed use of authority is often counter-productive, achieving compliance but not discretional effort.
- Teachers perform better when they enjoy their work and feel relaxed – leaders who can spread good cheer and empower teachers will be helping to motivate them.
- Teachers whose successes are recognized become more successful and more motivated – praise for teachers is as important as praise for their pupils (*positive strokes* in the jargon of neuro-linguistic programming).

From these statements it is not difficult to arrive at some general, though very important pointers on good practice in day-to-day behaviour for middle leaders.

Spend time getting to know the people in your team and then support them

When you become a middle leader it is worth spending time getting to know the people for whom you have a management responsibility. Your knowledge of the people in your team will help you to manage situations more easily, for example by being able to anticipate people's likely reactions to new ideas. As you get to know people you will become concerned for their welfare and as this begins to show it is likely to bring you greater loyalty than leaders who stand aloof. Showing that you are interested in colleagues as people and as professionals will encourage the members of your team to offer you the support you will need to do your job effectively.

Getting to know colleagues is sure to make you want to help them to do their best and this will make you a better leader. For example, a head of department who tries to support team members who are looking under the weather will not only help to prevent them 'going under' (thus saving work) but will also earn goodwill, which is likely to be repaid many times over. This makes sense, but the desire to support comes also from a genuine wish to help colleagues you have taken the time to get to know.

Of course, there is a fine line between being friendly and being a friend. Effective middle leaders are able to maintain a professional distance while still being supportive and caring. This is important as middle leaders who become 'over friendly' can find it difficult to be objective about their team members and also run the risk of being seen to have special relationships with some in their team. This can pose particular problems if a middle leader has to hold a colleague to account or conduct a challenging conversation with someone whom they regard as a friend.

Communicate clearly with your team and don't be frightened by debate

It is important that people in your team do not feel they are being kept in the dark about important new developments. Talk to colleagues about any plans or schemes and ask for their ideas. Remember that any initiatives you think up are unlikely to succeed without the support of a *critical mass* of team members. Always explain things clearly. People are more likely to cooperate if they know what they are supposed to be doing. If you are putting in place a policy generated externally, for example responding to new legislation, or initiated by senior leaders, involve your team as much as possible in deciding *how* the scheme will operate in your area. You want your team to be part of the solution not part of the problem and so you need to ensure they are actively involved in discussing how challenges are to be met and obstacles overcome.

A sense of ownership is really important if a new initiative is to succeed. Your team should not just be briefed about it but should have the chance to talk it through in a free and open exchange of views. This can act as a real safety valve, allowing people to share their worries and concerns. When there is no dialogue, people will be more likely to begin muttering in small groups and in these circumstances dissatisfaction can soon take hold.

Make decisions!

While it is important to consult people in your team and to keep them informed about important developments it is not necessary to involve all team members in every decision that has to be made. One of your responsibilities as a manager is to shield colleagues from trivia and minutiae so that they are free to devote their energies to their students. Colleagues would, quite rightly, be annoyed if you allocated teaching groups without consultation but there is nothing to be gained in consulting your team about whether or not to order another box of whiteboard markers!

Those decisions that require time, thought and consultation will still need resolution and expecting colleagues to attend many long meetings is unrealistic. Taking the time to make a good decision is one thing – being indecisive is quite another, and is fatal if you want to be an effective leader. Of course, involving people in making important decisions is good and getting people *on side* will increase the likelihood of success. However, not all decisions can be democratic and it is not always possible to get everyone in your team to be enthusiastic about every initiative. Finally, if you realize that a decision you made was wrong don't be afraid to admit it. Leaders who are open about their mistakes (unless mistakes are made all the time) earn more respect than those who insist on pushing ahead with flawed plans or who blame others instead of accepting responsibility when they are at fault.

Display self-control and be positive

Good leaders calmly find ways to solve problems and they do not make mountains out of molehills. Respect is more likely to be gained by being calm when things go wrong than by creating anxiety in others by exaggerating the impact of small mistakes they have made. You will soon lose the respect of colleagues if you constantly challenge them over minor matters and this will make tackling major issues more difficult. There is nothing constructive in interrogating members of your team about a missing set of pencil sharpeners! However, if stock control is an issue of concern then it should be put on the agenda for a team meeting so that all can have their say. Getting bogged down with insignificant day-to-day concerns prevents the more important issues being addressed. Team meetings cluttered up with minor matters can prevent the really important stuff – teaching and learning – being discussed. Indeed, over attention to detail can be a method employed, perhaps unconsciously, to avoid having to face more difficult decisions and can sometimes be a sign that the leader in question is suffering serious stress. Remember, as a leader you will never climb the mountain if you allow yourself to get bogged down in the mud in the valley.

Lead by example

You cannot expect other people to do what you are not able or prepared to do yourself. As a team leader you should set a high standard in the quality of the work you do and in your general attitude to your students and colleagues. You need to model what you expect from others. You cannot grumble about whole school initiatives and then expect people in your team enthusiastically to embrace new ideas you have. You cannot complain to colleagues about their lack of differentiation in lessons if you yourself always 'teach to the middle'. In short, you have to lead from the front.

Some leaders find it difficult to admit their own weaknesses. It is vital that you share your classroom failures as well as your successes with your team if you expect them to be open with you about their weaknesses. Creating a genuinely collaborative team ethos requires openness and critical self-reflection from everyone; this is much more likely to be achieved if the team leader makes it clear that they understand that nobody can be excellent at everything. This, of course, is not an excuse for poor performance, but the foundation stones of a team culture that enables all members to improve by learning from, and supporting, one another.

Be considerate and fair

The maxim 'treat other people as you would wish to be treated yourself' is an important one for middle leaders. This means more than simply being pleasant and friendly towards others, it means thinking about the impact your actions will have on their self-esteem and motivation. It also means not forgetting that members of your team also have responsibilities in other areas of school and are entitled to a family life. You cannot expect people to drop what they are doing to fit into your plans just because you are the team leader. Consult your colleagues before you arrange a trip or team activity so that you can choose a time and date that suits the majority. If you are fair with your team you will get more out of them and when there is a genuine crisis that requires them to change their plans at short notice, they are more likely to try and help you out.

One of the ways in which fairness becomes transparent is in the allocation of groups, rooms and duties to team members. It is very important that the criteria used are clear to everyone. A member of staff historically being allocated particular groups and rooms is not of itself a good reason for continuing the practice. It is a middle leader's duty to ensure that less experienced colleagues are nurtured and developed in terms of the range of groups and subjects they teach and that more senior colleagues experience their fair share of the 'challenging' groups.

Listen to people

The ability to listen carefully and, when necessary, sympathetically is an important skill for any team leader. Middle leaders should be willing to listen properly to the concerns of individuals in their teams and need to be accessible. This does not mean dropping everything at the precise moment someone mentions something to you; if necessary arrange another time that suits you both. It is important to remember when arranging such meetings that things usually take longer to discuss than you (or they) estimate they will. Being willing to give up time to help people is an important aspect of leadership and should not be regarded as a burden, even though it will take you away from other aspects of your role. You should regard time spent listening as a good investment as it really can help you to nip problems in the bud, and by supporting colleagues through difficult times you are helping to nurture the collaborative and supportive culture that will allow your team to flourish.

Middle leaders should also be skilled in assessing the mood of a meeting, by listening carefully to what is being said. When people are talking they should be given your full attention and when they have finished their contribution it is useful to sum up their ideas to make sure you and others have grasped fully what they have said. When new ideas are being proposed people's initial response can often be to focus on the negatives. This is understandable, as people are generally cautious when it comes to change, not least because extra work is likely to be involved. Be patient and allow people their say. It is amazing how soon a real debate will begin and, if the new idea is a good one, how quickly the proposals will be embraced. Trying to force your ideas on people without debate is counter-productive and undermines collaboration and trust.

When policies or targets are imposed from above it is important to involve your team in the 'how' even if the policy or target itself is non-negotiable.

Spread good cheer!

The ability to spread good cheer should be seen as an essential quality included in the person specification for middle leader posts! The importance of a positive outlook, especially for leaders, should never be under-estimated. In far too many staff rooms you will find disgruntled middle leaders being negative and cynical. No doubt individual cynics will have their personal reasons for their lack of enthusiasm, but they are being unprofessional and failing in their duties as leaders through their actions. Keeping up staff morale is a central role of middle leaders and it can be achieved in quite small, but very significant, ways.

Always give credit where it is due and always give praise and thanks when it is deserved. Often this will be done in a one-to-one situation but praising individuals in the presence of others (at a department meeting or a staff briefing) should occur when colleagues have special achievements worthy of sharing. Take pride in announcing what people in your team have achieved and never see their successes as a threat to your status. Leaders should be judged, at least in part, by what they have allowed and encouraged those in their teams to achieve. It is especially important to praise newly qualified teachers in the presence of a third party as you are trying to build their confidence and get their skills recognized by your team.

Praise, thanks and attention provide what are called *positive strokes* and these help to build up morale and confidence. We all want to be appreciated and valued but, sadly, it often feels like the media and government have little that is positive to say about teachers. This can undermine morale and self-confidence and makes it all the more difficult to motivate staff. It is true that success breeds success and it is also true that negative talk can create failure or at least sap enthusiasm. By spreading good cheer and publicizing achievement middle leaders help to keep up the morale of their teams and help individuals to feel valued and appreciated.

With the above foundation stones in place you will build up much good will (picture an emotional piggy bank) and this will make it easier to handle difficult issues when you have to (such as the poor performance of a colleague). Also, if you are consistent, fair and professional in your day-to-day behaviour, you will find your team accepts more readily the use of a different leadership style, when necessary.

Summary

A number of different management and leadership models have been shared to shed light on approaches to leadership in schools. Some leaders have a tendency towards being *task-orientated* while others are more *people-orientated*. The most successful leaders are those who can combine effective planning for the achievement of clear goals, with a style of managing people that is supportive and motivating. This is especially important for middle leaders in schools, who regularly find themselves having to lead their teams towards goals set externally by senior leaders or national policy makers.

Leaders usually have a 'preferred' or 'natural' style as a result of a combination of personality, training, institutional culture and immediate context. All leaders are capable of learning new skills and it is possible for determined leaders to enhance their performance and use approaches other than the one they are naturally strong in. To do this, though, they must be open, honest and self-critical. They must involve others in appraising their performance so that they begin to see themselves as others see them. Only then will they be able to begin to develop those aspects of their leadership that need development.

Good leaders see it as a duty to develop the skills of people in the teams they lead. By using the abilities of others, effective leaders can often compensate for weaknesses they acknowledge in themselves. Middle leaders should not feel threatened by others in their teams who have skills and attributes they lack, but should see these people as a rich human resource to be used to the benefit of the school and the children in the school. It is very often leaders who are unsure of their abilities who find humility difficult. Those who are confident about their strengths and abilities will have less difficulty in helping others shine and develop.

Effective middle leaders motivate their teams by the way they behave on a daily basis.

Adair (1997: 20) sums up the approach required very neatly:

> The six most important words…
> 'I admit I made a mistake.'
> The five most important words…
> 'I am proud of you.'
> The four most important words…
> 'What is your opinion?'
> The three most important words…
> 'If you please.'
> The two most important words…
> 'Thank you.'
> The one most important word…
> 'We.'
> And the last, least important word…
> 'I.'

Understanding different leadership styles and when to use them

Introduction

In chapter 3 an approach to leadership involving the modelling of expectations through day-to-day professional behaviour coupled with empowerment and autonomy for colleagues was encouraged. While this approach is likely to work well with committed and capable fellow professionals, there is no guarantee that it will succeed with *all* teachers and support staff in your team. Some may not have the levels of skill required to respond effectively to empowerment and there may even be colleagues who simply don't want to embrace the positive culture you are trying to establish. This is when *situational leadership* becomes important as a way of dealing with individual colleagues with different levels of professional competence and commitment.

If you are to be fair and consistent with all members of your team it is important to remember that 'there is nothing so unequal as the equal treatment of unequals' (Blanchard 1994: 33). Teachers know this to be true in meeting the needs of their students; it is true also for leaders addressing the performance and/or professional development needs of people in their teams. Effective leaders need to be flexible in how they manage individuals, choosing their approach depending on the situation and individual they are dealing with. Their analysis of how to proceed will be based on the goals that have to be achieved and knowledge of the people in their team. Formal evidence from data analysis, lesson observations or appraisal review meetings may determine what is needed but decisions will also arise instinctively, based on day-to-day observation and discussion with colleagues. Being able to use different styles effectively is dependent on well-developed inter-personal skills and emotional intelligence.

The need for flexibility

From the models presented in chapter 3 it is possible to see that most people as leaders are likely to have a particular approach or style that comes most naturally to them. Their preferred approach might work well with some colleagues but not others. If their approach shows extreme traits (e.g. over controlling or laissez-faire) it will be counter-productive and inhibit the creation of a high performing team. A look at a case study will help to illustrate how particular ways of working can prevent teachers performing as well as they might. If this happens, the middle leader must take at least some of the blame.

Case study

Below are the imaginary reflections of two newly qualified teachers. They are set out in the form of a conversation between the two.

What do their views tell us about the leadership style of their heads of department?

'Well, my first half-term at Leafy Glades Comprehensive certainly has been a baptism by fire. I feel ready for a good rest. Don't misunderstand me, the pupils are generally fine. There are a few lively characters, of course, but I met youngsters worse than them on my final placement. It's the department that leaves a lot to be desired!'

'What do you mean? Don't you get on with your head of department?'

'It isn't as though my head of department isn't supportive. In fact, he's very friendly indeed. It's just that he doesn't seem to have got his act together and, as such, the department seems really disorganized. I do get on with my head of department; he's not at all aloof, but he doesn't really behave like my head of department on placement.'

'What do you mean?'

'Well, on teaching practice my head of department was my mentor and gave really good, practical advice. I thought that this would continue during my first year of teaching but Chris, my new head of department, just leaves me to get on with it. He asks me how I'm doing but we never really talk in detail about my teaching because the meetings I should be having with him are usually cancelled. I've no idea how well I'm doing really. Chris praises me but he seems to praise everyone all the time, so I don't read too much into that. Another thing, I've asked for a departmental handbook on several occasions, only to be told that it is being rewritten, and the so-called schemes of work I was provided with are little more than lists of topics. Frankly, I feel the schemes I wrote on my placement are better, but I can hardly tell Chris that.'

'What about the other teachers in the team, are they just as bad?'

'It's difficult to say as I hardly see them. You see, there's no real departmental base and the History teachers only seem to get together once a fortnight when departmental meetings are scheduled.'

'At least you have regular meetings, then?'

'Yes, but they don't accomplish much. There's no agenda, people seem to wander in at whatever time they like so we never start the meetings on time. In fact, the head of department is usually late himself. He's usually been talking to some student about their work. That's part of the problem, I think, he tries to be helpful to everyone, but his organization is weak. He doesn't seem to have any sense of priorities. For example, when a meeting does eventually get underway people will chip in with all kinds of issues and anecdotes and the really important things seem to get forgotten. I find it very frustrating and I get anxious about the lack of clear decisions. The others seem to cope with it, though. They've been at the school a long time and just seem to do their own thing. I think I'd call it "muddling through". I do feel dreadful speaking about Chris like this, as he really is a very caring person. His heart is in the right place. He even sent me a card at the end of my first half term, thanking me for my hard work.'

'That is nice. I don't think Julie, my head of department, would do that. She sounds like the complete opposite of your Chris.'

'What do you mean?'

'Well, the department really is very well organized. You'll remember how impressed I was with that when I went for interview at Green Meadows; detailed schemes of work, the same text books for everyone to use, immaculate wall displays and so on. But Julie is not what I would call a warm person. I don't think I could turn to her if I had a personal problem and she is rather thin with her praise.'

'That's so different to Leafy Glades, I wish we had some clear direction on which books to use.'

'Yes, but it can go too far. I feel as though I have no freedom to experiment. After all, part of being a teacher is using your judgement about what a class needs. I used to enjoy preparing teaching materials on placement but Julie doesn't encourage that. In fact, she observed a lesson where I'd organized brilliant group work but she said I should have stuck to the textbook. That left me feeling rather deflated.'

'Is Julie very traditional then?'

'I'm not sure. I think it might have more to do with not wanting her team to deviate from agreed schemes of work. This comes across in meetings. They are so well organized but rigid. We always have an agenda and everyone turns up on time but there isn't any real discussion. People listen to Julie giving instructions; there's no real debate. I think people find it difficult to challenge Julie because she seems to work so hard. She prepares such detailed documents and schemes I just can't believe she has time for any life beyond school.'

'My head of department certainly has a social life. He's quite happy to share that with colleagues.'

'Julie is a perfectionist. She's devoted to her job and she expects everyone else to be the same. I've felt under pressure this term because of it. She seems to be scrutinizing my work more closely than my mentor on placement did, which hasn't exactly boosted my confidence. In fact, on one occasion I hadn't remembered to return a set of textbooks to the store room and she got really quite shirty about it.'

'I've just had a funny thought.'

'What's that?'

'Maybe we'll be heads of department one day and NQTs will be pulling us to pieces like this.'

'Yes, but hopefully we'll learn from the likes of Chris and Julie and make a better job of things.'

Reflection

While Chris and Julie are imaginary characters, leaders similar to both of them do exist. Chris displays many of the characteristics associated with a laissez-faire manager and Julie seems strongly task-orientated. Both have strengths as well as weaknesses.

Make a list of their strengths and weaknesses. Would you like to work for either of them? If not, why not? Do you recognize any of your behaviours in Chris or Julie?

There may be other points you have noted that could be added to Table 4.1 and 4.2. The interesting thing is that both leaders are failing to develop their teams, provide effective support and usefully involve colleagues, despite their very different styles. Both leaders could improve. Chris needs training in organization and communication as a priority, and Julie needs to be helped to explore people management and team building. Before this could happen, of course, both would need to be genuinely self-critical and want to improve their performance. We should also note that the senior leaders at Leafy Glades and

TABLE 4.1 Chris: Strengths and weaknesses

Strengths	Weaknesses
• Caring • Kind • Thoughtful • Presents a human face to colleagues	• Lacks organizational skills • Lacks time-management skills • Fails to prioritize • Fails to usefully involve colleagues • Fails to provide *useful* support • Fails to give a sense of direction • Fails to develop team members

TABLE 4.2 Julie: Strengths and weaknesses

Strengths	Weaknesses
• Hard working and efficient • Good at administration • Good organizational skills • Gives clear instructions • Has a clear sense of direction	• Lacks flexibility • Lacks empathy • Fails to build confidence in team members • Fails to provide *useful* support • Fails to develop team members • Fails to usefully involve colleagues

Green Meadows seem to have been less than effective if two middle leaders with such easily identifiable weaknesses exist.

Situational leadership

According to Blanchard (1994), situational leadership theory is based on the notion that there is no single 'best' style of leadership. Effective leadership is task-relevant, and the most successful leaders are those that adapt their leadership style to the level of capability of the individual they are attempting to lead or influence. Effective leadership varies, not only with the person being influenced or managed, but also with the task, job or function that needs to be accomplished.

As you get to know your team you will make judgements about both their level of skill (ability, knowledge, and aptitude) and level of commitment (confidence and motivation). A simple diagram such as Figure 4.1 can help you visualize where team members are. When plotting their positions do remember that individuals could well end up in different boxes for different aspects of their work. However, some generalizations are possible. NQTs will typically

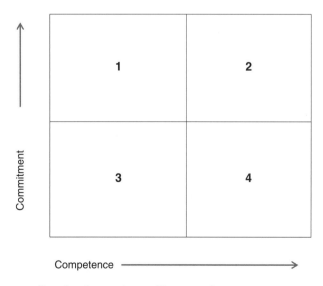

FIGURE 4.1 The commitment and competence of team members.

be found in box 1 as they will be enthusiastic and committed but lacking in refined skills. In box 2 will be your high-performing teachers who show both high levels of competence and commitment (use them to coach others). Box 4 will contain experienced teachers who have a high degree of competence but have lost their enthusiasm for the job (try making them responsible for supporting NQTs with very specific tasks). In box 3 will be your most challenging teachers. It is teachers from this box who prove very difficult to develop and who are likely candidates for formal capability procedures if your efforts to help them improve have no impact (see chapter 11).

Action point

Categorize your team in terms of the 4 boxes in Figure 4.1.

If anyone is in box 4 a difficult conversation is needed (see chapter 11).

In broad terms, leaders select from a combination of directing, supporting, coaching and delegating when managing individuals in their team, depending on the level of their skill and commitment. A leader who is respected for being consistently professional will find it much easier to slip between the situational leadership styles outlined in Table 4.3.

All of these styles have their uses for middle leaders and experienced team leaders move so easily between them that individuals on the receiving end are often unaware of different approaches being used with different team members. If they are aware they are rarely disgruntled by it, as skilful managers are operating within a culture of trust and support that they have created. Indeed, in an effective team it will not just be the team leader who is using these styles but all colleagues, as they support each other.

A consideration of these four styles reveals a balance between directive behaviour and supportive behaviour. Directive behaviour involves telling people what to do, how to do it, when to do it, and then monitoring performance. Supportive behaviour involves listening to people, providing support and encouragement, and facilitating involvement in decision making. Different circumstances and different individuals require different combinations of directive and supportive behaviour but in general middle leaders try to move

TABLE 4.3 Situational leadership styles

Directing	Coaching	Supporting	Delegating
The leader provides very clear and specific direction and closely monitors results achieved	The leader directs and supervises but also explains decisions, encourages suggestions and supports progress	The leader facilitates and supports team members in decision making and accomplishing tasks	The leader delegates responsibility for decision making and task completion to team members

colleagues from requiring direction to accepting delegated responsibility. A good NQT mentor, for example, will often move through these four approaches (from left to right in Figure 4.3) as the NQT develops. In general the styles can be applied to team members as shown in Table 4.4.

Typically, a directing style would be used when inducting new teachers or support staff into certain departmental procedures or when providing absolute clarity about how something must be done. A coaching style might be used with colleagues who have been identified as under-performing in some aspect of their work or to raise an already good performance to an even higher standard (coaching within a classroom can be especially powerful for developing specific aspects of pedagogy or moving lessons from good to outstanding). A supporting style is used to encourage and motivate. It often means working with someone to ensure a task is completed to the standard required. Delegation is used with capable and committed colleagues and is especially useful for providing ambitious and competent people with experiences that might help them gain promotion to leadership posts. However, it is important to remember that people's level of competence and commitment can vary with different aspects of their jobs. It is quite possible, for example, to find very competent and committed teachers who nevertheless lack well developed ICT skills or data analysis skills and may need coaching or supporting in this area. Equally, newly qualified teachers may bring high levels of ICT skills into a department, even though they will need directing in departmental procedures. The key thing for the leader is to be flexible and use an approach that is *fit for purpose.*

The same situational leadership styles can be applied when working with teachers and support staff; middle leaders must not be reluctant to develop support staff. They are usually keen to do the best they can for the students they support and welcome clear guidance and direction, especially when they are new to their role. Time spent with support staff should be regarded as an investment that will pay dividends in the future. Ofsted (2010) found that – when effectively deployed and developed – teaching assistants can make a clear difference to students' outcomes.

Middle leaders who have to deal with members of their teams who are under-performing usually find this the most stressful and difficult aspect of their work. Helping all colleagues to improve their performance can be very rewarding but struggling colleagues who resist support pose a particular

TABLE 4.4 Situational style and characteristics of team member

Style	Characteristics of team member
Directing or telling (provides clarity)	Low level of competence and low level of commitment
Coaching or selling (builds competence)	Basic level of competence and variable level of commitment
Supporting or participating (builds commitment)	High level of competence but variable level of commitment
Delegating (empowers)	High level of competence and high level of commitment

challenge. Middle leaders who fail to address their development needs let down not just the struggling colleague but the students in their care. Further guidance for situations where there are serious weaknesses in the work of a team member is provided in chapter 11.

Consciously using different styles of leadership

We discussed in chapter 1 that middle leadership is about more than managing and organizing a department or team; raising standards and strengthening teaching and learning are now crucial. This involves building a clear vision and working with and through team members to achieve goals. The styles used by effective leaders in all walks of life are well researched and have been actively disseminated through the National College for Teaching and Leadership (formerly NCSL) for some years. These styles are:

> **Coercive, Authoritative, Affiliative, Democratic, Pace-setting, Coaching**

Coercive

The aim when using this style is to seek immediate compliance. The leader uses lots of directives rather than directions, expects compliance, controls tightly, monitors regularly, relies on negative corrective feedback, and imposes lots of sanctions with few rewards.

This style is useful for simple straightforward tasks that are non-negotiable, for example, clearing schools when a fire alarm sounds. It is sometimes used when efforts to use more inclusive styles have failed.

Authoritative

The aim of this style is to provide long-term direction and vision for staff. The leader develops and articulates the vision (with opportunities for team input) and sees selling the vision as important. Colleagues are presented with clear evidence, analysis and appeal to moral purpose. The authoritative style involves setting clear standards and monitoring against these. A balance of positive and negative feedback is used by authoritative leaders.

It is useful when a team leader is moving a department in a new direction or when a new initiative is being discussed and introduced.

Affiliative

The aim of using this style is to create harmony amongst staff in a team. The leader is most concerned with promoting friendly interactions, placing an emphasis on staff personal needs rather than objectives/standards, caring for the whole person and avoiding performance related confrontations. Affiliative leaders tend to praise personal characteristics as much as performance.

This style is useful for getting to know staff and understanding how things are done. It is a useful default style for day-to-day behaviour but long-term the affiliative style used alone *can hold back progress as it fails to offer challenge.*

Democratic

The aim of this style is to build commitment among staff and generate new ideas. The leader encourages participation and seeks consensus; the aim is commitment through ownership. The style is commonly found in small and very high performing teams in the creative industries.

In schools it is useful when the vision is clear but actions for getting there are not so clear or more ownership by followers is required. Aspects of the democratic style are useful day to day and can be very effective when combined with the insistence on high standards associated with the pace-setting and authoritative styles. The use of the democratic style alone can result in acceptance of the mediocre.

Pace-setting

The aim of this style is to accomplish tasks to a high standard and/or to bring about rapid change. The leader leads by example, demonstrates high standards, expects others to know the rationale behind what is being modelled, is apprehensive about delegating, has little sympathy with poor performance and rescues a situation when there are difficulties.

This style is useful when managing change that must be accomplished quickly. It will work short term if team members have the skills required to perform to the level required.

Coaching

The aim of coaching is to support the long-term professional development of others. The leader helps staff identify their unique strengths and weaknesses, encourages staff to establish long-term development goals, reaches agreement on the way ahead, provides on-going advice and feedback and may trade immediate standards of performance for long-term development.

Coaching is useful when working with newly qualified teachers and those who need to improve aspects of pedagogy. Done well coaching can significantly improve teachers' performance as well as their self-belief. Unlike some of the other styles, coaching is associated with successfully embedding the changes in behaviour being encouraged.

Further guidance on how to use each style is provided in Table 4.5. Coaching will be explored further in chapter 11.

TABLE 4.5 Different leadership styles and when to use them

Coercive	Authoritative	Affiliative	Democratic	Pace-setting	Coaching
Most effective when: • Applied to relatively straightforward tasks • Used in crisis situations • Deviations from policies and procedures will result in serious problems • All else has failed with underperforming/problem employees	*Most effective when:* • A new direction or the development of new standards is required • The leader is perceived to be the 'expert' • Team members or people undertaking new tasks depend on the leader to give guidance	*Most effective when:* • Used as a part of a repertoire, this includes democratic, coaching and authoritative • There is a lot of interpersonal conflict within the department • Giving personal support to others • Getting diverse or conflicting groups to work in harmony	*Most effective when:* • Team members are highly competent • Team members possess critical information • Other people have clearer ideas about the best approach • Authoritative style has already been used to create a compelling vision	*Most effective when:* • Team members are highly motivated, competent, know their jobs and need little direction • Quick results are required • Acting as a role model to develop a similar team	*Most effective when:* • Colleagues acknowledge a difference in level of performance and where it should be • Give behavioural feedback to others to improve performance • Support team members in their professional development
To increase effectiveness: • Give direct orders • Set strict standards for behaviour and performance • Be decisive – the leader is in charge and must communicate what is required both verbally and non-verbally • Establish procedures that will provide quick and direct information concerning current events and their impact • Point out what behaviour does not meet the expected and agreed standards • Insist on adherence to the policies and procedures	*To increase effectiveness:* • Communicate the vision, targets, policies and procedures clearly to colleagues; make sure that all are clear about the core purpose of the department or school • Ensure that the goals and targets are reflected in everyone's expectations and actions • Clarify the vision and make it explicit at every opportunity • Solicit input from others, asking for ideas, thoughts, feelings and concerns in order to develop the vision • Provide specific, behavioural feedback on a regular, on-going basis • Explain the rationale behind decisions and actions	*To increase effectiveness:* • Build personal working relationships • Demonstrate concern and support for people and trust them to perform well • Try to understand and express concern about how others might feel • Encourage people to respect the individuality of others and accept them for who they are • Act to resolve interpersonal conflict	*To increase effectiveness:* • Hold information-sharing meetings to keep everyone involved and informed • Manage meetings well, including agendas, managing time, drawing reticent people in and holding back dominant individuals • Share decision making with teachers to encourage high performance • Build consensus through listening to views before coming to a decision	*To increase effectiveness:* • Model behaviour required of others • Insist on excellence • Be sure that when tasking a colleague with a role that it is something they can handle well • Let the team know that as long as they are meeting their performance targets they will be allowed to get on with their day-to-day activity. Support/guidance is available	*To increase effectiveness:* • Create development opportunities regularly • Actively support the development plans of others – especially career paths • Provide on-going developmental feedback, give balanced feedback in behavioural terms and make suggestions about areas of improvement • Negotiate performance targets and plans with colleagues • Strive to understand the longer-term aspirations of others and why it is important to them to achieve their targets

Emotional intelligence

Since the early 1990s Daniel Goleman and others have published research results to suggest that leaders' feelings play an important role in what they do and the decisions they make. Emotional intelligence means having the ability to manage one's own emotions while being sensitive to the needs of other people. Emotional intelligence includes not only our emotions, but the moods and feelings we display during personal interactions. Mayer and Salovney (1997: 12) define emotional intelligence as 'the ability to perceive emotions, to access and generate emotions so as to assist thought, to understand emotions and emotional knowledge, and to reflectively regulate emotions so as to promote emotional and intellectual growth'. George (2008) suggested that there are four dimensions of emotional intelligence: expressing emotions, using them to improve decision making, knowledge about emotions, and managing emotions. A middle leader's emotional intelligence skills are vital for managing and motivating their team and are used when deciding which leadership style to use with a particular colleague. In the application of the style great subtlety and nuance can be involved.

Emotional intelligence is often misunderstood, which can result in some people believing they are not 'naturally' equipped to be emotionally intelligent. Firstly, people who use emotional intelligence well are not pleasant all of the time. They will certainly be positive and upbeat and will understand the importance of spreading good cheer. However, there will be occasions when they are challenging and engage in difficult conversations. Emotional intelligence involves a heightened sensitivity to the needs of other people and sometimes having a challenging conversation is what is needed to assist a person in being effective. Secondly, people who use emotional intelligence well do not always express their feelings openly. Instead, emotionally intelligent leaders learn to manage feelings and express them appropriately. For example, middle leaders who regularly allow their anger or frustration to show in an outburst of emotion are not likely to be highly respected by their team. Thirdly, emotional skills are not fixed. They can be developed and refined through repeated use. For example, new middle leaders often fear confronting under-performance in others, believing they will not succeed with their challenge or they will not be emotionally resilient enough to manage the aftermath. Once they have succeeded in managing a challenging conversation effectively (by managing their emotional state and being very aware of the emotional state of the colleague being challenged) their self-belief grows and they are no longer daunted by the prospect of challenging others when necessary. The more they challenge the more successful they become at it as they learn and practise the emotional rules involved.

So-called 'competency frameworks' have been produced as a means of unpacking in some detail what emotional intelligence involves. The Consortium for Research on Emotional Intelligence in Organizations (www.eiconsortium. org) has distilled the findings from various sources on emotional intelligence into a framework, which I have modified to suit a school context (below).

Reflection

Use the framework below to reflect on your own use of emotional intelligence. Produce a plan for working on areas you currently find most challenging.

Personal competence

Self-awareness

Emotional awareness: Recognizing one's emotions and their effects
People with this competence:

- Know which emotions they are feeling and why
- Realize the links between their feelings and what they think, do, and say
- Recognize how their feelings affect their performance
- Have a guiding awareness of their values and goals

Accurate self-assessment: Knowing one's strengths and limitations
People with this competence are:

- Aware of their strengths, weaknesses and areas for development
- Reflective, learning from experience
- Open to candid, evidence-based feedback, new perspectives, continuous learning, and self-development
- Able to show a sense of humour and perspective about themselves

Self-confidence: Sureness about one's self-worth and capabilities
People with this competence:

- Present themselves with self-assurance; have presence
- Can voice views that are unpopular and go out on a limb for what is right
- Are decisive, able to make sound decisions despite uncertainties and pressures

Self-regulation

Self-control: Managing disruptive emotions and impulses
People with this competence:

- Manage their impulsive feelings and distressing emotions well
- Stay composed, positive, and unflappable even in trying moments
- Think clearly and stay focused under pressure

Trustworthiness: Maintaining standards of honesty and integrity

People with this competence:

- Act ethically and are above reproach
- Build trust through their reliability and authenticity
- Admit their own mistakes and confront unethical actions in others
- Take tough, principled stands even if they are unpopular

Conscientiousness: Taking responsibility for personal performance
People with this competence:

- Meet commitments and keep promises
- Hold themselves accountable for meeting their objectives
- Are organized and careful in their work

Adaptability: Flexibility in handling change
People with this competence:

- Smoothly handle multiple demands, shifting priorities, and rapid change
- Adapt their responses and tactics to fit fluid circumstances
- Are flexible in how they see events

Innovativeness: Being comfortable with and open to novel ideas and new information
People with this competence:

- Seek out fresh ideas from a wide variety of sources
- Entertain original solutions to problems
- Generate new ideas
- Take fresh perspectives and risks in their thinking

Self-motivation

Achievement drive: Striving to improve or meet a standard of excellence
People with this competence:

- Are results-oriented, with a high drive to meet their objectives and standards
- Set challenging goals and take calculated risks
- Pursue information to reduce uncertainty and find ways to do better
- Learn how to improve their performance

Initiative: Readiness to act on opportunities
People with this competence:

- Are ready to seize opportunities
- Pursue goals beyond what is required or expected of them
- Cut through red tape and bend the rules when necessary to get the job done

Optimism: Having a positive mind-set and 'can do' attitude; being persistent in pursuing goals despite obstacles and setbacks
People with this competence:

- Persist in seeking goals despite obstacles and setbacks
- Operate from hope of success rather than fear of failure
- See setbacks as due to manageable circumstance rather than a personal flaw
- Show resilience

Social competence

Social awareness

Empathy: Sensing others' feelings and perspective, and taking an active interest in their concerns
People with this competence:

- Listen well and are attentive to emotional cues
- Show sensitivity and understand others' perspectives
- Act based on understanding other people's needs and feelings

Developing others: Sensing what others need in order to develop, and bolstering their abilities.
People with this competence:

- Acknowledge and reward people's strengths, accomplishments, and development
- Offer useful feedback and identify people's needs for development
- Mentor, coach, and offer opportunities that challenge and develop people's skills
- Find ways of celebrating the success of individuals in the team

Maximising potential through diversity: Cultivating opportunities through using the talents of all
People with this competence:

- Respect and relate well to people from varied backgrounds and with different skill-sets
- Understand diverse worldviews and are sensitive to group differences
- See diversity as opportunity, creating an environment where diverse people can thrive
- Challenge prejudice, bias and intolerance

Political awareness: Reading a group's emotional currents and power relationships

People with this competence:

- Accurately read key power relationships
- Detect crucial social networks
- Understand the forces that shape views and actions
- Accurately read situations and organizational and external realities

Social skills

Influence: Using effective tactics for persuasion
    People with this competence:

- Are skilled at persuasion
- Fine-tune presentations to appeal to the listener
- Use a range of strategies to build consensus and support

Communication: Sending clear and convincing messages
    People with this competence:

- Are effective in registering emotional cues and attuning their message accordingly
- Deal with difficult issues straightforwardly
- Listen well, seek mutual understanding, and welcome sharing of information fully
- Foster open communication and stay receptive to bad news as well as good

Leadership: Inspiring and guiding groups and people
    People with this competence:

- Articulate and create enthusiasm for a shared vision and mission
- Step forward to lead as needed, regardless of position
- Guide the performance of others while holding them accountable
- Lead by example

Change catalyst: Initiating or managing change
    People with this competence:

- Recognize the need for change and work to remove barriers
- Challenge the status quo
- Champion the change and enlist others in its pursuit
- Model the change expected of others

Conflict management: Negotiating and resolving disagreements

People with this competence:

- Handle difficult people and tense situations with diplomacy and tact
- Spot potential conflict, bring disagreements into the open, and seek resolutions
- Encourage debate and open discussion
- Orchestrate win-win solutions

Building bonds: Nurturing productive relationships
People with this competence:

- Cultivate and maintain extensive informal networks
- Seek out relationships that are mutually beneficial
- Build rapport
- Show concern for colleagues

Collaboration and cooperation: Working with others toward shared goals
People with this competence:

- Balance a focus on task with attention to relationships
- Collaborate, sharing plans, information, and resources
- Promote a friendly, cooperative climate
- Spot and nurture opportunities for collaboration

Team capabilities: Creating group synergy in pursuing collective goals
People with this competence:

- Model team qualities such as respect, helpfulness, and cooperation
- Draw all members into active and enthusiastic participation
- Build team identity and commitment
- Protect the group and its reputation; share credit

Summary

Effective leaders need to be able to deal sensitively with people, recognizing individual needs and taking account of these in securing a consistent team approach. This involves the flexible use of directing, coaching, supporting and delegating with team members, depending on the particular individuals and the specific issues being dealt with. Successful middle leaders move between styles with sensitivity and tact, so as to help the professional development of their colleagues and task accomplishment. Effective leaders are very self-aware and understand the emotions of those in their teams. They use their emotional intelligence to inform the subtle and nuanced application of styles from coercive, authoritative, affiliative, democratic, pace-setting and coaching according to need.

5

Working together
Building a high-performing team

Introduction

Many teams exist in the average secondary school. Some teams are permanent, for example departments, faculties, year teams and the SLT, although membership changes as a result of staff being promoted, staff retiring or internal restructuring. Other teams are temporary, for example working groups established to write a particular policy document or plan a school production. Some teams operate very formally, for example governing bodies, whereas other teams can be quite informal, a group of colleagues who have taken on responsibility for organizing staff social events, for instance. Some teams have limited membership, for example the SLT usually comprises the head, deputy heads, assistant heads and the bursar. Other teams may offer open access, for instance a working party on behaviour. Membership of some teams is voluntary but membership of other teams is contractual. In secondary schools most teachers belong to at least two teams, a subject team and a pastoral team.

Some teams are more effective than others. Indeed, it would be fair to conclude that many teams are not really teams at all but simply groups of people placed together because they teach the same subject or are responsible for classes containing pupils in the same year group. In such groups the activities of individuals frequently limit, rather than enhance, the effectiveness of the whole. There may be jealousies between members, information suppressed and cooperation withheld because members see themselves as being in competition with each other. Alternatively, there may be apathy and indifference resulting from a lack of team vision or sense of direction.

A major challenge for middle leaders is to transform a group of people they have responsibility for, lumped together under some functional umbrella, into a successful team. Teams thrive best in collaborative cultures (see chapter 2) and in situations where the team leader is committed to the development of each individual (see chapters 4 and 11). Even then, there is still much effort and skill needed in creating and maintaining a genuine team. Where really effective teams do exist, the support that team members receive from each other, the

rapport that exists and the sense of working for common goals is very powerful. In fact, a successful team becomes very visible to others working in the
school and it is not unusual for pupils to notice and comment upon this. It is
a real achievement when the 'can do', positive spirit generated by a successful
team is absorbed by pupils and begins to influence their behaviour.

What makes a group of people a team?

Vision and sense of direction

Having shared goals is the first thing that distinguishes teams from groups.
This is why it is so important that the team leader has a clear sense of direction.
This should be provided partly by the vision or mission of the school, with the
team leader's job being to translate the vision into something meaningful at
team level. A clear sense of direction will also come from the team leader being
certain about what the team is uniquely contributing to the education of young
people. If you are in charge of History then what is your vision of excellent
History teaching? What can your subject uniquely contribute to the education of young people? If you are a year head what is your vision of successful
pastoral care? What uniquely can form teachers contribute to the education
of young people? These questions are fundamental and need to be discussed
and answers agreed upon by team members. Shared ownership of the vision
brings both a sense of direction and an under-pinning philosophy to the work
of the team.

The behaviour of the team leader

It is important that leaders are able to give their teams space for development,
can listen to the views of others and can encourage participation. Team leaders
should encourage collaboration by adopting a democratic style as often as possible. They must be self-critical and committed to the idea that their authority
comes more from their behaviour and the example they set than from their
title. Team leaders will want individuals in their team to progress and develop
and will be skilful at directing, coaching, supporting and delegating, as appropriate. The team leader will be visible and accessible and will strive to build the
self-esteem of all team members.

The extent to which people pull together

A team exists if members embrace the team vision and work together to
achieve it. The result is team members becoming interdependent, with particular strengths of individuals recognized and used to the benefit of the whole
team and the pupils. Team members also support each other and just as the

leader looks for opportunities to develop each member so members look for opportunities to develop other members and the team leader. This does not mean that there are never any disagreements. Open debate is encouraged and is one of the things that helps to clarify team values and the direction the team is going in. Team successes are celebrated publicly as are the achievements of individual team members. It is not unusual to hear laughter coming from meetings of successful teams. This indicates a relaxed rapport has been achieved and is in no way at odds with a team's serious purpose.

Open lines of communication

Team members talk to each other about issues and there is an atmosphere in which positive and negative feedback can be given. People are open-minded to other people's arguments and new ideas are encouraged and debated. Individual team members are assertive but not aggressive and conflicting viewpoints are seen as normal. Indeed, lively debate is seen as a constructive feature of decision making. While lines of communication are open there are also clear procedures for holding meetings and making decisions.

Regular reviews of progress

Teams are not frightened of reviewing progress. Successes are celebrated and failures are analysed so as to build on good practice and avoid repeating mistakes. All team members are involved in development planning and target setting.

An effective team combines creativity and energy to produce an output greater than the sum of its parts – this is known as *synergy*. You may have experienced synergy as part of a team putting on a public performance such as a show or maybe during an Ofsted inspection. What probably sticks in your mind is the real sense of working together for a common goal. Synergy is what good team leaders try and create in the everyday work of their teams.

A quick checklist for considering how well a team functions is provided by Hardingham (1985) using the acronym PERFORM. This has been modified to suit a school context in Figure 5.1.

The team life cycle

As well as understanding the difference between a team and a group, it is useful to understand the different stages that teams go through as they develop. Research has shown that these stages are fairly predictable. Recognizing them can be especially helpful to new middle leaders as taking over a team can often

Productivity	Is the team getting enough done? Is there evidence that the work being done is raising pupil achievement?
Empathy	Do the team members feel comfortable with one another? Do they encourage one another to succeed?
Roles and goals	Do they know what they're supposed to be doing?
Flexibility	Are they open to outside influence, willing regularly to review roles and keen to innovate?
Openness	Do they say what they think? Are meetings lively with plenty of debate?
Recognition	Do they praise one another and celebrate achievement?
Morale	Do people want to be in this team? Do team members spread good cheer?
Common indicators of problems in these areas are:	
Productivity	A team leader in a bad temper; performance targets not met
Empathy	No coffee at team meetings; tension between members
Roles and goals	Puzzled faces in meetings; unfinished tasks
Flexibility	Annoyed outsiders talking about the 'fortress mentality'; failure to embrace new ideas; complacency
Openness	Silence in meetings
Recognition	Backbiting; jealousy; splinter groups
Morale	No laughter at meetings; everyone looking for new jobs; people clock-watch and religiously stick to 1265 hours and contractual duties

FIGURE 5.1 Effective team checklist.

result in the initial stages of team formation being played out, even when most team members are not new.

Stage 1 – Forming

At this stage the newly created team is a group of people who are getting the measure of each other. They are concerned with 'who fits where'. Group members may exhibit self-conscious politeness, embarrassment, stilted communication or false enthusiasm.

Stage 2 – Storming

At this stage team members' different personalities and approaches to work can begin to clash. There is concern over 'how we work together' and a certain amount of 'juggling for position'. Group members may come into conflict and there is likely to be heated debate and discussion. Nevertheless, things begin to be achieved.

Stage 3 – Norming

At this stage the 'rules of the game' become clear and the members of the team begin to exhibit group behaviour. Goals are focused on effectively and a more relaxed and purposeful atmosphere emerges.

Stage 4 – Performing

The team now settles into a comfortable way of working and decisions and agreements are reached more easily. There is a feeling of confidence and achievement, with individuals in the team clear about roles and responsibilities.

With some teams in school these stages are easily recognized. Working parties, formed with a specific goal in mind, often follow this pattern. For established subject or year teams the cycle can be iterative, with teams switching between stages as they encounter new issues to resolve. In some ways the organization of schools around the academic year, with the long summer break, encourages teams to make a fresh start each September, especially as there are usually some newly appointed colleagues joining teams at this point. It is very important that middle leaders create opportunities for newcomers to contribute to team activity so that norming is accomplished quickly. Sadly, some teams never seem to develop beyond the storming stage.

Newly appointed middle leaders often feel vulnerable when taking over an established team. A successful team culture or ethos may have existed under the previous leader and some members will feel anxious by the prospect of the inevitable forming, storming and norming that will occur. A new leader is likely to be compared with the team leader they replace as new roles and ways of working evolve, making it a stressful time. It is important that new team leaders behave with tact and integrity and do not fall into the trap of feeling they have to dominate others in order to prove their leadership capabilities. As was noted in chapter 3, a calm and professional approach is the way to earn respect from fellow team members.

Belbin's work on effective teams

Being a highly effective teacher (see chapter 3) is not easy. A single person cannot be all things to all people and rarely has all the qualities needed to be excellent in terms of both people and task management. Effective managers, therefore, draw upon the strengths of members of their teams to compensate for weakness they are aware of in themselves. The importance of using the strengths of all team members is summed up neatly in the phrase 'none of us is as smart as all of us'. Dr Belbin's work on team effectiveness is both fascinating and influential, providing useful insights into how *the whole can be greater than the sum of its parts*.

Through his work at the Management College, Henley, Belbin learned to recognize individuals who made a crucial difference to teams. He identified eight clear team-types and to these individuals he gave names. He went on to relate observed team behaviour to psychological traits, using psychometric tests. Belbin and his colleagues then constructed balanced teams containing the eight identified team-types. When set management challenges the balanced teams consistently performed more effectively than teams with random membership. When there were fewer than eight team members then people tended to play more than one role, as necessary.

Belbin's work provides convincing evidence that getting team composition right can be as important as appointing the right individual to be leader. While it is not possible easily to change the composition of teams in schools, a consideration of the team-types that exist in any team may be a very fruitful starting point for analysing the reasons for the under-performance of a particular team. A consideration of Belbin's eight team-types should enable middle leaders to recognize themselves and others in their teams. It is important to remember that the names Belbin chose for team-types are less important than the characteristics associated with them and no one type should be seen as superior to any others.

Chairman

Traits: stable, dominant, extrovert. S/he may not be the leader of the team so 'chairman' is a misleading term – but s/he certainly has team leadership qualities.

- Presides over the team and coordinates its efforts to meet targets
- Intelligent but not brilliant and not an outstandingly creative thinker
- Has self-discipline and integrity
- Has good authority and is often charismatic
- Not domineering but in control in a relaxed way
- Trusts people and is not jealous
- Recognizes the strengths of others and uses them to create a team
- Easy to talk to and a good listener
- A good communicator
- Capable of making decisions once everyone has had their say

Shaper

Traits: anxious, dominant, extrovert. S/he is likely to be the task leader, even if the chairman is the 'social leader'.

- Full of nervous energy
- Impulsive and impatient
- Easily frustrated

- Often has rows but does not harbour grudges
- Tries to unite ideas into feasible projects
- Self-confident on the outside but full of self-doubt
- Competitive
- Critical of vague and muddled thinking
- People often see the shaper as arrogant
- Can make a team feel uncomfortable but does make things happen

Plant

Traits: dominant, high IQ, introvert. Belbin discovered that an ineffective team could be improved by 'planting' one of this type in it.

- Full of original ideas and proposals
- Very imaginative in solving problems
- More concerned with major issues than detail
- Even though introverted s/he is forceful and uninhibited
- Can be prickly and critical of the ideas of others
- Bad at accepting criticism of own ideas

Monitor evaluator

Traits: high IQ, stable, introvert. Likely to be serious and not very exciting – main contribution is dispassionate analysis rather than creative ideas – the monitor evaluator will stop the team embarking on misguided projects.

- A constructive critic and clear thinker
- Not highly motivated
- Slow to reach a decision
- Can assimilate and interpret large volumes of complex written material
- Can be tactless when assessing the judgements of others
- Can lower team morale by being a damper
- Dependable but lacks warmth
- Judgement is rarely wrong

Company worker

Traits: stable and controlled, a practical organizer who turns the team's plans into manageable tasks.

- Sorts out objectives
- Logical
- Disciplined

- Has integrity
- Doesn't like rapidly changing situations
- Very well organized
- Efficient and systematic
- Can be over-competitive
- Always understands policies and knows what should be being done

Resource investigator

Traits: stable, dominant, extrovert. A very likeable member of the team – relaxed, sociable and enthusiastic.

- Tends to drop ideas as quickly as they are taken up
- Gathers information from outside the team
- Makes friends easily
- Diplomatic
- Quick to see the relevance of the ideas of others
- Ineffective without the stimulus of others
- Good under pressure but over relaxes when it eases

Team worker

Traits: stable, extrovert, low in dominance – very aware of the feelings and needs of team members and senses emotional undercurrents – helps to keep team morale up in a low key way.

- Knows about the private lives of team members
- Popular and likeable
- Good communicator and listener
- Loyal and supportive
- Promotes unity
- Dislikes friction and personal confrontation
- Uncompetitive
- Helps team unity
- Works behind the scenes to keep peace

Finisher

Traits: anxious, introvert – the finisher worries about what might go wrong and checks details almost obsessively

- Communicates sense of urgency to others
- Good self-control

- Intolerant towards casual members of the team
- Compulsive about meeting deadlines
- Can lower morale of team by spreading anxiety
- Can miss the bigger picture by concentrating on detail

Some years after his initial research, Belbin modified role titles and identified one extra role (Belbin 1993). These changes are summarized in Table 5.1.

Middle leaders in schools can probably recognize the behaviour of members of their teams from the points above and it would probably be beneficial, given the right team ethos, to conduct a fuller assessment of team members as a team development exercise. The important thing is that people identified as being a certain team-type should feel neither inferior nor superior as a result. For success, there is a critical role for each team-type and middle leaders should ensure colleagues are used appropriately. If teams are assessed and appear unbalanced in terms of the range of team-types identified then this should be discussed openly. Knowledge is power and although people can't change their personalities they can modify behaviour associated with their personality, if this is necessary to improve team performance. Clearly, any attempt to use Belbin's ideas would need to be handled with sensitivity and it would be unwise for a newly appointed middle leader to look to Belbin as a panacea for problems being encountered with team behaviour. However, an established team, led by a self-critical and respected middle leader, might well be able to

TABLE 5.1 Belbin's team roles

Title	Role	Characteristic
Chairperson	Coordinating	Calm, self-confident
Shaper	Team leading	Highly strung, 'driven'
Plant	Innovating	Thinker, innovator, individualistic
Monitor-evaluator	Critical thinking	Sober, unemotional, able to assess, judge and evaluate
Implementer	Getting work done	Practical, common sense, organizing ability
Team worker	Personal relationships	Socially orientated, responds well to people
Completer	Keeping group on its toes	Orderly, painstaking, determined
Resource investigator	Keeping in touch with people outside the organization	Extrovert, wide contacts, likes making links
Specialist	Providing knowledge and skills in rare supply	Single minded, self-starting, dedicated

use Belbin's ideas as a way of gaining both individual self-knowledge and becoming a more effective team.

The materials needed to assess a team using Belbin's approach to profiling are available commercially, but there are other possibilities if your aim is to engage your team in some detailed self-evaluation of personality traits and preferred ways of working. This could be done in a very thorough way using a psychometric questionnaire such as the Myers-Briggs Type Indicator or in a very lighthearted way using a device such as 'Packtypes', where people's traits are thrown up through a card sort exercise and then associated with a breed of dog. A quick internet search will locate all of these tools and more; the point about using any of them is that greater self-awareness can aid understanding and productivity in a team by helping individuals reflect on their own behaviour and strengths and understand how others see them.

What can go wrong with teams?

All kinds of things can go wrong with teams. Team leaders will only improve team ethos and performance by reflecting honestly and critically on the behaviour of their team. A good starting point is to consider your own behaviour – a good team leader usually manages to produce an effective team; a poor team leader usually blames other team members when things are going badly.

Meetings

For many people 'teamwork' and meetings go hand in hand. It is important to realize that meetings can easily wreck, rather than build, teams if they are unnecessary, unproductive and badly managed. Further advice is given later in this chapter, but it is worth mentioning at this point that the leader is not automatically the best person to chair every team meeting. It is true that most people assume the leader will chair team meetings because being the chair goes with the role. However, there may be occasions when another member of the team acts as chair, enabling the manager to become one among equals. This is one practical way of encouraging both collegiality and staff development. Whoever chairs a meeting, it is important to ensure that 'action points' are recorded, with named individuals clear about what they have agreed to do and by when.

Conflict

Conflict in teams can occur in situations where there is rivalry between colleagues or fundamental differences of philosophy. Conflict associated with the 'storming' stage of team development is likely to pass, but if conflict is sustained, repetitive and hurtful to individuals it will undermine the team and prevent the growth of a collaborative team culture. This kind of conflict is quite different to the healthy debate and exchange of ideas associated with dynamic teams. Sometimes conflict can result from personality clashes, where two team members dislike one another intensely. This kind of temperamental incompatibility is best dealt with by speaking to each individual separately about the problem to agree a way forward. Defining their roles clearly can also help, as can praising each one for the particular strengths they bring to the team.

Complacency

In some teams there is little or no debate, little reflection and much defensiveness against criticism or challenge. Such groups have convinced themselves that the team is always right and are only shaken from their complacency by something like a damning Ofsted report. It is most likely that such teams have seen little movement of staff over the years and have not been challenged by senior leaders through the appraisal process, target setting and departmental reviews. Complacency is a dangerous thing and this is one reason why appointing a new middle leader from outside the school in some circumstances makes more sense than promoting someone from within the team. A new manager joining such a team would need to work hard to change the culture and should not, in the short term, worry too much if team members seem nostalgic about the team they have lost.

Techniques that help teams to develop and succeed

Treating team members appropriately, as outlined in chapter 4, is important for getting the most out of individuals. However, as we have seen in this chapter, a team is more than the sum of its parts and there are certain practical devices that can assist in getting group members working as a team.

Brainstorms (thought showers)

Most teachers are aware of brainstorming – the generation of as many ideas as quickly as possible by a group of people – and many teachers use the technique effectively in their teaching. Brainstorming can be a useful team-building tool because it can be fun, it encourages contributions from all team members and it creates the kind of 'clean communication' that helps teams to become dynamic and creative. When a brainstorm goes well it builds confidence and gives a team a real sense of achievement. Brainstorming sessions are especially useful for helping to integrate newly appointed colleagues into a team. If brainstorms are to be successful it is important to remember that every idea is recorded; no idea is evaluated at the brainstorm stage and the team leader does not have to be the scribe.

The PEP talk

PEP stands for 'Planning Effective Performance'. It consists of three simple questions: What did we do that worked well? What did we do that didn't work well? What shall we do next time? PEP talks should focus on moving forward and should avoid recriminations. PEP talks can be long or short depending on the event or issue under review. They can be used to evaluate almost any team activity: field trips, public events and new courses are just three examples. Of course, it is vital that, having engaged a team in the PEP talk process, conclusions reached are acted upon. If they are not then people will simply become cynical and put no real effort into the process when it is used again.

Development plans and action plans

Development planning is now well established in schools and the cycle of *audit – plan – implement – review* is used with varying degrees of success. Development planning must be a collective activity. Sharing views about what has been achieved and deciding together on objectives, individual responsibilities and success criteria is crucial to team effectiveness. It is also vital if teachers are to feel both empowerment and accountability. There are various tools than can be used to engage the team actively in the process (see chapter 8).

Self-assessment and reflection

As a middle leader it is important to reflect on your capacity for creating an effective team. I have included a number of scaled questions below, which should help you identify your strengths and weaknesses. These questions are based loosely on a series of questions by Maddux (1986) and modified to suit a school context.

Action point

Circle the number that best reflects where you fall on the scale.

The higher the number, the more the characteristic describes you. When you have finished total the numbers circled and look at the comment that goes with your score. Don't despair if your attitudes have generated negative comments. The important thing is to plan to modify your behaviour so that you are doing all you can to create an effective team.

If I could appoint a new member of my team I would select someone with good inter-personal skills ahead of someone with excellent academic qualifications.	7 6 5 4 3 2 1
I help my team develop a sense of ownership by involving them in problem solving, policy writing and goal setting.	7 6 5 4 3 2 1
I try to provide team spirit by encouraging colleagues to work with new team members on certain tasks.	7 6 5 4 3 2 1
I talk to people openly and honestly and encourage the same kind of communication in return.	7 6 5 4 3 2 1
I always try and keep my word. If I have promised a colleague something I always deliver because their trust is important to me.	7 6 5 4 3 2 1
I use activities such as brainstorms with my team as a means of generating trust and respect between team members.	7 6 5 4 3 2 1
I try and use directing, coaching, supporting and delegating as appropriate to individual team members.	7 6 5 4 3 2 1
I understand that conflict within groups is normal, but work to resolve it quickly and fairly before it can become destructive.	7 6 5 4 3 2 1
I believe people perform as a team when they know what is expected and what the benefits are.	7 6 5 4 3 2 1
I am not frightened of tackling team members who under perform.	7 6 5 4 3 2 1

What your score indicates

- A score between 60 and 70 indicates a positive attitude towards colleagues and the type of attitude needed to build and maintain a strong team. You appear to be an empowering leader, capable of raising and maintaining morale.
- A score between 40 and 59 is acceptable and with reasonable effort you should be able to lead an effective team. Even so, you should think carefully about your approach. Are there ways in which you can be even more positive with members of your team?
- A score below 40 means you need to examine your behaviour towards colleagues and reflect critically on your management philosophy. Do you praise enough? Do you empower? Do you act with integrity? Do you recognize the need to team build? Are you publicly enthusiastic?

Team meetings

Meetings are essential to the effective operation of a team. Sadly, far too many take place that are unproductive or even dysfunctional. Organizing successful meetings can be a demanding aspect of middle leadership and one that is sometimes a source of considerable stress to the inexperienced.

However, *effective* meetings have several advantages: they allow for clear communication; they improve staff skills in decision making; they provide a sense of involvement among team members; they improve job satisfaction; they increase commitment; and they ensure that leaders and their team are 'speaking the same language'. The essential thing is to make meetings productive.

Why meet at all?

The number of meetings held in a school will reflect the size and culture of the school. In most schools a schedule of meetings is drawn up before the academic year commences to ensure that all teams (academic, pastoral, key-stage etc.) are provided with fair and adequate meeting time within the 1265 hours of teachers' contracted time. This usually means having a rota of regular meetings. The advantage of this approach is that teams have regular scheduled meetings; the disadvantage is that there are some times in the year when meetings are not really needed and other times when additional meetings are needed because a team's workload is not evenly distributed throughout the year. For example, subject teams often require additional meetings when moderating GCSE course work. Ideally, there should be a schedule of meetings, with team leaders empowered to decide whether or not it is necessary to meet rather than feeling obliged to meet because of 1265 hours.

In a team where colleagues feel valued and trusted, there is likely to be flexibility over meetings, with meetings that are additions to those identified on the schedule being called *if necessary*. The important phrase here is *if necessary*. When colleagues can see the need for a meeting and when the meeting is conducted in a way that produces clear outcomes there will be little resentment about attending. However, when people are forced to attend irrelevant and unproductive meetings simply because they are on a schedule, a '1265 mentality' can result in which teachers are unwilling to attend meetings not on the schedule. This mentality is associated with the Newtonian culture described in chapter 2 and needs to be avoided at all costs.

If you decide to hold a meeting do all members of your team need to attend? If you are considering major issues or are brainstorming new ideas on policy and philosophy the answer is clearly 'yes'. However, there is little point in colleagues attending a meeting about the 'A' level syllabus if they are not and will not be involved in teaching it, for example. Thinking about the order of your agenda can help. By having information-giving and whole-team issues first all colleagues in the team can be involved, but then only those people connected with the agenda items that follow need remain. However, do bear in mind the points made about agenda writing given below. Try and make as many meetings as possible about teaching and learning. Meetings that deal purely with administrative matters can get bogged down with minor details and a weekly bulletin is a better way to communicate routine matters anyway. By focusing on pedagogy your meetings become central to your core business of ensuring high quality provision for students.

Different types of meeting

If meetings are to be effective then all team members need to understand their function. Middle leaders are required to plan, lead and participate in meetings that may have one or more of the following functions:

- To inform
- To decide
- To generate ideas
- To problem solve
- To consult
- To negotiate
- To plan
- To allocate
- To motivate

It is very important to be clear about the purpose(s) of a meeting and the balance within it. For example, it would be inappropriate to use a sixty-minute meeting simply for information giving. Likewise, in a meeting devoted to generating ideas (strategic discussion) it would be unproductive to get bogged down in the minutiae of how a new policy might work in detail (operational discussion). Strategic discussions would be best kept to one meeting with operational considerations for another. In this way more will be achieved.

Steps to effective meetings

Before the meeting

1. Plan the meeting carefully by asking the following questions:
   - Who should attend?
   - What is the purpose of the meeting?
   - Where and when will it be held?
   - How many items will be on the agenda?
   - What briefing papers are needed?
2. Prepare and send out the agenda and briefing papers well in advance of the meeting (a week is usually fine). Think carefully about the agenda. You might want routine business first because you only need certain colleagues to stay on and discuss later items that directly concern them. It is equally

possible that you have a major issue to discuss that concerns everyone. Should this be the first item on the agenda? If it isn't then there is a danger that routine matters and announcements will use up valuable time needed for discussing the major issue, unless the meeting is very tightly chaired. Ensure that there are not too many items on any one agenda; between three and five is usually a manageable number for a meeting of an hour. As team leader it is vital that you have prepared yourself for each item on the agenda so that you can provide clear thinking and answer any questions posed by the team.

3. Try to hold the meeting in a pleasant room and get there early to arrange the chairs. Different types of meeting work best with different seating arrangements (see below) and so you must ensure that the seating is *fit for purpose*. Providing refreshments is always appreciated by colleagues and helps to set a relaxed tone, as well as preventing late arrivals using the excuse that they were desperate for a drink and had to wait for the kettle to boil! Don't time your after-school meetings to start immediately the school bell goes. Give people ten minutes to gather their thoughts. A fifty-minute meeting that begins promptly at 3.40 is likely to be more productive than a sixty-minute meeting that is supposed to start at 3.30 but never does. A sloppy start to a meeting sets the wrong tone.

At the beginning of the meeting

1. Always start on time; this sets an appropriate businesslike tone and means you are more likely to finish on time. Remember, there is no conflict between having a relaxed and collaborative team ethos and being businesslike in meetings. People appreciate meetings that are run properly.

2. Clearly define roles within the meeting. Who is acting as chair, who is taking minutes and is anyone providing a specialist input? Although it is assumed that the team leader will be chair this doesn't have to be the case for every meeting. A team leader may wish to give a colleague the experience of running a meeting as part of their development, for example. If the meeting is a decision-making meeting where a vote is being taken the team leader might think it fairer to allow a colleague to chair so that they can express a view from the floor, with no danger of showing bias in the way they handle the discussion. It is a good idea to rotate minute writing as this spreads the work load, gives experience to newcomers and prevents the chair of the meeting giving a particular 'flavour' to the decisions made. On a practical note it is actually quite difficult for one person to effectively chair a meeting and make notes, however brief.

3. Review, revise and order the agenda. It may be that since the agenda was issued something urgent has occurred that needs addressing in preference to some routine items on the agenda, or a colleague who was due to contribute an item to the meeting may be ill, for example.

4. Remind colleagues of the time at which the meeting will end and, if necessary, remind them that there are time limits on certain agenda items. This helps to focus people's minds and, with effective chairing, prevents the meeting wandering off track.

5. Always review the action points from the previous meeting. If people are used to meetings being closed with clear action points and opened with a review of these it is more likely that they will be efficient in completing the action agreed. It also means that if action points have not been achieved some thought can be given to how best to move things forward. Being accountable to the team is an important aspect of the collegiate culture and being supported towards achieving goals is more likely if these goals are regularly reviewed.

6. If there are guests at your meeting or if you are chairing a meeting for the first time it is polite to ask all participants to introduce themselves. If you are chairing a one-off meeting it is important to ask all participants what they hope to get out of the meeting.

During the meeting

During the meeting the chairperson must adopt a style *fit for purpose* (see below), but whatever the nature of the meeting it is important to:

- Keep to time
- Keep people on task
- Ensure action points are clear

At the end of the meeting

1. Remind people of action points agreed upon during the meeting: who, what, when?

2. Set the date and time of the next meeting and develop a preliminary agenda. It might be that some non-essential items from the current meeting have been deferred or that a team member is going on a course and needs an opportunity to report back at the next meeting.

3. Evaluate the meeting. This does not mean asking everyone to complete a questionnaire! It simply means giving people the chance to say whether or not they feel the aims of the meeting have been met. If people feel disgruntled that an issue has not been adequately debated it is better that they say so rather than leaving the meeting unhappy and uncommitted to a decision made.

4. Close the meeting crisply and positively. Generally, it is important to finish on time or even a few minutes early. However, on occasions members may decide to prolong a meeting by an agreed amount so as to get business finished or to prevent the need for another meeting. There is a big difference

between meetings regularly overrunning due to being badly chaired and an occasional meeting being extended due to unforeseen difficulties with a particular item. Remember, though, that for some colleagues extending a meeting may be very inconvenient as they might have other commitments to meet. It is not fair to exclude people from participation simply because they cannot alter their domestic arrangements at the drop of a hat.

5. Clean up the room and rearrange the furniture.

After the meeting

1. Liaise with the minute taker, if appropriate, to ensure that the minutes are accurate and efficiently written up and distributed. With most colleagues you will simply need to thank them for taking the minutes but do nothing else, whereas with a new team member they may feel happier if you have seen the minutes before they are distributed to other colleagues. Keep the minutes brief by reducing each item on the agenda to outcomes: the agreed action points – who, when and where? In some schools a standardized pro-forma for minutes exists and administrative staff type minutes of meetings up. This is an excellent idea for two reasons. Firstly, a regular moan from teachers is that they do too much administration – here is one simple way senior leaders can be supportive in reducing administration. Secondly, minutes in a standardized form are easier for senior colleagues to digest and need only contain essential information, namely the agreed action points but not unnecessary detail about who said what. In schools where no such arrangements exist middle leaders would be advised to act together to explain the benefits of such a system to senior staff.

2. Monitor action points, as necessary, and begin to plan the next meeting. Some colleagues will not need to be reminded about what they have agreed to whereas others may benefit from questions on progress asked informally and others may need more overt support. As with so many other aspects of leadership, knowing your staff is essential and being flexible in your leadership style will pay dividends.

Some thoughts on chairing meetings

The success or failure of a meeting rests on how effectively the meeting is chaired. Usually, though not always, the team leader will be the person who chairs team meetings. The chairperson must fulfil a number of functions that make up the role. Firstly, there is a leadership role. This involves setting guidelines, exercising authority, summarizing discussions, insisting on facts before opinions and countering limited vision that can come sometimes result from a group being well established and comfortable. Secondly, there is a gate-keeper role. This involves protecting the weak and vulnerable, encouraging the nervous, motivating the uninterested, controlling the dominant and managing ramblers and jokers. Thirdly, there is a referee role, which involves keeping cool, staying neutral and managing conflict, while at the same time allowing healthy debate. Finally, there is an administrative role, which involves organizing the physical setting, keeping to time and ensuring notes are taken.

Effective chairing of meetings requires effective inter-personal skills. The chair must ensure that the atmosphere of the meeting is conducive to discussion and that members feel valued. Middle leaders need to develop skills in managing teams during meetings. This means taking the lead, establishing acceptable behaviour and setting a good example. A sense of humour is very useful for diffusing conflict in a meeting and careful planning should avoid many problems. A middle leader who has created a good team ethos with a culture of support, cooperation and debate usually manages meetings well. There is an element of the chicken and the egg in this, however, as it is often well managed meetings that have contributed to a positive team spirit in the first place.

Sometimes it is beneficial to have a facilitator rather than a chairperson, depending on the purpose of the meeting. If the aim of the meeting is to generate ideas or problem solve then a facilitator should be used. There are good reasons for the team leader not acting as facilitator and for a more neutral colleague to perform the role instead. It is almost impossible to run a fair, non-manipulative meeting when you have a personal investment in the subject matter. It is extremely difficult to objectively lead a group that is considering whether or not to discontinue a course that you introduced and have faith in, for example. Even if you try not to influence the group your body language is likely to reinforce those who hold the same views as you. Quite unintentionally, you might end up dominating the floor in your role as chairperson. A possible solution is to invite a fellow middle manager to act as a facilitator. They should, of course, have no preferences regarding outcomes of the meeting.

The facilitator needs to operate differently to a chairperson. They must be a neutral servant of the group and should not contribute or evaluate ideas. However, like a chairperson they must encourage all participants, protect individuals from personal attack and help the group arrive at a consensus. Facilitators make use of the following techniques to achieve their aims:

- Flip charts for recording ideas
- Brainstorming
- Boomeranging questions back to group members
- Taking 'straw polls' to see if a line is worth pursuing
- Using 'negative voting' to see what options cannot be lived with
- Sub-dividing the group for discussions
- Using open questions
- Using rounds to hear what everyone thinks

Some thoughts on seating

The arrangement of seats and tables sets the stage for a meeting and can influence what will happen. A circular pattern encourages a sense of warmth and togetherness. It is easy to make direct eye contact with everyone else and there is a sense of equality from the chair not being the focus of attention. The circle can be useful for informal discussions. However, whatever the mood of the group, it will be heightened by the circle. If anger or aggression is in the air, this negative energy will be aimed directly at individuals and can lead to heavy encounters. If the pattern is an oval, one person's energy is focused on the person opposite and is thereby critically restricted. When everyone faces towards the person at the end of the table the collective energy is aimed at one individual, which is not conducive to problem solving but is fine for a formal information-giving session.

One of the most effective ways to get a group to focus on a task is to seat the participants in a semi-circle facing the question written on a flip chart and facing the facilitator. The energy of the group is now directed towards the common problem. Ideally, the semi-circle should face away from the entrance to the room so that people coming in or leaving don't disrupt the flow of the meeting. The semi-circle is ideal for presentations and problem-solving sessions.

Reasons why meetings are unproductive

There are a number of common problems encountered in all kinds of meetings. The list below covers many of them. Some of these problems can be solved by effective preparation and chairing, but others will only be remedied by building the kind of team culture that has been encouraged throughout this book.

- Everyone going off in different directions at the same time
- Attacks on individuals rather than their ideas
- People find it difficult to join the flow and participate
- Confusion over who is doing what in the meeting
- Abuse of power by chairperson to achieve personal objectives
- Too much information given in too short a time
- Going over the same old arguments again and again
- Lack of commitment from members, complacency or negativity
- Lack of clarity over objectives
- Hidden agendas
- Problem avoidance – 'everything's fine'
- People not listening to what is being said or only hearing what they want to hear
- Poor meeting environment – people can't hear, can't see, are too cold or too hot
- Lack of openness and trust

Problem people

Some meetings are ineffective or have a negative feel because of the behaviour of particular individuals. Tight chairing will solve many problems but if certain people are persistently difficult it becomes necessary for the team leader to consider strategies for dealing with them individually. All participants of meetings display, at various times and in varying degrees, some of the following negative behaviour:

- Arriving late and stopping the meeting so that they can catch up
- Leaving early and disrupting the flow of the meeting
- Popping in and out of a meeting to receive messages and phone calls
- Having only one thing to say and constantly repeating it
- Constantly putting new ideas down – 'that will never work'
- Using nonverbal communication that is very dramatic – headshaking, rolling eyes, madly scribbling notes
- Contributing nothing and appearing totally disinterested or, worse still, engaging in a separate activity such as reading a book or marking
- Constantly whispering to a neighbour
- Talking too much and dominating a meeting
- Launching personal attacks on group members or the chair
- Interrupting what people are saying and rephrasing things for them
- Introducing gossip, anecdotes or rumours into a discussion
- Using status, qualifications or length of service to argue a point
- Telling the chair how to run the meeting

It is important to think about how to deal with colleagues who are too shy to contribute in meetings, those who dominate meetings and those who are immature and distract others during meetings. Some basic tips are provided below.

- *Silent and shy colleagues* can be encouraged by having their achievements recognized. This builds self-esteem. The team leader should try and bring the shy person into discussions, perhaps by asking for comments on areas that are one of their strengths. Any contributions made during meetings should be rewarded with positive words and encouraging body language. As their confidence grows ask them to prepare a contribution on a topic that interests them and is relevant and provide feedback afterwards, in private of course. Sometimes discussion can be improved by sub-dividing a group and asking smaller clusters of people or pairs to report back to the whole group. A pair of shy people could be put together at these times. If a leader is deeply concerned by a person's lack of participation this should be discussed with them in private but done with sensitivity so that the shy person does not feel guilty about their lack of involvement.

- *Dominant and self-opinionated colleagues* can be given specific tasks to do that will prevent them dominating. Taking minutes is the obvious example. The use of sub groups during discussions could allow dominant people to be clustered together. Essentially, though, over-bearing people need to be handled well by the chair who should insist on contributions being made through the chair and be assertive when self-opinionated people are dominating the meeting. This does not mean using put-downs but involves politely thanking them for their input and immediately bringing other people into the discussion before the dominant person continues with an argument or starts on a new point. Ultimately, encouraging everyone in a team to contribute and be assertive is the way forward. If dominant people are also aggressive managers need to discuss their behaviour with them in private.
- *Colleagues who 'clown around' and distract others* exist in some teams. They have a tendency to make light of serious issues by whispering to other colleagues or making inappropriate jokes. It is important to arrange seats in such a way that whispering becomes difficult and small groups cannot separate themselves from the main body. Analyse your reactions to the clowning to see if you are making the situation worse and reward positive contributions with praise. If necessary, establish ground rules for the conduct of meetings with the whole team and confront bad behaviour publicly. If it becomes necessary to address the behaviour through a private meeting do ensure that there is plenty of praise for the positive things this colleague contributes to the team.

It is worth remembering that bad behaviour in meetings is unusual and that managers who have cultivated a collaborative, open and positive culture rarely encounter difficulties in meetings. If team leaders feel the dynamics in a meeting are unproductive then it may be helpful to invite a trusted outside observer to watch a meeting and provide feedback that the whole team considers together with a view to improving matters.

Reviewing your team meetings

Good managers reflect on all aspects of their practice. It is a good idea to find out from other team members what they think about the meetings you run. The Meeting Review Form below (Table 5.2) based on a design by James Sale (1998) could be used to provide feedback, which could act as a basis for discussing meetings with others in the team and setting targets for improving meetings, if necessary.

TABLE 5.2 Meeting review form

1	Agenda received in advance	1	2	3	4	5	6
2	Meeting in suitable environment	1	2	3	4	5	6
3	Meeting kept to time	1	2	3	4	5	6
4	Documentation available	1	2	3	4	5	6
5	Decisions taken	1	2	3	4	5	6
6	Action points agreed	1	2	3	4	5	6
7	Participation of all team members	1	2	3	4	5	6
8	Appropriate leadership style adopted	1	2	3	4	5	6
9	Minutes clear and useful	1	2	3	4	5	6
10	Planning and review integral	1	2	3	4	5	6

1 = poor, 6 = excellent

Case study

Read the following comments and consider why the meeting in question was de-motivating for this participant.

'Another meeting for Year 9 tutors this evening…what a waste of time – the same old boring items. Why we have to sit and listen to Sue, the head of year, going through a catalogue of things she has had to deal with this week I don't know. She seems to assume we want to know about everything she's been doing; perhaps she just wants us to know what she does for the extra money she gets? I certainly get fed up of her moaning – I thought managers were supposed to be positive and full of optimism!

The arrangements for Open Evening are exactly the same as they were for the last one so why do we have to listen to them all over again. Surely she could have told Peter, a new tutor, about these at some other time. He was asking so many questions it must have wasted ten minutes.

I know I should take more interest but I'm not really bothered about what the new arrangements might be if we get the building extension. The finance isn't in place yet so I can't really get enthusiastic about what might never happen anyway.

New job descriptions – that was an important item but Sue didn't give us any opportunity to discuss the matter. She'll probably land me with some extra responsibility – as if I don't have enough to do already. She also glossed over the issue of new admissions. There are now thirty-two students in my tutor group but

I'm sure we have a policy of no more than thirty to a class. I think I'll have to ask the union rep' about this as Sue was not very forthcoming.

To make matters worse it was freezing in the meeting room tonight but no one dared to mention it – again. I suppose I should have said something if only to get it in the minutes. But then I never see the minutes so I wouldn't know for sure that Sue had put it in.

It was very embarrassing when Clive was asked to tell us about the drama work he'd thought of for his class. He obviously wasn't expecting to be asked to speak about it and he was quite coy at first. At least people showed some interest in what he was doing, which seemed to put him at his ease.

At the end of the meeting Sue asked if she could change next week's meeting to Tuesday. I felt really angry – she knows how difficult it is for me to change child-minding arrangements. It wouldn't be so bad if our meetings were productive! On my way out I passed my pigeonhole and found the agenda for the meeting I had just left. It must have been posted this afternoon as it was the first I'd seen of it. I screwed it up tight and ceremoniously tossed it in the bin to help relieve the tension I was feeling.'

Reflection

This unfortunate teacher has a lot to feel annoyed about and it is not surprising she is feeling tense. Sue's handling of the meeting can be criticized on several grounds:

- The agenda was not provided in advance
- The room was cold
- Clive had not been warned about having to speak
- Irrelevant items were included – Sue's work load and hypothetical building issues
- Time was wasted answering questions for a new colleague who could have been seen at a different time
- A major issue – admissions – was glossed over with no opportunity for discussion
- Job descriptions were given out but not discussed – this should have been done with individuals on a one-to-one basis
- The time of a scheduled meeting was changed at short notice

Apart from failing to organize the meeting efficiently, communication in general seems to be poor, members of Sue's team are not encouraged to assert themselves and there is certainly no culture of collaboration in evidence. However, colleagues were supportive and interested in what Clive had to say and they seem to cooperate with Sue despite the shoddy treatment meted out by her. From this short extract we can conclude that Sue lacks basic management skills and is failing to motivate, communicate and organize. Thankfully, there are probably few managers as incompetent as Sue in real life!

Summary

A team is more than a group of people placed together because they have some aspect of their work in common. A team is characterized by:

- Members sharing a vision
- Members being interdependent
- Members knowing what the team's goals are
- Members understanding what their unique contribution to achieving the goals is
- Members communicating openly
- Members supporting and trusting one another
- Healthy debate between members
- Relaxed but purposeful relationships

A successful team is creative and flexible and the achievements of the team are greater than the achievements of individuals in the team working separately would be. A successful team is likely to be led by a leader who encourages collaboration and empowerment, who trusts and praises individuals in the team and who is receptive to new ideas and opportunities.

Productive, well chaired meetings can help to create a purposeful team spirit and greatly increase the effectiveness of a department or group. Equally, badly organized and poorly focused meetings lower morale and sap energy. A tongue in cheek way of understanding what makes an effective meeting is to consider what makes an ineffective meeting and then pledging to do the opposite. These are a few suggestions:

1. Run long meetings and invite people for whom the issues are irrelevant.
2. Meet regularly when there is nothing to do.
3. Don't get things too clear, e.g. what has been decided – then you have a good reason for holding another meeting.
4. Don't set a finish time – people have nothing else to do and the head is sure to be impressed by the long hours your team puts in.
5. Leave your mobile on in meetings. You need to read texts and answer calls as it shows how much in demand you are.
6. Never create an agenda – people might think about the issues in advance.
7. Be late for meetings – keeping people waiting is a clear sign of your importance.

8. Never discuss one topic fully when you can confuse people with several.
9. Don't hurry decisions – if you wait long enough the problem might go away.
10. Don't have relevant papers to hand – you can all sit and wait for the photocopier.

6

Team building and departmental improvement

Case study by Stuart Ash

The situation

My school, a small rural comprehensive, had been placed in Special Measures in January 2008 following a particularly poor summer of results. Morale was low; behaviour was poor in all areas of the school and staff and students had assumed the habit of blaming everyone else for the school's failing without accepting responsibility for their own part in its downfall. One particularly surprising aspect of the situation was that no one seemed to see it coming.

In the English faculty, there was a never-ending rotation of supply teachers filling the gaps created by illness, maternity and resignation. Results at the high performance end were satisfactory, although boys underperformed; results in the lower performance band were well below national averages and students generally felt very negative about their experiences in English. The school had seemed to lose faith in the very students that came through the doors and expectations of their performance and behaviour were painfully low. There was no meaningful curriculum structure in place and monitoring and tracking of students was cursory at best. Lessons lacked vigour and students were mostly content to watch videos or complete wordsearches and make posters in those lessons delivered by supply teachers and subject non-specialists. In short, things were bad.

In order to begin making the necessary changes for departmental improvement, we first had to actually accept that change was necessary. This was, in many ways, the most difficult of all the challenges we faced: we all had to accept our involvement in the 'failings' of the department but at the same time avoid pointing the finger of blame at anyone in particular. The truth of the situation was, the overall achievement of students was unsatisfactory and a significant proportion, mostly boys, was not making sufficient progress. As uncomfortable as it may have felt on many occasions, we had to keep returning to these facts, confronting our shortcomings and thinking about what we were doing to make things better. And this, for us, was at the heart of the improvement: recognizing where things simply weren't good enough and then doing something about it.

Establishing vision and aims

With the spotlight firmly placed on core departments and the pressure exerted from above for a quick turnaround in results, it can be difficult to see things clearly in such high-pressure situations. As a departmental team, we needed to act calmly and with a sense of purpose in the situation. We had to hold no emotional attachment to any aspect of the department and talk about our change priorities in purely pragmatic terms. With an eye on the past we had to look positively into the future.

To begin with, we conducted some faculty visioning exercises, thinking about how we wanted the department to look in five years' time. All our discussions had to be based around positive images of the department without any consideration to perceived obstacles. The visions of the future could be anything from a description, a picture or a word, to a list of results or figures. Once we had begun to think about the kind of department we wanted to be part of, we could then think about the steps needed to move towards that vision. By focusing on positive images and how they can be achieved, we could then see each and everyone's involvement in the forthcoming changes but easily avoid the habit of seeking a place for blame and being reactive to recent poor performances.

In order to make swift improvements we had to keep things simple and have clarity about all of our aims. In order to do this, we began to define what appeared to be our key principles and the core aims of our department following our vision exercises. It was vital to us to have a core purpose and ensure that everything we did as a faculty supported these aims. This then simplified the process and gave clarity to the work that we did as a team in the complex environment of a school in an extremely difficult situation.

As a result of our discussions, we decided on the following aims and principles.

The core aim:

■ To raise student progress, achievement and attainment

The key principles behind our core aim:

■ Great teaching
■ Positive relationships
■ A quality curriculum
■ Accurate assessment and feedback

In the often chaotic world of schools and education, it can be easy to lose sight of the things that actually matter and in this situation in particular we had to see our purpose in the most simple and straightforward terms. It is all too easy to let panic take hold and then keep relentlessly throwing different ideas, initiatives and strategies into the mix in an effort to solve a difficult and multifaceted problem. In many of the departments I have worked with, this becomes all too evident in their aims for improvement: throw everything and anything at the problem and then hope that something sticks. Sometimes this approach may work as an initiative clearly takes hold and has a positive effect. However, more often than not, it results in jaded teachers suffering from exhaustion brought about simply by the pace and size of the change. Simplicity was absolutely key as it allowed us to focus purely on what actually mattered: what goes on in the classroom and what progress the students are making. And these key ideas formed the central structure around which all faculty meetings and communications were built.

The improvement process: From vision to reality

Having the key aims and core principles in place gave us the clarity of vision to now move quickly in making some substantial changes. It also meant that we were no longer seeking to blame but taking proactive roles in the forward movement of our department and the progress of our students. It brought a greater clarity of thought from all members of the team and helped form the basis of all developmental work.

Great teaching

Of course, at the core of all great departments is great teaching. It was vital that everything we did together avoided distracting us from actually what matters: delivering great lessons. Together everything we did had to ultimately have a positive impact on what took place in the classrooms. If it didn't, then we didn't do it. It really was as simple as that! We encouraged this question in conversation and in meetings: what has that got to do with what happens in my classroom?

I purposefully avoided the Ofsted terminology of 'Outstanding' as it is a word that is now inextricably linked with the judgement of a performance. This wasn't about performance. This was about delivering great lessons and seeing students make great progress over a period of time. I didn't want the teachers in the department to be invited into each other's lessons to simply watch performance lessons: they would have been a waste of time both for the teacher planning and the teacher observing as they would not have offered a realistic reflection of what was taking place day in, day out in the classroom.

We encouraged a more open door policy in which teachers went in and out of one another's classrooms as a matter of habit. It was then a more useful discussion point to consider what we had seen taking place in other lessons. It was these moments that were more likely to influence what we did and how we did it in our lessons in future. Once we had become used to seeing each other more frequently in classrooms, we began to feel a lot more comfortable that no snap judgements were being made about what was taking place at any one time.

Meetings could then centre round the concepts of pedagogy in a far more relaxed atmosphere; teachers could feel comfortable that discussions were not taking place in order to reach any kind of conclusion about the quality of the teacher, but far more about the learning that was taking place in the classroom. We could share good practice and some great ideas that could be taken easily from classroom to classroom, but we could also be open about those things that didn't quite work and could be best forgotten about.

As a result of these discussions, we then built a lot more of the work in our classrooms around talk. We focused on developing the students' skills in conducting quality conversations in lessons and got the students to reflect on their performance in group work. We wanted students to have the confidence to express their ideas in other ways than simply writing in exercise books and give students whose literacy skills were below those of the others in class the chance to shine. With a greater emphasis on the expression of ideas it allowed us to move away from the more formal aspects of assessment and actually listen and respond to the students' ideas in real time. This type of formative assessment was particularly effective in helping improve the boys' contributions and engagement in lessons.

As a faculty, once we felt a great deal more confident about what was taking place in our classrooms and less likely to feel castigated by a poor judgement, we were able to ask the students more openly what they felt about their experiences in English. Rather than avoid criticism, we actively created opportunities for students to let us know what they thought of the lessons. It was vital that we did this not just in English lessons, but around the school at different times of the day. We also pursued more formal feedback in the shape of student voice questionnaires, but just as importantly, stopping students in the corridor to ask them if they had English that day and what they thought of their lessons at the time. By getting as much feedback as possible, it could continually feed into the work that we were doing and let us know if we were moving in the right direction. We also made every effort to speak to parents about what was being said at home with regards to English lessons. If things were changing (for better or for worse) then we could guarantee that conversations of one kind or another were taking place around the kitchen table. We wanted to get the students talking and we wanted parents to ask their children about what was happening. By getting them involved, we could all feel part of the journey.

Positive relationships

One of the most difficult aspects of this kind of wholesale change can be the impact it has on personal relationships. I cannot deny that things were not always a bed of roses between the members of the faculty. It is understandable that in times of great change and immense stress such as these we all from time to time become agitated, frustrated and sometimes plain angry. This was true for all of us at one point or another but it was integral to our success as a faculty that we remained a team and understood that teams are built around positive relationships.

The nucleus for these positive relationships was always the faculty meetings. It was vital that we kept these meetings as positive as possible and avoided any fractious interactions. The meetings had to be calm and purposeful with an all pervading sense of good humour throughout: it was in these meetings that our ethos and values as a faculty were established. With the nature of work in schools, a large proportion of interactions take place in passing on corridors or through quickly written e-mails. These meetings had to be a time in which conversations could take place with breathing space for all; a time for ideas to be thrown around and plans put in place for classroom based improvements. To return to an earlier point: if it doesn't have an impact on what happens in lessons, then don't talk about it. It is the job of the faculty to get an agenda together before the meeting, which outlines the key points for discussion and these agenda items should all be about teaching and improving the provision for students in the subject. Once the faculty got into the habit of discussing teaching, it was unlikely that teachers would want to return to talk about systems and structures.

As the meetings began to take shape and developments were taking place, it was then everyone's responsibility to take a role in making things happen. And to maintain positive, warm relationships within the department, everyone had to get involved. If one member of the team decided that something was not their responsibility, then there was a corrosive effect in which soon no one wanted to take responsibility for what needed to be done. We had to create a work ethic that meant if something needed doing, then we would just do it. As a faculty leader, the best I could do in this situation was simply lead by example. So whenever a job needed doing, I would roll up my sleeves and simply get stuck in. From moving books to picking up rubbish and cleaning whiteboards, I was involved. No job was too small: if we kept an eye on the small stuff, it seemed that the big stuff just followed.

Every week we published a departmental bulletin, which outlined the different activities taking place in the department. This was an opportunity to share good practice and to take notice of all the extra work that was taking place by teachers in and around lessons. It was also a place to get all the functional, day-to-day notices out of the way so that they didn't clog up the meetings where pedagogy was the central tenet. In this sense we managed to optimize our time together and ensure that we were able to discuss the things that really mattered and to spend time building our team and strengthening relationships.

One of the observations we made about the department before and during the time in Special Measures is how professionally introverted the teachers had become in the department when things weren't going well compared to the professional openness success seemed to bring. Building strong, warm relationships is a way of creating teams and moving forward together.

A quality curriculum

The curriculum has to afford all teachers the opportunities to thrive and to build on their own personal strengths as a classroom practitioner. This means that the curriculum needed to be simple, coherent, flexible and well-resourced. As a team of staff with different interests, outlooks and beliefs, it felt vital that the curriculum should allow us to express ourselves in the classroom and therefore encourage students to do the same.

With this in mind, we constructed a curriculum that focused on the acquisition of skills. As much of what had gone beforehand had become very content based, the new curriculum structure focused more on developing skills. These skills could be delivered through topics, but the emphasis had to be based on the students becoming better at actually 'doing' rather than 'knowing' something. This meant that there were greater opportunities built into the curriculum for students to prove what they had improved at and a wider range of methods to track that improvement beyond written assessments or tests.

We kept everything as simple as we possibly could in order to allow for greater flexibility within and between classes and groups. If students wanted to repeat something or move groups to try an alternative approach, it was most easily achieved through a simple and transparent curriculum structure. All too often it seems to me that faculties create unwieldy curriculum systems, which seem to be more of a straitjacket than a way of supporting students' growth in the subject.

The curriculum needed clarity in order to allow teachers to approach lessons with their own ideas. We created a bank of central, online resources towards which all teachers were encouraged to contribute and once a spirit of sharing had been established, the resources grew organically as ideas flooded in over time. With more resources available to pick and choose from, the more time was given over to quality lesson planning and assessment by the teachers.

Accurate assessment and feedback

A contributing factor to the school falling into Special Measures had been the staff's failure to recognize when students were underperforming against their target or predicted grades. It was clear that there was a distinct lack of robust assessment taking place and this became a central component to the changes in our faculty. We needed to make sure that assessment was used in the right way to help drive attainment but also to give teachers information about their classes and the relative performance of students in order to inform planning.

We created assessment packs for all students in Years 7, 8 and 9 with half termly 'capture points' to generate six 'working at' levels across the year for all students. These levels were then collated centrally and used to analyse the performance of students in each of the classes. In this way teachers were responsible for the continual progress of all students regardless of level or year. Previously, results were only used retrospectively and were often a surprise or disappointment for both teachers and students. With frequent capture points, students and teachers were able to accurately reflect on the progress of individuals and groups in different skills areas. This in turn could then inform future planning and give students robust feedback on particular areas of strength or weakness.

The levels and work generated by these assessment tasks were then used in faculty meetings to discuss the progress of students in an objective manner. In this sense, it removed any discussions about the perceived capability of students and ensured we all reflected on skills and performance. In meetings we frequently returned to the level descriptors in our discussions and used work produced by the students in the assessment tasks to discuss student performance. This in turn informed our future planning and long-term plans for curriculum structure and content.

As a result of these frequent assessment tasks, students became far less concerned or worried about levels as they knew they were not a reflection of ability but a mark or level applied to a piece of work they had produced. Grade predictions for students are now far more accurate in the department as a result of these frequent discussions and teachers have used the available data to compare different groups year-on-year to reflect on their own performance in a proactive manner.

Assessment had at one time seemed a dirty word, but students and teachers have grown to enjoy the tasks and value the information produced. Fundamentally, assessed tasks allow you to see how you are getting on and make any necessary corrections before it's too late.

Impact, evaluation and the future

Having established our aims and begun working according to our key principles, the momentum of the department began to move in the right direction. Once this started to happen it all seemed so much easier and ultimately a far happier place to be. Success breeds success and, as can be seen in Table 6.1, when we began to challenge ourselves and our students effectively our hard work and their hard work paid off and performance improved dramatically. There has been a year-on-year improvement as the department continually

TABLE 6.1 GCSE English results 2008 to 2012

A* – C Grades

2008	46%
2009	55%
2010	79%
2011	87%
2012	91%

aims to learn from and build on previous results. We have used the data drawn from examination results to continuously reflect on our practice. Rather than look at results as a picture of past practice, we have used the results to determine our curriculum and methods in current and forthcoming years. In this way, we can pass on the successes of one year into the next but we can also learn from under-performance and consider different approaches and methodologies. The results also show the continuing impact of a more secure Key Stage Curriculum developing students' skills in preparation for the terminal exams. This open and honest approach to using data is critical to improving outcomes, but it will only succeed if actions follow analysis and reflection.

Conclusion

We have come a long way as a professional team in recent years and our students have benefited enormously as a result. However, we have been careful not to become complacent. This can happen when things stop changing and the forward momentum has been lost. Despite the fact that our results are now in most respects outstanding, we continue to discuss all aspects of the students' performance and how we can make changes and improve. Change is one of the hardest parts of school improvement but remains one of the most motivating. The comfort of the everyday is not always a positive and in many ways, regardless of exactly what we did, it was simply our willingness to embrace change that helped us move forward. We continue to reflect on our performance and the work of the students, but ultimately we look forward and work to make our department a better place for all.

7

Clarity and focus
Getting communication right

Introduction

Communication is an activity that takes place when a message is transferred satisfactorily from one party to another. For communication to take place there has to be a source, transmission through channels and a receiver. Middle leaders have to communicate with a wide range of client groups and need to make their chosen style and language (spoken or written) *fit for purpose*. They therefore need the ability to make points clearly and understand the views of others. This phrase is useful as it reminds us that communication should be a two-way exchange; negotiation in communication is often vital if the message is to be fully received, accepted by the parties concerned and acted upon.

Poor communication lies at the heart of many misunderstandings and disputes that arise in secondary schools. Even in teams that have cultivated a positive ethos and where collaboration is well established, team leaders often have to make decisions 'on the hoof' and failure to inform colleagues of these can cause resentment. Of course, occasional failures of communication will be tolerated if the foundation stones of good leadership are in place, but when poor communication becomes habitual it can undermine good team relationships. In other teams it can be the failure to communicate clearly and effectively that is the barrier to creating a sharing and supportive team culture. In teams where comments like 'I always seem to be the last person to find out what's going on in this school' and 'what exactly are we doing before the next team meeting then?' there is clearly cause for concern.

One problem is that communication skills are frequently taken for granted. It is assumed that colleagues who speak the same language need only the time, effort and sincerity to communicate successfully. As communication is a fundamental teaching tool newly appointed middle leaders often feel they don't need to develop this skill. This is not usually the case; leaders do need to analyse and reflect on their communication skills as on all other aspects of their leadership. Just as teachers refine their classroom style over the years so team leaders learn how to communicate with greater proficiency as they become more experienced. If you are aiming at becoming a middle leader or are a newly appointed middle leader this chapter should help you to avoid making basic mistakes with communication and thus help you to establish yourself more smoothly in a management role.

Middle leaders and communication networks

Middle leaders operate extensive communication networks. A typical communication network for a head of department is shown in Table 7.1. It will be slightly different for other middle leaders.

As a head of department you do not have to communicate actively with all the groups all the time, but you should be aware of the range of 'client groups' you may have to make contact with. Generally speaking communication will be more formal with people in the 'occasional' category than with people in the 'daily' category. However, there may be exceptions to this rule: regular contact with colleagues in other schools may result in a very relaxed approach to communication, for example. Also, much will depend on the personalities of the particular people in each group. There may be some people who change categories over time. For example, student-teachers may need to be seen every day in the early stages of their training but less regularly as their skill levels develop.

Networking, the activity of developing professional contacts, is endemic to organizations. It is quite useful for middle leaders in secondary schools to share information, ideas and concerns with colleagues in similar roles from their own school and other schools. Being aware of what other year heads think about a particular policy proposal that will impact on your role as year head is perfectly legitimate, for example.

TABLE 7.1 Communication network of a head of department

Daily communication	Regular communication	Occasional communication
Members of department	Head of faculty	Parents
Learning support staff	Other heads of department	HE and FE establishments
Students in your classes	Your line manager	Other schools
(trainee teachers)	Senior leaders	Local community
	Governors	Local industry
	Pastoral heads	Exam boards
	Pupils beyond your own	HMI
	classes	Ofsted
	Administrators	LA advisors
		The media
		Past students

Formality of communication increases

Making communication effective

Effective communication is more likely to occur in collaborative team or school cultures, where people are valued, encouraged to voice their opinions and supported than in hierarchical institutions. When people feel trusted, secure and confident they are much more likely to admit to not understanding messages given or to engage in debate as a means of achieving agreed meanings. In more rigid teams and schools a climate of closed communication is likely to exist, with greater competition between team members and control maintained in part through suppression of information. Two contrasting communication climates are outlined in Table 7.2.

There are various communication flows that exist within institutions and teams (Lewis 1975). Two contrasting arrangements are the chain and the all-channel model illustrated in Figure 7.1. The chain is associated with hierarchical cultures with a line-management approach. Communication tends to be instructional, which can work with simple tasks, but morale tends to be low at the end of the chain. The all-channel model seems most effective for complex tasks and would be the favoured approach of leaders wanting to generate a collaborative culture in which the views of professionals are encouraged and valued. Encouraging an open communication climate in your team is important and the team meeting is the obvious place for the all-channel model to be encouraged.

Effective communication involves making appropriate use of a variety of communication techniques: formal, informal, oral and written, *fitness for purpose* is the important thing. It is essential that the people you communicate with feel your choice of method is appropriate; this means being sensitive to people's needs. Two examples will illustrate this point.

Example 1

A head of department needs to tell a member of her team that she has had to change next year's timetable in a way that might not please him. She does this

TABLE 7.2 Communication climates

Open communication climate	Closed communication climate
• Communication encourages and values everyone, regardless of status	• Communication emphasizes differences in status
• Communication shows empathy and understanding	• Communication is impersonal
• Feedback and debate are encouraged	• Little discussion is allowed
• There is a focus on collective problem solving	• Decisions are made by a few who hold positions of power
• Statements are informative not evaluative	• Statements are judgemental
• Error is recognized and minimized	• People are blamed
• There are no hidden messages	• Messages hold hidden meaning

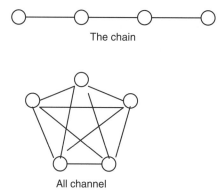

FIGURE 7.1 Contrasting communication flows.

in an e-mail. The information is communicated, but not in the right way. In this instance the head of department should have given the team member an explanation, which would have been best achieved in a face to face conversation.

Example 2

A year tutor receives a note from a parent, about an incident the parent would like to discuss. The year tutor sends a quick handwritten note back with the student concerned, saying that he will be in touch soon. This is an inappropriate response, which will reflect badly on the school, assuming the note ever reaches home. The parent deserved a telephone call (possibly from a secretary) to put them at ease. It is not unreasonable for the year tutor to delay a meeting, but the method used to communicate this was unprofessional.

Verbal communication skills

Most communication is verbal and this is theoretically a very efficient form of communication, which allows the transmission of complex information from one person to another. Thoughtful and reflective leaders can get the basics of this form of communication right by thinking about their listening and speaking, social skills and how best to create understanding.

Listening and speaking

Listening requires an awareness of bias, visual signals and vocal sounds.

Bias

Everyone's point of view includes bias of some kind. Being aware of this should help to prevent leaders from dismissing the views of others too readily. It is important not to make assumptions about the likely views of colleagues and so pre-judge their ideas or arguments. By being open minded and encouraging a range of ideas team leaders help to generate trust, real debate and collaboration from their team.

Visual signals

A visual sign is body language. People interpret the meaning of body language according to their own understanding, usually based on background, upbringing and experience. Even so, appropriate gestures can add considerable meaning to communication. Listening is obviously enhanced when eye contact is made with the speaker and people will be encouraged to contribute when they can see they have the full attention of the listener. A body turned away from a speaker or shuffling papers is very discouraging. Nods while someone speaks to you can convey reassurance.

Vocal sounds

Listening to the sound and tone of a speaker's voice enhances understanding. Sometimes there are hidden meanings that can be read from the tone being used. Speakers signal an emotional state through their voice more than their choice of words and it is important for a leader to tune into the message being conveyed. Speaking effectively requires tuning in to the listener's needs and pacing what is said accordingly. It is important for leaders to speak *to* people not *at* them. This means giving people the opportunity to respond to statements made so that a dialogue can take place. Speakers communicate warmth, interest and authority through their voice and those who vary their tone and rhythm are usually more engaging and interesting than those who don't. Appropriate use of humour is a good way to relax people and need not detract from serious points you are trying to make.

Social skills

Socially skilled information exchange occurs when the leader:

- Has clear goals to be achieved through the communication
- Behaves in a way that conveys a consistent overall impression; eye contact, facial expression, tone of voice and body language support the message being given in words
- Chooses an appropriate time and situation to convey the message

Creating understanding in the team

On key issues it is the leader's responsibility to open a debate, encourage colleagues' contributions and guide discussion so that a common understanding emerges within the group. This enhances a group's sense of purpose and clarifies the team vision.

Newly appointed leaders can feel very threatened when difficult issues are discussed and team members present their opinions forcefully, especially if there appears to be opposition to the views presented by the leader. Those committed to encouraging a collaborative culture turn such discussions to their advantage by attentive listening and setting a tone of tolerant discussion. Respect generates respect and it is a leader's duty to set the right tone. The key task is to achieve a balance between creative exchange of views and a free-for-all, where the loudest voice gets heard most. There are several important skills or techniques that leaders should develop in order to facilitate effective group discussions. Here are a few of them:

■ Insist that people speak one at a time through the chair. This prevents the loudest and most confident team members dominating discussions and encourages the participation of everybody.
■ Learn to keep a discussion on track. If there is too much digression from the main point then the leader should paraphrase what has just been said, making links to the key issue under discussion. This should be done in a non-judgemental manner so as not to discourage the colleague responsible for the digression. A good example of when to use this technique is when teachers introduce long anecdotes about particular pupils they have taught to illustrate discussion points.
■ Be willing to intervene if two or more colleagues become locked in a dispute. The leader's task is to take attention away from the disputing participants and focus on the issues that they raised. Encouraging the rest of the group to discuss the controversial issue in order to find a solution best does this. Changing the subject is not a good strategy as it leaves the issue unresolved and likely to flare up again at some point in the future.
■ If there are silences resist the temptation to 'jump in'. Silences give people thinking time. They can be used as a way of ensuring someone offers up a comment, which will then prompt discussion.
■ If there are dominant or opinionated people in your team use techniques like asking the whole group what they think after someone has made a challenging comment or giving time for discussion in pairs and then taking responses from each pair. These techniques can dilute the influence of dominant people and draw others in.

Barriers to effective verbal communication

Communication is ineffective when the receiver ends up with a different understanding to that intended by the transmitter of the message. This can be caused by poor communication skills on the part of the sender but barriers to effective communication also arise as a result of a climate of mistrust. For example, if leaders make a habit of saying one thing but doing another it should not be surprising if their messages cease to be accepted at face value. The most common barriers to communication are:

- *Semantics* – Words and phrases can have different meanings and can be interpreted differently by different people. It is very important, therefore, that everybody uses the same definitions. In teams and departments this means discussing what words and phrases mean. For example, does everyone have the same understanding of what is meant by 'assessment for learning', 'bullying' and 'behaviour for learning'? Parents sometimes need words used regularly by teachers explaining the difference between a test and an exam, or the difference between achievement and attainment, for example.
- *Status* – In schools and departments that are hierarchical status can become a barrier to effective communication. Junior colleagues can feel reluctant to ask for clarification if a communication is unclear because they fear looking stupid in the eyes of older and more senior colleagues. This is one reason why it is so important to build an ethos of trust and support in a team, which means no one is ever embarrassed to admit they don't understand something.
- *Cultural and gender differences* – If leaders are insensitive to differences of interpretation of words and non-verbal signals that can result from gender or cultural differences they will not be effective communicators. Putting people at their ease is necessary if a relaxed team ethos is to be built; this means team members being sensitive to the feelings and expectations of others. Physical contact is an example of behaviour that can produce very positive or very negative responses depending on the interpretation attached to it. The leader must set the tone by getting to know each team member individually and by showing appropriate respect and sensitivity.
- *Information overload* – When the timing and content of a communication is inappropriate people may fail to act on it. Even very loyal and hardworking colleagues reach saturation point and are simply unable to take more information on board. Too many items on the agenda of a team meeting can result in information overload, for example.

The importance of being assertive

Much has been made in this book of the need to encourage collaboration and openness in your team and in this chapter open communication has been advocated. In teams where members trust and support one another people are encouraged to be assertive. Being assertive means taking responsibility for our behaviour, having respect for ourselves and others and being honest. It allows us to say what we want or feel but not at other people's expense. It means understanding the point of view of other people and being self-confident and positive. It is not about winning come what may or getting our own way all of the time. Assertiveness is about handling conflict and coming to an acceptable compromise.

At some stage middle leaders are sure to encounter people who are aggressive and people who are passive. Being aggressive means getting your own way at the expense of others by making them feel worthless or incompetent. Being passive means ignoring your interests and allowing others to manipulate you by denying how you really think or feel. It is important that middle leaders are neither aggressive nor passive and that they encourage assertiveness in other team members. Not only is this morally right but it creates a stronger, more dynamic and more able team and ensures that honest communication occurs. Middle leaders should learn to recognize passive, assertive and aggressive behaviour in order to be able to respond appropriately (see Table 7.3).

TABLE 7.3 Passive, aggressive and assertive behaviour

	Passive	**Assertive**	**Aggressive**
Verbal content	• Rambling • Apologies • Self put-downs • Frequent justifications	• Clear statements • Distinctions between fact and opinion • Questions to find out opinions of others • Ways of resolving problems	• Boastfulness • Opinions expressed as fact • Threats • Blame put on others • Sarcasm
Voice and speech	• Wobbly • Soft • Monotone • Pauses • Frequent throat clearing	• Steady • Rich and warm • Clear • Fluent • Emphasizes key words	• Very firm • Cold • Strident • Loud • Abrupt • Emphasizes blaming words
Face and eyes	• Evasive • Looking down	• Smiles when pleased • Frowns when angry • Firm eye contact	• Scowls • Eyebrows raised in amazement • Tries to stare-down
Body language	• Arms crossed (protection) • Hand-wringing • Shrugs • Mouth covered	• Open hand movements • Sits upright but relaxed • Stands with head held up	• Finger pointing • Fist thumping • Sits upright • Stands tall • Strides around • Arms crossed

It is especially important to recognize signs of aggression when dealing with angry parents. Responding inappropriately to these signs could be potentially very dangerous. How we listen, how we respond and our body language can help us to diffuse conflict situations. Whenever a parent, colleague or pupil has what they regard as a grievance it is important to listen, show understanding and ask questions. If you feel their anger is misguided it is tempting to state your position firmly but it would be wrong to do this when they are full of anger. By listening and showing empathy a dangerous situation can be diffused; there will be opportunities to explain your position later. By avoiding aggressive body language yourself you help to calm the anger in others.

This does not, of course, mean you have to 'give in' to unreasonable people. Your aim will be to come to a joint agreement on action and this is more likely to be achieved by allowing a person who is 'worked up' to have their say first. Once an angry person has calmed down and you have convinced them of your concern and sincerity things can begin to move forward. It is important that any grievance is fully investigated and, once the facts are known, your position can be stated firmly and an appropriate way forward negotiated with the parent (or colleague or pupil) concerned. The important thing is that by using appropriate communication skills in a heated situation you have prevented an escalation of anger into violence. Remember, listening shows cooperation, showing understanding indicates you care and asking questions allows you to gain control. Good teachers use these techniques with pupils and effective leaders use them also.

Written communication

Middle leaders in schools need to be able to communicate clearly in writing. They are accountable to a range of different client groups and need to think carefully about the needs and expectations of the audience they are communicating with. As with many other areas of management *fitness for purpose* is the important consideration: an e-mail to a colleague will clearly be written in a very different style to a report for governors, for example.

Formal written communication

Middle leaders are usually involved with communicating in writing (on paper or electronically) with the various groups listed in Table 7.1. The range of documents they will have to prepare will include: worksheets and booklets for pupils; memos and minutes for colleagues; reports for senior staff and governors; progress reports for pupils and parents; a departmental or team handbook; schemes of work; mark schemes; departmental evaluations; student data and tracking reports; development plans; materials promoting courses; press releases; and a range of letters to various people.

The tools of written communication are sound grammar, accurate spelling, structure and punctuation, though communication by e-mail and especially text does allow for less formality and different conventions. In formal documents each sentence needs to be effective and it makes sense to use the following steps: pre-writing; drafting; revising; editing; printing.

Pre-writing

This stage involves the gathering of ideas, for example by brainstorming a series of developments chronologically or listing the advantages and disadvantages of a particular proposal.

Drafting

This stage involves the initial production of the document. You need to focus and structure the ideas you generated in pre-writing into an order and format that will make sense for your chosen audience.

Revising

Revising involves reading your document carefully to determine whether it delivers its intended message for its intended audience. At this stage you may add new material, delete inappropriate material and rearrange the order of information to achieve maximum effect.

Editing

You now need to check spelling, grammar, punctuation and tone to ensure that the finished document is accurate and polished.

Printing

Ensure that pages are numbered and that the front cover does justice to the contents. It is a good idea for subject departments to develop a 'house-style' in order to market themselves both internally and externally (see next section).

E-mail and text communication

Communication has been revolutionized in recent years, making contact with stakeholders easier and quicker. A few examples of things that were unheard of twenty years ago that are now commonplace will illustrate this point: automated text messages to parents if students are absent from schools; electronic records of students' lunch time food choices; interactive school websites with access to policy documents, schemes of work and homework details; e-surveys of parental views; school e-mail addresses for all teachers. The list goes on.

Technology can, of course, greatly improve the operation of a school but it is also potentially overwhelming and can create expectations that are impossible to fulfil. There are also dangers with communication being so rapid and middle leaders need to be aware of these:

- E-mails can be sent 24 hours a day. This does not mean it is reasonable to expect instant replies. Don't get annoyed with colleagues if they haven't responded to the e-mail you sent at midnight by the time you reach school the next day.
- E-mails can be responded to very quickly. However, a rapid response might be an ill-considered response or the language used might sound blunt – some e-mails are worth pondering over before you press 'send'.
- Do you really need to copy everyone in? The more people copied in, the more e-mails begin to feel overwhelming. A colleague might not bother to read a really important e-mail from you because they are so used to receiving trivia or being copied in unnecessarily.
- There are occasions when using e-mail with a parent can be useful, but try and keep this to a minimum. It is often much better to pick up the phone so the message you give can be explained properly. Short and pithy communication lacks subtlety and can sometimes cause offence.
- Be careful not to allow technology to become more important than people. If you are reading your mobile while having a conversation with a colleague you are being rude and are probably making them feel unimportant. It is a good idea to insist on phones being switched off during meetings. Likewise, insist on teachers and support staff having phones off when they are in class.
- If you have reason to communicate with students by e-mail always use your school e-mail account and follow agreed school policy. Never allow discussion to move away from school business. Under no circumstances give students your mobile phone number. If you become aware of teachers or support staff communicating with students in this way you need to intervene as there could be a child protection issue.

Communication and marketing

Many teachers still feel marketing has little to do with schools and education. They associate marketing with the commercial world and with persuading people, often by exaggerated claims, to part with their money. Marketing, they feel, is *gloss at the expense of substance*. If schools see marketing simply as *promotion* then there is a real danger that their marketing will simply become an 'add on' and that their glossy brochures will bear little resemblance to the reality of everyday school life. However, schools are increasingly under the spotlight and in some areas competing with other schools to maintain their student numbers. Therefore, it is important they communicate their strengths and achievements effectively. Likewise, departments in secondary schools are to an extent competing for pupils at Key Stage 4 and Key Stage 5 when subject choices are made. It is sensible, therefore, for a department to generate a positive image.

Many schools go further with marketing, though, seeing it as an integral part of the school's ethos and using marketing to help with quality assurance. Marketing in such schools is characterized by the following attitudes:

Marketing is more than promotion

Marketing is seen as a process not an event. The clients (mainly students and parents) are involved in the process. They are asked their views about the quality of services provided through market research and their opinions are taken into account when planning for improvement. In such schools it is quite normal for students to be consulted through questionnaires and interviews about courses, preferred teaching and learning styles and pastoral support. They try to focus on the services they provide through the eyes of the users rather than simply as providers, in an effort to improve quality and satisfaction (see Total Quality Management chapter 1). Marketing is not an 'add on'; it is part of the continuous process of school improvement.

Marketing is internal as well as external

Marketing is traditionally associated with conveying the right image to those outside the organization. In the case of schools this means prospective pupils and parents, the local community, prospective staff, the LA, Ofsted, FE/HE and so on. Schools taking marketing seriously realize that communicating effectively with internal clients is equally important. This doesn't just mean existing parents but includes current staff, pupils, governors and any regular visitors or helpers. Promoting the achievements of the school or 'talking up' the department is done continually and helps to maintain a positive ethos and a feeling of success.

In order to communicate an effective image the staff (teaching and others) and governors must have a 'corporate perspective'. This means being clear about the vision and goals of the school (and department/team). This is helped by spending time on developing a coherent view of the school, agreeing its aims and values and making sure these are reflected in development plans before producing marketing materials. There is little point trying to promote a product that is ill defined or the suppliers have no faith in; similarly those who work in a school must believe in the quality of the education they are providing and feel confident about 'selling' their excellent provision. This is why it is vital to create a shared school vision as the foundation for school development and marketing. This idea works at department level also.

Marketing is everyone's job

Even though a senior member of staff (possibly the bursar or business manager) may be the marketing coordinator it is important that everyone working in a school sees marketing as their job. The way a receptionist deals with parents or the manner in which a teacher handles a complaint from a student are aspects of marketing. Indeed, a single incident badly handled can undo much that has been achieved in creating a positive image of a school. At departmental level it is easy to see that an ineffective teacher of Year 9 classes will have much more impact on pupils' likelihood of choosing the subject for GCSE than publicity leaflets created by the department. If departments are providing stimulating lessons and positive experiences and outcomes for students marketing their courses should be relatively easy.

Reflection on marketing

To an extent middle leaders will be influenced in marketing by the school marketing policy. For example, in some schools heads of department are free to make contact with the local media in others they must go through the marketing coordinator. Whatever policy is in operation the following questions are worth asking. They are not in any order of priority and the list is not an exhaustive one. Nevertheless, they should raise awareness of the numerous ways in which an image of themselves and their team is being created and ways in which their work could be more 'client focused'.

- Does the way I deal with colleagues beyond my immediate team reflect well on my area and on me?
- Do my letters, e-mails and memos create a professional image for my area? Do we have a 'house style'?
- Do I take enough care with the appearance and content of documents I produce for people?
- Do the display boards in my area create a good impression of the work of my team and students?
- Does my area have a corporate identity?
- Do we produce accessible and interesting course guides for students, especially when they are choosing between courses?
- Do we use flyers, posters and newsletters to promote the work and achievements of our area?
- Do we use the school website effectively to promote our area?
- Do we involve students in evaluating courses?
- Do we use students to promote our area to other students and parents?
- Do we make use of the local media in promoting the newsworthy things we are engaged in?

- Do I keep senior colleagues informed about all the good things colleagues in my area are engaged in?
- Do I use team meetings and staff briefings as opportunities to celebrate achievements and praise the work of colleagues in my team?
- Do we praise students enough and do we publicize achievements of pupils in our area more widely, for example through assemblies?
- Are we welcoming to visitors?
- Do we create a good impression on parents' evenings?
- Are letters and reports to parents of a high enough standard?
- Do we listen to our students?
- Do we systematically garner students' opinions?
- Are we accessible to students?
- Do I take student complaints seriously?
- Do we evaluate events such as parents' evenings and trips in order to capture how they could be even better next time?

It may be that you are the leader of a team providing a very good education to your students but simply not sharing your achievements widely. It is just as important not to be shy about announcing the achievements of your team as it is not to exaggerate their successes and make false claims. Informing others of the successes of staff and pupils in your area is important for several reasons:

- As a middle leader you should be keeping senior managers informed of developments in your area. They need to know what colleagues are doing so that when they evaluate their performance or write references a clear picture exists.
- The public praising of colleagues for their successes raises self-esteem and increases motivation.
- The public praising of students for their successes raises self-esteem and increases motivation.
- The public sharing of achievements in one area of school can encourage other areas of school to reflect on their own achievements.
- It is important that all pupils and parents know about the successes of their school even if they are not directly involved. This increases confidence in the institution and is good marketing.

Reflection – Departmental documents

Over the past quarter of a century schools have been made increasingly accountable and middle leaders need to ensure they can provide a range of stakeholders with information they might require. In most schools there will be agreements about what information needs to be held at team level and which needs to be lodged with senior leaders. If you are a head of department could you answer 'yes' to the following questions?

- If a new pupil arrived from abroad would you be able to provide her parents with written information about your department and about the curriculum/syllabus she would be following? Would you be able to provide a scheme of work that would help the pupil and her parents understand your curriculum model or GCSE syllabus?
- If a Local Education Authority adviser arrived in school and wanted to see information about the organization of your department would you be able to provide it? Is your handbook up to date? Do you have a staffing structure/ responsibilities diagram in it? Are there copies of your team's current timetables available? Is your departmental development plan up to date, including an indication of progress made with targets since they were set?
- If you were asked by an Ofsted inspector about attainment and achievement in your subject would you have clear data to support your claims? Are you able to show how different groups of students (male, female, high ability, SEN, FSM, looked after, vulnerable) are performing in your subject? Can you prove that interventions you have in place for students identified as not achieving in line with expectation are working? Do you have clearly logged 'case studies' of some students to show how your team typically tries to meet the needs of 'complex' or 'challenging' students and pupil-premium students?
- If a parent wanted to know how her son was doing in your subject would you be able to show her? Are you able to show how he is doing compared with national expectations for pupils of his age? Are you able to show how he is doing compared with other pupils in your school? Are you able to demonstrate progress being made over time by him? Detailed and clear tracking of all students is essential.

Documents relating to all of the above ought to exist. If they don't then planning for their introduction ought to become part of your development plan. It is likely that assessment and data is handled at a whole school level and that models for demonstrating value-added or comparing departmental performance are organized by a senior member of staff. Even so, the data generated ought to be with your department (possibly refined for different audiences), as your team needs to be considering it in planning for future improvements in performance.

It is not necessary to go over the top with documents. Some heads of department can show beautifully produced, detailed documents that are more gloss than substance and do not reflect what is really happening in their subject or are even confusing to readers. Simple, clear documents written with the audience in mind are best. Quality in the classroom from all team members is a head of department's primary aim. Clear planning, agreed schemes of work and systematic assessment procedures are important foundations of quality in the classroom. Documents for internal use relating to these areas must be in place. However, departments must also have a range of documents to meet the needs of clients. A concise handbook, a leaflet or flyer promoting the work of the department and a 'pupil-speak' version of syllabi and assessment criteria are essential. It does not have to be the head of department who produces all these, of course. Tasks relating to documents can be agreed when the development plan is being written. Once in place, documents should be reviewed and updated annually.

Summary

Communication is central to the operation of an effective school and it is important that middle leaders are skilled in communication techniques. An open and supportive team culture in which colleagues feel valued and secure is likely to promote open communication between members. Team leaders need to encourage new members to be honest and open by being clear and supportive in their own style of communication and by providing opportunities for newcomers to contribute and express their views.

Middle leaders are involved in communicating with a wide range of people and must be able to adapt their style accordingly. Effective communication involves a range of strategies from informal discussions to formal written reports. Skilled communicators consider *fitness for purpose* when deciding which communication technique to employ. By seeing all people communicated with as 'clients' (internal and external) team leaders begin to think about the need for clarity and quality in their communications. Considering what it would be like to be on the receiving end of your own communications is something middle leaders need to do, however busy they may be.

Verbal and non-verbal communication involves listening and observing. Being an effective listener is very important and encourages others to be open in their communication. As a middle leader you need to be assertive but not aggressive and you should encourage and develop assertiveness in your team members. If people feel both relaxed enough and confident enough to speak their minds a more dynamic team with shared and understood goals is likely to develop. This is far better than a passive team with no dynamism or a team that accepts what you say to your face but then moans and undermines your ideas behind your back.

As schools become increasingly self-sufficient and concerned about maintaining or improving their market position creating a positive image becomes a high priority. Middle leaders have their part to play in this and should ensure that their communications reflect well on their teams and the school. By publicising the achievements of their team and students middle leaders are helping to market their area and the school and to contribute to raising morale. As well as producing quality material for school brochures, flyers, newsletters and the media, middle leaders need to be mindful that every interaction they engage in with colleagues, pupils, parents and others is an act of marketing. Pupils going home disgruntled and complaining to their parents because an incident has been handled badly can produce negative publicity, which easily undermines the positive image being conveyed through the school's published materials.

8

Developing a vision and achieving it

Introduction

Over the last quarter of a century the determination of successive governments to drive up pupil achievement and make schools more accountable has resulted in wave upon wave of centrally directed initiatives being implemented in schools. This 'top-down' approach to change produced improvements in those things that can easily be measured but, arguably, created in some schools a kind of innovation fatigue and left many teachers feeling deskilled and demotivated. Many rank and file teachers in secondary schools (whether LA schools or academies) feel more monitored, more accountable and less in control than previous generations of teachers.

This feeling of lack of control comes in part from the fear of Ofsted inspection and what follows when a school is classed as 'requires improvement' (or worse – 'notice to improve' or 'special measures'). The desire to 'keep Ofsted happy' can lead to decisions being made which, in poorly led schools, are not well thought out or appropriate; knee-jerk reactions to inspection frameworks. This need not be the case. Effective schools and departments are, of course, mindful of any changes in Ofsted inspection requirements and strive always to ensure the best possible outcomes for pupils. However, their work and provision is informed by a clear vision and set of core values rather than by Ofsted per se. These schools and departments understand that if they get the curriculum and pedagogy right for their students and if they create learning environments in which students can thrive then the outcomes for all students will be impressive and that if this is the case they have nothing to fear from inspectors. In such schools leaders and teachers feel they can shape educational provision in their own way and can control change rather than be controlled by it. Such schools use the impetus of national agendas or Ofsted frameworks to improve or develop themselves, ensuring their particular circumstances and context informs how they manage national changes. In these cases what is best for young people in that school or department is always the driving force.

Schools with the following features have been identified as most likely to manage change effectively:

- Trust, openness and collaboration
- Clear core values and beliefs
- Clear vision and commitment to raising standards
- Robust self-evaluation processes based on valid information streams
- Good staff-student relationships

As explained in chapter 2, academics have for decades studied organizations to uncover the characteristics that enable some to manage change successfully. Holly and Southworth (1989: 27) wrote about 'developing schools' in which the culture was enabling, promoting learning and growth for adult members as well as students. They described the culture as 'interactive and negotiative; creative and problem-solving; proactive and responsive; participative and collaborative; flexible and challenging; risk-taking and enterprising; evaluative and reflective; supportive and developmental'. These features were still recognized as important by Michael Fullan in *The Six Secrets of Change* (2008: 12), who also stresses the importance of decision making informed by transparency about results. 'The job of leaders is to provide good direction while pursuing its implementation through purposeful peer interaction and learning in relation to results'.

Change can be threatening and unsettling and can cause weariness and fatigue. Equally, introducing change can be an opportunity for learning, creativity and personal development. Effective leadership can make the difference between a cynical and lack-lustre approach to change and an approach characterized by enthusiasm and commitment. At subject and team level, middle leaders play a vital role in the change process and their level of success in managing change is dependent upon having a clear and shared vision, good inter-personal skills, a collaborative team culture, honest self-evaluation and effective planning and monitoring procedures.

Establishing a vision

Vision is a word that has become much used in education in recent years. For some, the ability of a head teacher to articulate a vision for a school means they have found a panacea for all ills the school might be facing. Of course, this is not the case. Successful school improvement requires more than just a vision, but it is true to say that a head teacher who can successfully galvanize a critical mass of staff around a vision of what success looks like has one of the key foundation stones for school improvement in place. Similarly, in schools where there is no vision, the vision is not understood, members of staff feel no ownership of the vision or individuals don't understand their part in achieving the vision, school improvement is less likely. All of this is true also for teams within a school. Of course, subject teams and year teams should be working towards an overarching school vision, but this must be translated into something meaningful at subject or year level. If a school stresses being 'inclusive' for example, the year leaders or heads of department need to be ensuring their team is clear about what being inclusive means in the context of their tutoring or subject teaching.

Beyond the school vision, it is important each team has a clear vision that is meaningful to them. For example, if I am Head of History as an absolute minimum I need to know that my team share a common view of what the unique characteristics of History are (why it is important), what high quality pedagogy in History looks like (the teaching and learning to aspire to) and what we are aiming for with our students (measurable outcomes). Put simply, a key part of my leadership is to create a compelling vision, translate it into action and sustain it.

While middle leaders will have their own core values and their own 'non-negotiables' around vision, it is important that they involve their teams in contributing to and shaping the vision. 'Buy in' is essential to success (see chapter 6). The key questions for discussion with teams are:

- What does this subject, well taught, offer students? (Or what does good tutoring offer students?)
- What does outstanding teaching in this subject involve? (Or outstanding tutoring for this age group?)
- How do we shape up currently in relation to our ideal?
- Where would we like to be in the future?
- What changes do we need make to move the faculty/department/team forward?

Middle leaders need to be able to reach for the stars while having their feet firmly on the ground; in other words their vision must be ambitious but also realistic. They must be clear about the direction of travel but must engage their teams in discussions about the best way to get to the agreed destination.

Reflection

- *Think of posts you have held to date. In which post(s) did you have (or not have) clarity about your role, the aims of your team and the values and vision of your school?*
- *Can you analyse why you had – or did not have – this clarity?*
- *Did having clarity help you in your role? Did lack of clarity hinder you?*

Getting staff involved

While some rare individuals have the capacity to be truly visionary and inspire others to follow them most middle leaders recognize that 'many heads are better than one' and that involving the whole team in creating and sharing a vision ensures a commitment to the agreed direction of travel.

One way to achieve a common vision with groups is for the subject leader to arrange a period of time without interruption (possibly off-site) when teachers and support staff can discuss what they hope the department will look like, say in five years' time, in terms of teaching and learning. Such discussions need a clear structure and one way to provide this is to offer statements that staff are invited to agree with, disagree with and add to. These statements will, of course, include the 'non-negotiables' the team leader holds dear. This can take place through discussion, card sorts, post-it activities etc. (see Figure 8.1 for an example

(This activity assumes you have at least eight people in your team; it is easy to work out how the idea could be modified for a smaller team.)

Stage 1 Getting started (20 minutes)

You will need A3 paper, marker pens, Blu-Tak and a flip chart

Ask the team to produce statements around their ideal team or department. Stimulate their discussion by having examples ready to share (your own non-negotiables, for example). 'All members of the team are confident and equipped to facilitate high quality learning' might be one statement provided as stimulus. Capture their statements on flip chart paper and cluster them into themes.

Stage 2 The Brainstorm Carousel (25–30 minutes)

You will need four pieces of flipchart paper, four marker pens in different colours, Blu-Tak.

1 Divide the team into four equal groups.
2 Write one of the themes from stage 1 or a clear vision statement from stage 1 on the top of each piece of paper, using the format: 'What will it look like, sound like and feel like if….. all members of the team are confident and equipped to facilitate high quality learning.'
3 Ask each group to brainstorm their responses. (3–5 minutes)
4 Instruct each group to move – clockwise – to the next group's sheet, taking their marker pen with them. Instruct them to read carefully the group's responses and to place a tick against any statement they agree with. They are not allowed to write comments on what the group has written on their sheet. They may add any ideas of their own. (2–4 minutes at each station)
5 Repeat the process until everyone is back in their home group. Allow 2 minutes for them to read any additions to their sheet.
6 Allow 2 minutes for feedback from each group; where there are three ticks, you have group consensus. Where you haven't, ask the group what you would need to change in order for them to be happy with the statement they didn't tick. Check the home group is happy with any amendments.
7 Use the sheets at each meeting for the first term to re-focus the team on the 'corporate vision'.

FIGURE 8.1 Activity: Creating a manifesto for change.

activity). The outcome should be a consensus around a clear understanding of what the department or team stands for and what they must strive to improve if they are to do their best for all students. Of course, a middle leader could simply announce these things at a meeting but the only way progress will be made is if colleagues have arrived at core values and vision for themselves. Furthermore, Hopkins (2001: 47) states that 'leaders determined to bring about improvements need to display behaviours that include ability to articulate values and vision around student-centred learning and achievement, and to make the connections to principles and behaviours and the necessary structures to promote and sustain them'. This reminds us that arriving at a vision is not enough; middle leaders must also model the values and principles they regard as essential.

Development and the change process

It is often said that change is now a constant in schools. However, some changes are more significant than others and their impact more far reaching. It is important that leaders and managers understand how change affects the individual. All change causes a certain amount of stress to people but it will not necessarily always be negative stress. Some people fear change more than others and this together with the extent to which a change is *desired* and *predicted* determines how stressful it will be. For example, taking up a new post can be stressful. This is because you are moving from what Plant (1987: 32) calls 'firm ground' to 'swampy ground'. You are stepping out of a position where you feel confident, you understand the culture and your role is clear into an altogether more uncomfortable position where you are uncertain about your role, relationships and responsibilities. However, because the new job was desired and success in securing the post boosted your self-esteem you will probably turn the stress into creative energy and work very hard to make a success of the post.

There are other occasions, of course, where change that was not expected or desired can cause great stress, which, at least in the short term, can lead to loss of self-esteem, decline in performance and depression. Some teachers don't manage to cope with the pace of change required when Ofsted puts a school into 'special measures', for example, and such teachers may choose to leave their posts or be forced to leave through capability procedures. To avoid stress, leaders and managers need to involve colleagues fully in decisions about change and the change process, starting with reaching agreement about vision. Once that is in place, the reason for changes becomes clearer. Change should not be seen as undesirable or unexpected and the greater the involvement of team members in decisions about the future the less likely it is that change will have a negative effect on them.

Everyone has a need for a certain amount of stability, both personal and professional. The stress factors of illness, moving house, getting married or divorced are well documented. A teacher experiencing stress outside work will be unlikely to embrace change in the workplace with enthusiasm. By recognizing the need for some stability leaders show understanding and provide support. People come from different backgrounds with different experiences and therefore cope with change in different ways and at differing speeds. Leaders need to acknowledge this when change is being introduced. They are more likely to be able to do so and control the pace of change if they are robust in their self-evaluation so that they have identified what needs to improve and decided how best to do it, rather than waiting for a judgement from above (from SLT) or from external inspectors (Ofsted) to force change upon them.

Of course, middle leaders cannot control the speed of change that is centrally imposed but they can make the change less threatening by providing support for colleagues and by ensuring that the change is controlled, directed and shared. When a collaborative and supportive culture exists in a team change can usually be accomplished smoothly. Indeed, in most successful schools bottom-up change is common, with discussion and the implementation of new ideas and ways of improving provision seen as quite normal.

Even so, change in schools ultimately concerns changes in individual practice, which some colleagues find more difficult to cope with than others do. It is likely that the implementation of a significant curriculum or organizational change will involve one or more of the following features:

- Changes in the structure and organization of the school; for example time-tabling or the shape of the school day
- Changes in pedagogy, for example understanding and implementing 'behaviour for learning' strategies
- Acquiring new knowledge, resulting from curriculum changes or expectations, for example all teachers being expected to develop students' literacy skills
- Changes in beliefs, values and practices on the part of some teachers, for example the introduction of streaming or the removal of course work at GCSE level

Managing development

Managing development in schools involves controlling and directing change in order to improve the service and nature of education provided and outcomes for students. A clear sense of direction and routes to follow are essential and effective development planning should provide these. Cyclical development planning is now well established in schools with middle leaders being actively involved in the process and critical to its success. Hargreaves and Hopkins (1991) argued that the merits of development planning are:

- It focuses attention on the aims of education
- It provides a coordinated approach to change
- It considers long-term vision and short-term goals

- It puts control of change into the hands of teachers
- Staff development becomes more focused
- The achievements of teachers in promoting change are recognized
- It becomes easier to report on the work of the school

While all these elements are still relevant, twenty years on – with school performance data now central to school improvement and inspection – we can add that development planning ensures key changes made are informed by robust evaluation of data. Also, with appraisal regarded as increasingly important and legislation giving appraisal processes more teeth, we can see that development plan priorities should inform target setting for teachers and support staff. Thus, development planning is used to drive through strategic priorities in a systematic way.

Although called different things in different institutions, schools should have a strategic plan, a school development plan and departmental plans. Together, these plans help schools to provide answers to several important questions:

- Where is the school or department now? (audit, often captured in a self-evaluation form or SEF)
- Where do we want it to be in three to five years? (strategic plan linked to school or department vision)
- What changes do we need to make and when? (yearly goals captured in development and action plans)
- How shall we manage these changes? (milestones and who is responsible for implementation)
- How shall we know whether our management of change has been successful? (What are our success criteria and milestones and who will monitor and evaluate impact?)

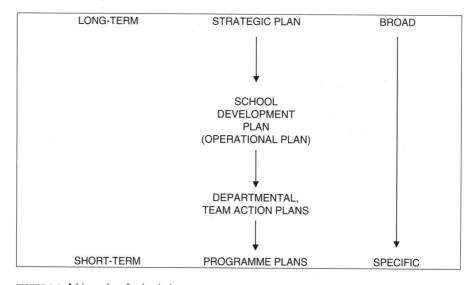

FIGURE 8.2 A hierarchy of school plans.

A strategic plan communicates decisions that have been agreed concerning the long-term (usually three to five years) development of the school or department. The strategic plan reflects the values, vision, mission, aims and policies of the school or department. These will shape the planning goals for the future.

A development plan prioritizes goals from the strategic plan. Typically, action points from Ofsted inspections can be found in development plans but they are not driven exclusively by Ofsted, and schools that self-evaluate effectively would have the areas identified for improvement by Ofsted already in their plans for improvement. Internal audits, pupil voice and external market research might also shape a school development plan. Hopkins and MacGilchrist (1998) noted schools increasingly using their development plans as a means of raising student achievement through focusing on the quality of teaching and learning. This practice is now absolutely central to school development planning, further developed through linking development priorities to teacher appraisal targets.

Departmental and team development plans will be strongly influenced by the school's strategic plan, by school development plan priorities and by Ofsted inspection findings. However, teams and departments may have areas for development that they themselves have identified and regard as important. Middle leaders must never forget that they are able to inspire and motivate colleagues by ensuring there are priorities agreed by the team in their plans.

Action plans turn relevant parts of the school's development plan into a working document for teachers. Action plans describe and summarize what needs to be done to implement and evaluate key priorities. They clarify what has to be done by assigning responsibility for action. Action plans show:

- Milestones and targets to be achieved in implementing a particular strand of the plan
- Resources allocated
- Individuals responsible
- Completion dates
- Success criteria

The action plan is thus a convenient guide to action. The better the quality of the action plan, the more likely it is that implementation will proceed smoothly. The more effectively all team members can be involved in drawing up the action plan the more likely it is to succeed.

Making a success of team planning

Middle leaders are more likely to achieve smooth and successful change if they can create a collaborative team culture in which individuals are constantly striving to improve the education they provide and by using well established development planning techniques. Team leaders operate within a wider school development planning context and so a clear understanding of the whole school approach to development planning is important.

The development planning cycle

Essentially, development planning is a cyclical process that involves audit, construction, implementation and evaluation. Prior to implementation it is important to discuss 'road blocks', especially things that have prevented targets being achieved in the past. In most secondary schools the audit and construction phases occur during the summer term when there is usually the opportunity for teams to spend more time together. Implementation usually takes place during the autumn and spring terms. Evaluation should be ongoing but with a more thorough evaluation at the end of the cycle, in the late spring term, which feeds into the audit. It is obviously the case that raising student attainment and achievement is a major aim, whatever the specific development plan targets, and an analysis of external exam results should occur in September and be revisited at the audit stage of the cycle. If schools are accurate in their assessment and tracking, external results should bring few surprises.

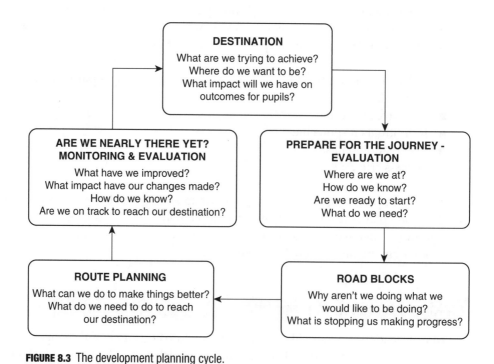

FIGURE 8.3 The development planning cycle.

It is, of course, impossible to address every issue that might require attention in a development plan. Development planning involves making decisions about which issues take priority, which areas will be maintained and which will be developed. Highly successful schools and departments are likely to include more maintenance and fine-tuning than new initiatives in their development plans. However, education operates in a rapidly changing world and it is unlikely that any team will ever be in a position where no change is necessary and no improvement is possible.

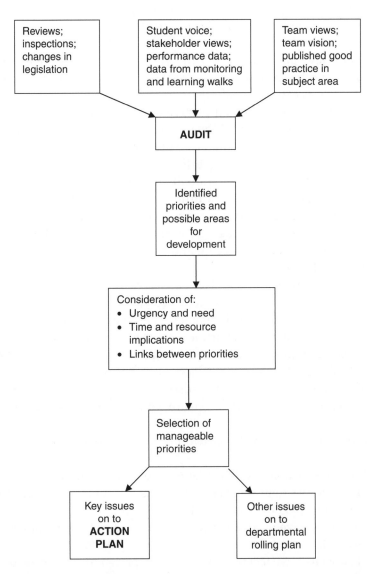

FIGURE 8.4 Construction of the departmental development plan.

The audit

The audit stage is extremely important and involves a review of strengths and weaknesses. It provides a good opportunity for team building with openness, reflection and constructive criticism being essential. The audit should be seen as an evaluative summary of the team's performance in the key areas of its work. The key areas of its work should be defined in relation to pupil performance, national legislation/inspection frameworks, whole school aims and mission and data from a variety of sources, including 'market research'. Increasingly, students' opinions are being used to assist team leaders in making judgements about the quality of the education they provide. While some teachers are still horrified by the idea of students assessing them in any way, others now happily accept the notion of 'young person as client' and understand that the vast majority of students provide useful and sensible responses when asked their opinion on matters such as what teachers can do to help them learn effectively. Teams where openness exists and colleagues are supportive are more likely to consider using student assessments as part of the evaluation and audit process. We all know that at options time students make judgements about courses and teachers by voting with their feet. We often become aware through anecdotal evidence of what the views of students are but the picture we get is a partial one. Investigating students' attitudes in a more systematic way, therefore, would seem sensible and the information gathered, if used sensitively, can help teams consider how best to improve their practice. It could be used to inform decisions on curriculum and pedagogy and also for individual staff reviews and appraisals.

A departmental audit involves consideration of strengths and weaknesses of the department. This can be done in a variety of ways from initial 'gut feeling' and brainstorming, to judgements based on consideration of generic criteria and checklists for departments, to systematic consideration of subject best practice findings (available from www.ofsted.gov.uk), chief examiners' reports and student surveys. Clearly, it is not possible to use every method every year, but using a valid yardstick by which to judge your department and a variety of sources to ensure your judgements are triangulated is important.

The audit should involve answering such questions as:

- What are we doing well in relation to our vision statement?
- How are we doing in performance terms compared with other schools nationally and other similar schools?
- How well have we done in relation to our development priorities over the last cycle?
- How well do we feel we would do if inspected in the very near future?
- What are we not happy with?

- What statutory policies affect us? What are the constraints?
- What are the opportunities?
- What should we try and change over the next year?
- What should we try and change over the next three years?

Performance indicators

A performance indicator is a piece of information that helps you to know how well a person, group or an organization is performing. It is very important to include performance indicators in the audit process. SATs, GCSE and 'A' level results should be analysed with reference to both student attainment and progress. Schools use various tools to assist this process, including Fischer Family Trust (FFT) data, Durham University's CEM tools (Alis and Yellis) and the 'A' level reporting system known as ALPS. With so much riding on data in inspections schools now use a range of measures to establish how well they are performing compared with other schools catering for students of similar ability and backgrounds. At middle leader level it is also important to know in detail how your department is performing compared with other teams in your school. This means knowing how well groups such as boys, girls, gifted and talented, SEN, looked after students, vulnerable students, students receiving free school meals are all performing. The current inspection regime, rightly, is concerned with identifying 'coasting' schools and departments where attainment may look good superficially, but on closer inspection progress is not good and/or specific groups of students do not perform well. At the time of writing, the progress of students who attract pupil-premium funding is of particular interest to inspectors.

Quantitative performance indicators by themselves rarely provide definitive answers but they do help teams to focus on the important questions to ask and areas to investigate. They draw attention to issues that deserve a closer look. Comparisons between one year and another, between subjects, between teachers of the same subject and with local and national norms help to focus teams on the key question: are we doing the best we can for *all* our students?

Middle leaders must be committed to raising standards in schools. The use of statistical information on student performance with teams and individuals is an essential part of the process. However, if such performance indicators are used only to blame and shame individual teachers it is likely that the collaborative and supportive culture that is so important for achieving success will be undermined. 'Total quality management does not seek to attribute blame, total quality management seeks to understand and control quality' (Smith 1996: 46). This reminds us that there is a balance to be struck between using data for individual accountability and using data as a tool for improving provision overall. Analysing student outcomes is likely to become increasingly important with performance related pay for teachers now on the statute books.

The development plan and the action plan

Once the audit has been conducted it is possible to translate the findings into a development plan or rolling plan and an action plan. Establishing priorities, and an order for dealing with them, is the way a team can control change rather than be controlled by it. When choosing between priorities in order to decide which issues should be dealt with urgently and which should be addressed in the coming years the following questions are important.

Urgency

- What is unavoidable (e.g. a legal requirement or some provision that is so poor immediate action is needed)?
- What will make the biggest difference to our students (e.g. addressing an aspect of under-performance through better teaching and learning)?
- What are the consequences of delay (e.g. students sold short or likely poor Ofsted inspection outcome)?

Manageability

- Can the development(s) be achieved in a reasonable timescale?
- What are the milestones?
- Do we need to deploy resources differently to achieve the identified priorities?
- Do we need outside support?

Roots and branches

- Have we got the right ethos, team structure and team skills to make the change work (the roots)?
- Are the changes needed a natural extension of what we have already started (the branches)?

Links

- Are priorities inter-related?
- Will tackling one make it easier to address another?

Answering these questions will help a team arrive at an action plan. Action plans should capture a long-term vision in manageable short-term goals. Action plans should set out success criteria, identify group and individual responsibilities and completion dates. Action plans state realistic targets to be achieved within a given time. Using a format such as the one provided in Table 8.1 helps to make action plan decisions easily accessible to team members and to senior managers and outside agencies.

TABLE 8.1 Action plan summary sheet

Action plan summary   Team/Dept. _____   Date _____

Overall objective

Why important (rationale)

Milestones	Action needed	Person responsible	Assisted by	Resources, CPD and costs	Success criteria	Completion date

When aiming to achieve complex objectives or where developments involve inter-related elements, it is important to undertake a critical path analysis. This involves agreeing a timetable for action and listing on it deadlines relevant to each stage of the proposed development. Summarizing these on a grid that shows the months of the year, individual deadlines and who is responsible helps to improve the management of development. Displaying this in a departmental office and highlighting elements achieved can be helpful.

Success criteria

Success criteria used in development planning should relate to specific targets. They should be capable of demonstrating that targets have been achieved. They should be used by teams during the review and audit stages of development planning in order to evaluate success. Of course, some success criteria will be more easily measured than others. If an objective is to rewrite a Year 9 scheme of work then the contents of the new document will provide clear evidence that the target has been achieved. If another target is to increase uptake of a subject at GCSE level then the numbers of pupils taking the subject compared with previous years may be used as success criteria. However, in this case demonstrating cause and effect may be more difficult. In order to recruit more students to GCSE classes you may have modified your Year 9 courses to generate more interest, marketed your subject more actively at option time and introduced a newsletter for your subject. Which of these initiatives produced the increase in students opting for your subject will be difficult to establish. Indeed, it is possible that other subjects becoming less attractive rather than yours becoming more desirable caused the change. Conversely, introducing the new initiatives in Year 9 aimed at increasing uptake may have been achieved (for example, there may have been a wonderful newsletter produced) but may not have had the desired effect of increasing uptake. This illustrates the difficulty involved in deciding on success criteria. It also warns us of the dangers of always seeking to demonstrate success in terms of only what is measurable in statistical terms.

Action point

Team plans should be clear in all aspects if they are to be fit for purpose. Table 8.2 provides a useful checklist for you to judge how useful your current development plan is. Evaluate your current plan, making a note of areas that you will improve when the plan is revised or redrafted.

Keeping developments on track

After the audit and construction stages of the development planning cycle are complete it is important not to assume that agreed action will simply progress

TABLE 8.2 How clear is your action plan?

1	Presentation / Clarity / Appropriateness	Yes	No	Notes
1.1	Is the plan easy to follow (e.g. are pages numbered and column headings on every page).			
1.2	Is there sufficient emphasis on the most important issues arising from evidence gathering and audit and why these are important?			
1.3	Are the action points expressed in terms of raising standards of pupil achievement and improving the quality of teaching and learning?			
1.4	Is it clear who has lead responsibility for each action and are deadlines set?			
1.5	Are actions manageable and are the outcomes achievable?			
2	**Resources**	Yes	No	Notes
2.1	Is each action costed?			
2.2	Have sources of funding been identified?			
2.3	Is teacher time included?			
3	**Monitoring**	Yes	No	Notes
3.1	Is it clear how progress with each action will be monitored?			
3.2	Is there an appropriate range of strategies for gathering different types of evidence (e.g. lesson observations and sampling work)?			
3.3	Does the evidence being gathered directly relate to the impact of actions on pupil achievement and the quality of teaching and learning?			
3.4	Is it clear who will do what by when?			
4	**Evaluation**	Yes	No	Notes
4.1	Are there clear criteria for judging success and are these quantifiable where possible?			
4.2	Are the success criteria expressed in terms of raised standards and improved teaching and learning?			
4.3	Is it clear how and when judgements will be reported by whom and to whom?			

on auto-pilot. Successful implementation needs support and sustaining commitment is a key task for team leaders. The enthusiasm of even the most competent and committed teachers can wane simply because of the pressures of everyday teaching.

There are simple but effective ways in which middle leaders can keep things on track. Firstly, an occasional, informal enquiry about progress to a teacher demonstrates that their efforts are appreciated and provides them with an opportunity to raise with you any difficulties they are encountering. Secondly, having progress reviews built into some departmental meetings means that individuals with responsibility for action will have to report the progress they have made to colleagues. This helps to prevent complacency and again provides an opportunity for identifying difficulties being encountered. Thirdly, an enlarged copy of the development plan summary should be displayed on your team notice board with targets achieved ticked or crossed out so that everyone has an idea of the progress being made.

If things are not proceeding to plan it is usually because time schedules are too tight, circumstances have changed, unexpected obstacles have been encountered or key colleagues have simply allowed matters to drift. Progress checks allow re-orientation to take place. Where a collaborative team culture exists, most problems can easily be overcome. If a major obstacle has emerged that the team was unaware of at the time of constructing the development plan it may be necessary to modify your targets. However, this should only be done if absolutely necessary. In rare cases, lack of progress may be down to failures of individual teachers in which case the middle leader will need to engage said teacher through a challenging conversation (see chapter 11). It is worth remembering that during the change process there can be initial excitement followed by a dip in morale as the hard work and challenges kick in. For example, implementing new pedagogy is difficult and, at first, some teachers can feel as if their lessons are worse not better. This is where the middle leader needs to show resilience, give clear support and consistent messages and work hard at maintaining morale. Martin and Holt (2002) provide an explanation of why change sometimes fails in a simple diagram (Table 8.3).

TABLE 8.3 Why change fails

Vision +	Skills +	Incentives +	Resources +	Action plans	= Change
******	Skills	Incentives	Resources	Action plans	**= Confusion**
Vision	******	Incentives	Resources	Action plans	**= Anxiety**
Vision	Skills	******	Resources	Action plans	**= Gradual change**
Vision	Skills	Incentives	******	Action plans	**= Frustration**
Vision	Skills	Incentives	Resources	******	**= False starts**

Source: Martin and Holt (2002).

Techniques for generating team involvement

Like visioning, and in effect a continuation of that process, successful development planning depends to a great extent on staff commitment and involvement. Much of this book has been devoted to the effective management of individuals and teams and the creation of a 'can-do' culture. The audit stage of development planning provides a great opportunity for a team to clarify its aims and philosophy and work together on deciding how the education you are providing can be improved. However, in a team where all members are not yet committed to the idea of continuous improvement or where teachers are simply suffering innovation fatigue generating interest in further development becomes a real challenge to middle leaders. The key is to create opportunities for staff involvement so that they feel ownership of the development plan. The imposition of change can never be as effective as the embracing of change.

Brainstorming, sometimes called thought showering, is one way of generating involvement. This involves starting with a blank piece of paper and accepting (initially without question or criticism) people's views on, for example, departmental strengths or what constitutes effective pedagogy.

Process analysis is another technique. This is a group problem-solving approach used for examining the operation of a process or procedure in order to identify ways in which it can be improved. Inducting Year 7 pupils, guiding Year 9 pupils at option time, preparing Year 11 for exams and organizing field trips are all examples of *services* that might be improved by process analysis. The benefits of the technique are that it fosters collaboration, it increases commitment and it helps a team to develop a coherent view of a complex process.

The technique is similar to preparing a flow chart and involves the group in critical review by mapping the main stages in the process, detailing what happens at each stage, evaluating each stage of the process and agreeing strategies for improvement. Process analysis needs to be conducted in an atmosphere free from blame and where everyone's opinions are considered. The team should sit in a horseshoe shape facing a wall. Recording ideas on large sheets of paper on the wall means that the information is clear and all can see it. Diversions and side-tracking become obvious and are likely to be corrected by the group. Individuals can see easily how they contribute to the whole process under review. By increasing understanding greater collaboration during implementation can be achieved.

When auditing the work of a team a *SWOT analysis* should be conducted, involving all team members. SWOT stands for strengths, weaknesses, opportunities and threats and it is a useful technique for summing up the status of your department or team in both a school and a national context. It helps a team to look to the future and avoid complacency. The team leader must prepare for the analysis by producing key questions that raise awareness of school and national issues.

Reflection: Evaluating your department

A departmental review survey is an excellent device for contributing to the review and audit stage of a department's development planning cycle. A possible survey is provided as Table 8.4. This covers a wide range of things and has some themes covered by more than one question to test for consistency in responses.

TABLE 8.4 Departmental survey

Relative personal priority (A)	Reflects this department (B)
1 = Top priority	1 = Strongly agree
2 = High priority	2 = Agree
3 = Fairly important	3 = Slightly agree
4 = Not really important	4 = Slightly disagree
5 = Low priority	5 = Disagree
6 = Lowest priority	6 = Strongly disagree

Number	Criterion	A	B
1	Schemes of work are agreed by the department as a whole		
2	Tasks are delegated fairly		
3	The department is receptive to new ideas		
4	Individual student targets are used effectively		
5	Schemes of work give detailed and clear guidance		
6	Opportunities for career development exist through appropriate delegation		
7	The department shows selectivity when considering innovations		
8	The department keeps abreast of recent developments in the teaching of the subject		
9	Marking is consistent and adheres to clear criteria		
10	Teaching and Learning is consistent and adheres to our T&L policy		
11	Designated roles in the department play to the strengths of individuals		
12	We use inclusive Teaching and Learning strategies in the department		
13	Students understand the marking criteria for assessments		
14	The schemes of work detail a *range* of teaching and learning styles		
15	The department is united in its attitude towards all key policies		
16	Resources are well organized and arranged		
17	Teachers are involved in making decisions on key issues		
18	The department has a sense of common purpose		

continued

TABLE 8.4 *Continued*

Number	Criterion	A	B
19	Appraisal is used to improve teaching and learning		
20	Tracking is used effectively to monitor the progress of individual students		
21	Effective use is made of in-class support for vulnerable students		
22	Teaching assistants are used effectively to support student learning		
23	Attainment data is analysed thoroughly to assist in raising achievement		
24	Able students are stretched and challenged		
25	Inter-personal relationships in the department contribute to effective team work		
26	Students are well prepared for external exams		
27	You feel able to raise issues that you feel strongly about		
28	The department has a clear vision		
29	There are systematic procedures for the moderation of assessments		
30	Departmental meetings focus mainly on teaching and learning and not administration		
31	Opportunities are created for colleagues to share good practice		
32	Effective support is provided in the department when behaviour problems occur		
33	Clear priorities for development are identified collectively		
34	Student achievement is celebrated		
35	Day-to-day routine tasks are efficiently organized		
36	The department understands clearly what needs to be improved		
37	Staff achievement is celebrated		
38	Student achievement is rewarded		
39	Students' work is well displayed		
40	The work of the department is effectively promoted		

The survey should be completed and handed in confidentially. Participants should be encouraged to use the whole range of scores available and not restrict themselves to 3s and 4s. When all the sheets are returned the scores can be averaged to produce two rankings: one on the basis of 'importance' (column A) and one on the basis of 'performance' (column B). Each descriptor can then be placed into one of four categories:

- Those high in both importance and performance rankings. These areas of success can be celebrated and analysed to see if the reasons for success can be replicated in other areas.
- Those high in importance but low in performance. These issues will need to be considered for inclusion in the development plan.

- Those low in importance but high in performance. These issues might be unpopular 'housekeeping' tasks or irritating time wasters. It is important to consider how necessary each one is.
- Those low in both importance and performance. These can probably be ignored.

Summary

The purpose of development planning is to improve the quality of teaching and learning and outcomes for students through successful management of innovation and change. Middle leaders are critical to the success of school development. By being systematic in their approach to development planning they can help to reduce the stress associated with change and can ensure that the aims and mission of a school are translated into practice through 'a logical progression from policy formulation to policy implementation within the planning hierarchy' (Giles 1997: 8).

Heads of Department and Heads of Year will principally be involved in the writing of development plans and action plans for their areas. These form part of the school development plan and contain targets relating to whole school aims as well as targets generated by the team relating to issues of concern that they have identified.

Development planning is a cyclical process involving audit, construction, implementation and evaluation. It involves planning for the maintenance of aspects of provision that are effective as well as planning to develop areas of weakness. It is important that planned developments are based on evaluation of data and are realistic and achievable, that people know clearly who is responsible, that clear timescales are agreed and that success criteria are established at the planning stage.

Collaboration, openness and critical reflection are essential when teams are evaluating their performance. Collective ownership of the development plan with key tasks shared between team members is important for effective implementation. Team leaders need regularly to review progress so as to avoid developments falling behind agreed schedules.

9

Leading professional learning

Introduction

Most leaders of subjects have usually gained promotion because they have a track record of effective teaching. They are good in the classroom and they love their subject. This is important as heads of department do need to be able to lead by example. Their own classroom practice should be such that they are respected as a teacher by their colleagues. This does not mean they have to be the best teacher in their department; effective teaching comprises many elements and it is unlikely that any individual will be the most accomplished in all aspects. If a middle leader is in the fortunate position of having outstanding teachers in their team, they should celebrate their capabilities and ensure they are used effectively to develop the pedagogy of other team members.

As a middle leader it is important that you are ambitious for teachers and teaching assistants in your team, helping them to be the very best practitioners they can be, not only to benefit the students but to help them feel satisfied and proud and to fulfil career aspirations they may have. It is important therefore to establish a culture of continuous learning and to make staff development a key aspect of your role. Leaders achieve great things through others. Effective subject leaders understand that they reach only some students through their own teaching; the rest must access high quality provision through other members of the team.

Effective teaching and learning

Part of a team's vision is likely to include providing students with high quality learning experiences. This requires agreement and clarity about what constitutes effective teaching and learning. In order to arrive at a consensus it is important to consider what is known through research about effectiveness in the classroom. It is also useful to know what your students think makes a good teacher and what classroom strategies most help them learn.

Ofsted inspectors tend to focus on outcomes for students when making an initial assessment of a school, believing that if outcomes are good it is logical that teaching must also be good. There is naturally a link between effective teaching and the performance of students but in order to help develop your team of teachers it is important to look more closely at what teachers actually do that has most impact on learning. Although specific teaching tools and techniques evolve and change (e.g. the use of ICT in the classroom), the basic qualities needed to be effective as a teacher remain fairly constant. Barber and Brighouse (1992), for example, associated the following qualities and characteristics with 'good' teachers:

- Good understanding of self and of inter-personal relationships
- Generosity of spirit
- Sense of humour
- Sharp observational powers
- Interest in and concern for others
- Infectious enthusiasm for what is taught
- Imagination
- Energy
- Intellectual curiosity
- Professional growth and understanding of how children learn
- Ability to plan appropriate learning programmes for classes/groups/ individuals
- Understanding of their curriculum in the context of the school as a whole

David Reynolds (1998) summarized research on effective teaching from a number of different countries. He noted great consistency in the research findings, with the following traits common to all successful teaching:

- Intellectual challenge through high expectations, exciting interest and appropriate questioning
- Strong classroom structures with a limited range of goals
- Efficient use of time with well-handled lesson transitions and good use of homework

In 2000 Hay McBer published a model of teacher effectiveness. They had conducted extensive research into what exactly successful teachers do, by talking to a number of 'star teachers', their pupils and their colleagues. They also observed these teachers at work in an effort to identify practices and characteristics common to all of them, even though they came from a variety of types of school and a range of geographical areas. The research confirmed much of what was already known about teacher effectiveness and concluded that a combination of interconnected factors contributed to overall effectiveness. These factors were classified as teaching skills, professional characteristics and classroom climate.

The full report can be found online (http://dera.ioe.ac.uk/4566/1/RR216. pdf) but the following summarizes what the research concluded about the teaching skills of the very best teachers.

- Effective teachers communicate *high expectations* directly to students. They encourage effort, accuracy and good presentation. They have differentiated objectives for students of different ability but are consistent in expecting all students to do their best. They use a variety of techniques to motivate students, draw on students' own experience in lessons and give them opportunities to take responsibility for their own learning.
- Effective teachers' *planning* is thorough and systematic. Each lesson is considered in the context of the longer-term scheme of work and takes into account what students learnt in the previous lesson and for homework. Account is taken of the needs of different ability groups within the class. Lesson intentions (expected learning outcomes) are shared with students and instructions given are clear. Lesson objectives are reviewed with the class.
- Effective teachers employ a *variety of teaching strategies*. Many activities are led by the teacher. Information is presented with enthusiasm and clarity and the lessons move at a brisk pace. Individual work and small group activities are common. The learning is often 'active'. The teacher uses questioning regularly and in a sophisticated way to help move students' understanding on.
- Effective teachers have a clear strategy for *behaviour management*. Their classrooms are places where a sense of order exists. They set clear expectations and boundaries for behaviour. They nip inappropriate behaviour in the bud. They make sure they know what is going on everywhere in their classroom (360° vision). In schools where there are significant numbers of students with challenging behaviour effective teachers have a very structured approach to each lesson, with regard to behaviour. For example, they stand at the classroom door to greet students. These approaches are used alongside the longer-term approach of getting to know the students well and making them feel valued as individuals.
- Effective teachers make good use of *time and resources* (including other adults in class). Lessons are started briskly, activities are well paced with effective transitions between activities, and there is time for review built in at the end of a lesson. The teacher's time is allocated fairly among students. Resources are organized efficiently in the classroom so that the lesson runs smoothly. For example, books and materials needed are set out in advance of a lesson to ensure time is not wasted and pace is maintained.
- Effective teachers use a range of *assessment* methods to monitor progress. Tests, competitions, questions in class and regular written work are all used. Students are encouraged and helped to assess their own work and set targets for improvement. Critical and supportive comments are provided on

students' written work, emphasizing the 'next steps' needed to improve. Effective teachers use the information gathered from assessment to inform planning, for example, to plug learning gaps.

- Effective teachers make good use of *homework*. This is set and marked regularly and is integrated into the work being covered in the lesson.

The professional characteristics identified in the report are defined as 'deep-seated patterns of behaviour which outstanding teachers display more often, in more circumstances and in greater degree of intensity than their colleagues' (Hay McBer 2000: 11). These characteristics include:

- Professional behaviour characterized by respect for others, self-confidence, creating trust and a willingness to challenge and support students.
- Clear thinking, enabling cause and effect to be recognized (analysis) and patterns and links to be made (conceptualization).
- Channelling energy into planning and setting expectations. These teachers are committed to improvement and are willing to seek out information that will help them to get the best out of their students.
- Leadership abilities demonstrated through motivating students, adaptability and flexibility and a willingness to hold their students to account for their achievement and behaviour.
- Good inter-personal skills leading to the formation of productive relationships with colleagues, effective teamwork and the capacity to influence other people.

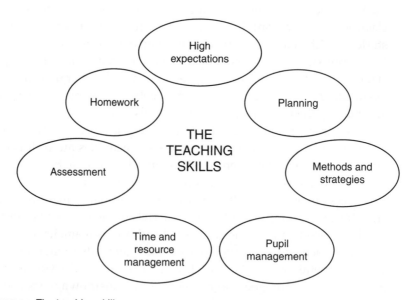

FIGURE 9.1 The teaching skills.

Finally, the report makes reference to 'classroom climate'. Essentially, the researchers tried to uncover what it feels like for a student to be in a good teacher's classroom and identify exactly what features that make up the ethos of the classroom help to motivate them. The following points were identified as being important:

- Clarity about the purpose of the lesson
- A feeling of order in the classroom
- Clear standards relating to behaviour
- Fairness (no favouritism)
- The opportunity to participate actively
- The opportunity to make decisions
- Students given support and responsibilities, as appropriate
- A safe classroom (free from bullying and fear)
- A stimulating classroom (where students' interest is developed)
- A clean and comfortable environment

At department level, most of these themes could be explored through discussion and, if appropriate, made a focus for improvement through teacher development. It would be possible to take a key theme, for example 'assessment' or 'homework', and agree a checklist of what effective practice looks like. This checklist could then be used by individuals to improve their own practice and also for monitoring purposes. Team discussions become even more powerful when they involve consideration of students' views, systematically gathered.

Student voice

Why it matters

While research evidence provides a comprehensive understanding of what makes a good teacher, it is extremely helpful in the context of your own school to consult learners about teaching and learning; after all, they are the clients!

Consulting students has become an important part of self-evaluation because it tells us about the quality of a school or classroom from the learners' perspective. Used well, 'student voice' helps teachers, school leaders, parents and students to be aware of and responsive to the conditions that support and detract from learning. Teachers in a self-improving department will inform their agenda for change from what students can tell them about learning and teaching. Some teachers may feel uncomfortable about entering into genuine, critical dialogue with students, since it might change the traditional power relationships. It is therefore important to take time to build a climate of trust in which teachers and learners can evaluate their work together in an open and constructive way.

Consultation is important because it can provide teachers with valuable evidence about:

- What it is like to learn their subject
- Students' satisfaction with the way they are taught
- How secure and safe students feel in their lessons
- How much progress they think they are making
- Whether they face any problems in the subject and what is done to resolve them
- What they know, understand and can do and the extent to which they are fulfilling their potential

Young people in school who feel they are being 'treated like children' quickly become disengaged and tend to develop a negative perception of themselves as learners. They may see learning in school as something they have to do, rather than a valuable and necessary part of their lives. Genuine consultation helps learners to feel valued as active participants in school, as opposed to (unwilling) 'consumers'. Consulting students can improve their achievement and commitment and help the teacher focus on key levers for improving teaching and learning. Companies and service providers consult their consumers because it helps them to tailor their products and services better. Similarly, paying attention to learners' perspectives has the potential to improve learning and teaching in schools. Teachers that have consulted students are generally impressed by the richness, the positive nature, insightfulness and the good sense of many of the students' ideas.

Reflection point

Use the bullets below to consider the current situation in your department or year group in relation to consulting students.

- *Do your students feel their views are respected or do you need to raise their expectations about what they can contribute? If so, would consulting them about learning make a difference?*
- *Have you used student consultation to find ways of improving the aspects of teaching and learning?*
- *If you have consulted students have you acted on the findings?*
- *Have you used student consultation to measure the impact of changes you have introduced in the curriculum and/or teaching and learning?*
- *Could student consultation data help you to identify the kinds of difficulties encountered by different groups of students and enable you to develop strategies to support these groups?*
- *Students suggest that having someone to talk to (an older peer or an adult) about their learning helps raise their confidence in themselves as learners. Are there*

students in your class who would find having a mentor or peer support helpful? Could some of your older students act as a mentor to others and benefit themselves from the process?

- *Do all your students understand how they could improve their work and what they are aiming for?*

Some themes for student consultation

The following are all possible areas for consulting students:

- Things that help them to learn/get in the way of learning
- How to deal with classroom noise
- Classroom rules
- How to involve parents/carers more in their learning
- What they would like more/less of in lessons
- Grouping and seating arrangements
- What topics they enjoy and why
- What makes a good lesson
- Best ways to start/end a lesson
- How they learn from each other
- What to do if they do not understand the work or miss a lesson
- How teachers can best support them in their revision for exams
- What feedback helps them to learn best
- What motivates them
- How confident they feel in their abilities as learners
- Their understanding of the criteria for 'good' work
- The impact of students' friendships on their learning
- How the way time is managed in school impacts on students' learning

Principles of consulting students

Consultation must take place in an atmosphere of trust and mutual respect. Whatever approach you use, it must be simple and accessible and it must generate insights that enable you to deepen your understanding of learning and make informed changes.

- Decide whether you want information to test a hypothesis or to measure the impact of changes you have introduced
- Ensure that the topic is not trivial – link it to the priorities identified in the departmental improvement plan
- Demonstrate a genuine desire to hear what students have to say
- Ensure a spread of students (range of ability, level of confidence, behaviour)
- Explain the purpose of the consultation to the students involved
- Make sure students know what will happen to what they say

- Students must be confident that expressing their opinion or describing their experience will not disadvantage them
- Give feedback to everyone who is consulted
- When actions are taken and decisions made, ensure that students are able to understand the wider context in which their views are placed
- Ensure that parents' attitudes to consultation are considered – the practices and values that consultation embodies can be in conflict with those of the home

Whom will you consult?

Make sure that the selection of students is appropriate to your focus, not just the more articulate, able or well behaved students. Ensure that you also gather the views of students who are less positive about learning those of minority groups.

- A year group
- Boys? Girls?
- Particular ability group
- A specific class
- Lower, middle, higher attainers (from one or across several year groups)

Who will carry it out?

- Teachers
- Teaching assistants
- Subject leader (you)
- Link governor
- Your line manager
- Researchers
- Local advisers or consultants
- Students as researchers

How frequent will the consultation be?

- At the end of a block of work
- Consultation with each class on a termly or yearly basis
- In response to a specific initiative (e.g. changes to the curriculum)
- At pre-planned review points to assess the impact of changes in teaching and learning or curriculum

What form will the consultation take?

There are three basic forms of consultation:

- Direct consultation – students are asked directly for their views in talk or writing

- Prompted consultation – a stimulus is used to 'prompt' students to express their views
- Mediated consultation – students express their views through art or drama and then talk about what they wanted to communicate

Direct consultation

Ask students directly about their experiences or views, through interviews, group discussion or through open or closed questions in a questionnaire or checklist. Students may respond in writing or what they say may be recorded. On questionnaires they may tick boxes to indicate a view that is similar to theirs or to indicate the extent to which they agree or disagree with a range of statements. Direct consultation is effective when students have something to say and want to say it – for example, the things that help them to learn and that get in the way of their learning, what activities they like/dislike.

Prompted consultation

This approaches students' thinking and feelings by a less direct route. It is helpful when students are not confident about expressing their opinions, the topic might make them feel uneasy or students do not know where to begin. An advantage of prompted consultation is that you can start with things that other students have said about the topic. This encourages students to offer their own views.

Examples of prompted consultation:

- A card with a statement by a student from another school or another country to stimulate a response
- A video clip or photograph of a differently organized classroom
- Another department's 'mission statement' or list of 'rules'
- The results of a questionnaire that the whole class has completed can be a useful prompt for further discussion

Mediated consultation

Rather than relying on words and comments, students communicate feelings or summarize experiences through drawings, taking photographs, making a video or creating and performing a role-play.

- Students role-play a typical teacher-student scenario
- Students photograph places where they feel most comfortable working
- Students role-play classroom scenarios in which their concentration is undermined by other students' behaviour

Some useful tools to support the garnering of students' views are provided as appendices. If you have joined a team with no experience of this, encourage your team to experiment individually with student voice so that they begin to feel at ease with the idea. Gradually, you can discuss and agree more systematic surveys to inform policy and practice across the department. Table 9.1 provides a summary of various types of consultation and their benefits. The important thing, of course, is to act on your findings. As with tracking data, student voice data it is only of any real value if it results in changes to provision that improve the student experience and impact on their learning.

Acting on findings

The wealth of knowledge gained from research about effective teaching is pretty much reflected in the Teachers' Standards (2013). It is unlikely that

TABLE 9.1 Ways of consulting students

Consultation tool	Context and fitness for purpose	Potential advantages	Potential disadvantages
Questionnaires	A versatile tool that can serve a range of purposes, generally used in whole school context but may refer specifically to classroom, out of hours learning or other contexts for learning	Provide quantitative data; are quick to use; easy to analyse; offer a broad overview; are anonymous; can also be used to gather qualitative data	Can limit responses; are usually open to a variety of interpretations; may encourage random answers rather than considered reflection; are context sensitive and not hugely reliable
Individual interviews	May be used for a variety of purposes and be conducted by external critical friends, teachers or by students interviewing one another, often older pupils interviewing younger peers; training is an important prerequisite	Can provide in-depth insights in a context where there is anonymity and no need to conform to classmates' or teachers' expectations	On the part of the interviewee, requires verbal skills, a willingness to open up and trust the interviewer; can be uncomfortable and exposing for pupils; relies on high-level interviewer's skills; is time-consuming and not very cost effective
Group interviews	Used to cover greater ground and in less time than individual interviews; well-handled, allows for rich dialogue, consensus and challenge	Students, teachers and parents may be more relaxed in a group setting; ideas are sparked and insights gained that might not emerge from an individual interview; more cost effective than individual interviews	Dangers of peer pressure and conformity to mainstream views; difficult to quantify unless voting or other recording systems are used

TABLE 9.1 *Continued*

Consultation tool	Context and fitness for purpose	Potential advantages	Potential disadvantages
Focus groups	Used, and often confused, with group interviews but they have a more structured protocol, usually led by someone with trained expertise	Is able to extract the maximum information by virtue of its tight structure	Requires expertise in managing a group and relies on training
Group card sorts	Card sorts come in many forms but usually involve a group choosing or prioritizing items that they agree on as representing their view of practice	Its hands-on format benefits people who are more reserved or less articulate; stimulates dialogue	May allow stronger members of the group to dominate; the end result may be meaningless without a record of the dialogue leading up to it
Sentence completion	Providing a prompt such as 'I learn best when…' can be a helpful starter for students but also for a range of other users (e.g. teachers or parents)	Provides the stimulus for an open-ended response and can tap into feelings	Low in reliability as it depends a lot on context, recent events and feelings at the time
Drawing and paintings	Very useful with young children but can also be powerful when used with adults to portray their school, their job, or their relationships, for example	Is creative; no right and wrong answers; generates insights less easily accessible through paper and pencil or conversation; pupils are more likely to talk about things they have created themselves	May be highly ambiguous, difficult to analyse and requiring high inference, unless used as a basis for a more extended individual or group interview
Photo evaluation	Usually used for whole school purposes, for example students work in groups with a camera to record places around school that are threatening/ unthreatening or show the school in a good/ bad light	Allows a school to see itself through a different and graphic lens; is an enjoyable activity for students; can be empowering	Is limited by the medium to what can be seen and by the perceptiveness of those with the camera; may be threatening and reveal things some people would rather not have exposed

continued

TABLE 9.1 *Continued*

Consultation tool	Context and fitness for purpose	Potential advantages	Potential disadvantages
Spot checks	An instrument that gives immediate feedback on what is happening at a given moment in the classroom or elsewhere, such as in study support or homework, for example	Gives an instant snapshot of pupil engagement and feelings and provides the basis for a rich conversation about teaching and learning	Can expose practice and accentuate differences in teachers' and students' perceptions, which may be discomforting
Role play	Used to recreate a situation, replaying it through drama to illustrate a student's perception, or to examine some detail or aspect of the event	Enjoyable; a break from pencil and paper routines. Can be very revealing in holding up a mirror to a teacher or to the school	Requires skills and confidence on the part of the players and can meet with resistance; is limited to what can be represented in this medium
Diaries and logs	Keeping a record of events, successes, problems raised, solutions found, can be used by students, teachers, middle or senior leaders, governors or parents	Provides an on-going record for self-evaluation; can be rich in detail and insight	Diaries and logs are necessarily subjective and portray things through a single lens

students will deviate in their views from these findings, but student voice will add tones and textures that reflect their experience and the local context. As a team leader you will use the Standards (and other data including student voice) to inform the objectives you set colleagues as part of the appraisal process (see chapter 12). Information about effective practices and behaviours can also be useful in supporting lesson observations and discussions aimed at identifying particular aspects of practice individuals or the team need to improve. This is especially powerful when team members have agreed together what good practice looks like and what should, therefore, be looked for in observations. Once the use of student voice becomes part of the culture of your department you will be able to use it more strategically to support evaluation and inform development planning (Figure 9.2).

Teachers' professional learning

Improving provision and pedagogy can only happen if teachers and support staff are themselves effective learners. This is why so much emphasis has been

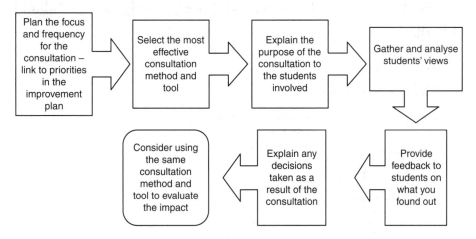

FIGURE 9.2 Systematic use of student voice.

placed in earlier chapters on establishing a reflective learning culture at team level. Such a culture cannot be established easily and, once in place, still needs nurturing. It is never possible to guarantee that all team members will become reflective practitioners, but there are approaches and structures that can be used to encourage this approach.

One size doesn't fit all

In the past, most teachers were subjected to a 'one size fits all' approach to professional learning (then called in-service education and training or INSET). This typically involved time on a staff training day being used to enable the entire staff to listen to some outside expert hold forth on a key priority the school needed to work on. The problems with this approach were that it was undifferentiated and learners tended to be passive. By failing to take into account the prior knowledge of participants, some listeners were soon bored while others struggled with the concepts being presented. The use of an external expert meant the school's context was often ignored and a didactic delivery style meant listeners had little opportunity to engage critically with the issues presented. This lack of engagement meant understanding for some was superficial.

Professional learning (or continuing professional development, CPD) is now more creatively and effectively managed in many schools. There are greater efforts to balance using external experts with colleagues in school with expertise or highly developed skills. Similarly, there is now a better balance between training linked to whole school priorities and development opportunities more closely aligned to individuals' needs, based on the use of audit tools and data from lesson observations. Another major shift has been the move towards learning 'in situ' resulting from the realization that training and development will only have impact if the learning of something new is followed by putting it into practice (Table 9.2). This shift towards more practical and personalized professional learning is important as it offers opportunities for more rapid development of the school workforce and real impact on pedagogy.

The shift isn't accidental. It is based on an understanding of what works with adult learners. Middle leaders planning learning opportunities for their team need to bear in mind what Earley and Weindling (2004) noted about adult learners:

– They require a climate of trust, respect and collaboration
– Their previous experience has to be taken into account
– They need to accept the need to learn
– They are biased towards problem solving as a learning activity
– Practical relevance is important for commitment
– They need intrinsic motivation to learn effectively

If you take over a team where professional learning has been neglected you might find some teachers very resistant to changing the way they teach. They might be fearful of moving out of their comfort zone, their ways of working

TABLE 9.2 Training and evidence of impact

Training method	Level of impact			
	General awareness of a new approach	Understanding of how to implement the approaches in a new context	Internalizing the new approach	Able to apply the new approach in a range of contexts
Presentation of the approach through workshop or reading	Evidence			
Modelling of the new approach by demonstration or video	Evidence	Evidence		
Practice in nonthreatening settings, e.g. simulated	Evidence	Evidence	Evidence	
Constructive feedback on performance	Evidence	Evidence	Evidence	Evidence
In-class support such as coaching by peer or expert	Evidence	Evidence	Evidence	Evidence

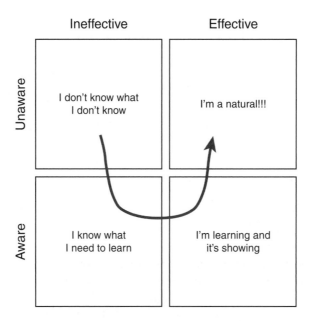

Ineffective   Effective

Unaware

I don't know what
I don't know

I'm a natural!!!

Aware

I know what
I need to learn

I'm learning and
it's showing

FIGURE 9.3 The four stages of learning.

could be so entrenched seeing something better is really challenging and they are possibly unaware of just how inadequate their current practice is. They will need to be shifted out of what learning theorists call a state of 'unconscious incompetence' (Figure 9.3) if progress is to be made. You may well face resistance initially but by creating a culture in which talk about learning is central you will begin to erode people's entrenched views, an important first step towards change.

Talk is important

At team level, leaders should be balancing the need for professional learning to support development plan priorities with strategies that allow individuals to improve specific aspects of their classroom practice. First, though, a more open approach towards improving pedagogy can be developed by encouraging talk about teaching and learning. This can be done in various ways. Here are some of them:

- Ensuring most time spent in team meetings is focused on discussion of how to improve teaching and learning (routine administration and notices can be passed on by using a team bulletin).
- Conducting individual interviews with team members (not linked to appraisal) to talk specifically about pedagogy, identifying strengths that could be shared and areas of practice that could be further developed.

- Having team meetings in different teachers' classrooms so that they can lead on some aspect of how they organize their environment to maximize learning.
- Asking all team members to be on the lookout for interesting articles about teaching and learning, which they can share with the team.
- Regularly e-mailing team members with some interesting article or saying about effective teaching and learning and then discussing these in team meetings.
- Agreeing joint meetings with another department to share ideas on teaching (most classroom practice can be applied to almost all subjects with slight modifications).
- Providing opportunities for learning walks with another team member to spark discussion about what is happening in other areas of school.
- Enabling observations of other teachers to take place, with a key focus that will be discussed afterwards. Use might be made here of a checklist created following analysis of student voice surveys.
- Using video clips in team meetings to analyse effective classroom practice.
- Using joint planning as means of collective sharing and learning.
- Arranging for colleagues to visit other schools to investigate specific aspects of provision.

At first, talk about teaching and learning might be a little cautious. Some people will be reluctant to express their ideas and beliefs about teaching for fear of being judged by others. The more talk is built into routines, the more disciplined people will become about listening and contributing. This can be encouraged, as with students, by the use of talk partners or seating people in a circle, so that everyone gets a chance to be heard. As with gathering pupil voice data, though, the important thing is to move from talk to action, for example by allowing teachers to experiment with new approaches. One of the most powerful ways this can be encouraged is by the use of coaching. While this can be heavy on time, there is clear evidence that the impact from effective coaching is long lasting, unlike some other forms of professional learning.

Coaching

Coaching for teachers is usually concerned with improving classroom practice. When we coach the effectiveness of what we do depends on our belief about human potential. The expression 'to get the best out of someone' implies that more lies within the person waiting to be released. Unless the coach (or leader or teacher) believes that people possess more capability than they are currently demonstrating, he will not be able to help them reveal it. As Whitmore (2013: 14) explains, to be successful coaches must 'think of people in terms of their potential, not their performance'.

At its simplest, coaching is about enabling people to grow. It involves a one-to-one relationship in which the coach supports a colleague to identify, focus on and achieve specific targets. Through a series of discussions, 1:1 or in small coaching groups, the coach helps the individual teacher to explore:

– Pedagogical skill goals, personal goals or career goals
– Their current practice and context
– The changes they want to make
– The actions they want to take to make the changes
– Their experience during the learning process
– The progress made

Good coaches are good listeners, good observers and positive thinkers. They make an effort to know, accept and respect the goals and interests of their colleagues and, in the end, establish an environment in which the colleagues' accomplishment is limited only by the extent of their talent. Confidentiality is essential if the relationship is to work effectively. This enables individuals to speak freely and trust that anything said will be treated with absolute confidence.

A cycle of actions is necessary to enable coaching conversations to develop in a productive manner.

There are some key qualities that coaches develop over time. These are at the heart of effective coaching and also have relevance to the classroom and many other contexts. Coaches should aim to become excellent in the following areas:

> Observing – Listening – Questioning – Probing – Summarizing

In a pure coaching relationship the coach focuses on drawing out solutions from the learner rather than offering advice and guidance. This is different to mentoring, where a more experienced colleague supports someone at a point of career transition. A mentor will sometimes quite legitimately make recommendations or suggestions based on their own experience. For example, a newly qualified teacher's mentor may well give very practical advice on behaviour management if the NQT is unable to work out what action they might need to take.

In a subject or pastoral team it is excellent practice to use more experienced and effective colleagues as coaches. The main aim of the coaching is to release potential and by so doing improve practice. There might be occasions therefore when a coach slips from coaching into a mentoring style in order to assist this process by offering more directed guidance. Of course coaches want their colleagues to develop their own solutions to problems and they will develop questioning techniques to help this but, occasionally, they may need to offer guidance based on their experience and understanding. The important thing

TABLE 9.3 Phases in successful coaching

Phase	Purpose
Contracting	• Establish the purpose of the relationship • Establish the ground rules • Build trust
Building rapport	• Develop a deeper understanding of the learners context • Develop an understanding of how the individual is motivated • Develop an awareness of the values and roles the individual thinks are important
Understand the situation	• Make sense of the data (from lesson observation) • Develop shared understanding about the classroom environment • Gain an insight into intentions and goals • Start to develop the outcomes
Gaining commitment	• Discuss different classroom strategies and teaching scenarios • Begin to understand the individual's perceptions of using different scenarios and strategies • Consider how the changes in pedagogy will impact on students and how they will respond • Establish why the intended changes to practice and/or behaviour are important
Testing hunches	• Move from analysis to action • Focus on the intended changes and their outcomes • Be specific to context and to classes • Establish milestones • Offer ideas *but not solutions* • Seek robustness by linking ideas to specific lessons
Feeding back	• Check for progress against agreed actions and review practice (through further observations) • Check that the agreed changes are being implemented. The plan may need to be adapted • Agree the way forward
Action planning	• Make clear links between the changes in practice and personal development as a teacher • Be clear about how changes will be recognized • Ensure that the next meeting is carefully planned • Think through where you will re-enter the cycle

is that the coach works in a way that is 'fit for purpose' in that it enables the learner to make clear steps forward towards the goals they have agreed.

Lesson observation

Coaching, of course, involves lesson observations and these should be a very positive experience for the teacher concerned. However, in far too many schools teachers have come to associate lesson observations with monitoring and accountability. It is necessary, of course, to have some observations for monitoring purposes. A head teacher needs to be aware of the quality of teaching and learning across their school and middle leaders need to observe their teachers as part of the appraisal cycle. Beyond this, it is important that middle leaders encourage the use of *lesson observation* for development and encourage their team to 'take control' of observations. There are many ways observations can be used to assist teachers' professional growth:

- In some schools small cameras or a system called IRIS Connect allow teachers to record their own lessons for later viewing and analysis. This is very unthreatening to teachers as only they see the recording.
- Peer observations can aid understanding of practice. Here two teachers who trust each other agree to observe and feedback on each other's lesson. Such observations are best when a pre-agreed schedule around a particular theme is used, e.g. questioning techniques or group work strategies.
- Short observations of a part of several lessons, e.g. starters or plenaries, can be a powerful way to learn. Having a sharp focus helps the observer concentrate on just one aspect of pedagogy.
- Observing lessons in a different subject can be powerful as the subject content doesn't get in the way and attention can be paid purely to the teaching and learning taking place.
- Joint observations involving a middle leader and a colleague can help to ensure consistency of judgements about teaching and learning. Very powerful learning can come from analysing together what has been seen.
- Watching recordings of parts of lessons as a team can help to develop a common language and understanding around pedagogy.
- For colleagues finding particular students difficult to manage, observing those students taught by other teachers can be very helpful.

Learn, learn, learn

There is no doubt that coaching and lesson observations are very powerful methods of achieving deep learning and understanding. However, they are not the only way for teachers and support staff to learn. As a middle leader you should encourage and support your colleagues in their learning journeys. If they are motivated through desiring career progression so much the better. Of course, you have a limited budget for professional learning but some sources of development (often the most powerful) can be arranged 'in-house' and cost nothing in monetary terms. In effective schools a broad range of development opportunities, other than attendance on courses, should be available to all staff. Examples include:

- Learning through collaboration with others, both in school and with colleagues from other schools, e.g. through joint planning or sharing resources.

- Being a mentor or being mentored. Good mentoring relationships allow colleagues to learn from experiences of each other.
- Being a coach or coaching others (see above).
- Peer networks enable groups to share experiences, information and good practice with colleagues from other schools.
- Professional learning teams set up, for example, to analyse and interpret pupil data or solve a specific challenge by seeking to identify and implement solutions collaboratively.
- Learning from highly skilled teachers such as Specialist Leaders in Education (SLAs) through observing them teaching and planning with them.
- Joint planning with colleagues within school and across schools.
- Visits to other schools to observe lessons, discuss practice, provide a demonstration lesson, shadow colleagues etc.
- Working in partnership with higher education institutions and other schools to research an aspect of teaching or learning. This also includes reading academic and professional journals and might, or might not, be part of planned study for a qualification.
- Make use of on-line learning opportunities and forums.
- External training events and courses organized by exam boards, local authorities, teaching schools and private providers.
- Job shadowing within school, across schools and in industry, to further career development.
- Starting a professional portfolio helps individuals to plan a career path, and allows individuals to record, reflect, analyse and self-evaluate.
- Professional subject associations often provide up-to-date information relevant to specific subjects through journals, websites and conferences.
- Taking on additional responsibilities such as being an exam marker or moderator, becoming a governor representative, contributing to an academic or professional journal, taking part in interviews, leading staff development, developing policies.
- Taking part in nationally recognized courses e.g. NPQH or MA.

Removing barriers

There are no doubt people who will read this chapter but conclude that most of what is being suggested is impossible to arrange due to lack of time and/ or money. Time and money should not be allowed to be an excuse for doing nothing. There are many things recommended in this chapter that can easily be put in place for very little cost. The more ambitious ideas are worth fighting for. Most heads will be receptive to middle leader requests if you go to them with a solution not a problem. Be professional. Make your case. Meet the head teacher armed with a plan so you can be very clear about what you are trying to achieve, how much it will cost and what the measurable benefits will be. If you can involve outside experts, e.g. a local authority adviser or a teacher training department this will strengthen your case. A coaching programme jointly planned with the local authority, focused on moving teachers from 'good' to 'outstanding', using a methodology easily replicated in other departments would be a difficult package for any head teacher to resist.

Action point

Some teachers will talk more freely about learning if this is structured around a very practical idea. As a middle leader you could encourage everyone in your team to try out an 'idea of the week'. For example, if you wanted to improve plenary sessions as part of embedding AfL, you could ask all the team to try out an idea with one class and then report back at an agreed meeting. The idea could be something as simple as making use of 'exit tickets'. This requires the teacher to give each student an index card near the end of the lesson and get them to write their answer to a key question on it before they leave. The teacher can then analyse the responses to assess how well a concept has been understood and to inform the next lesson.

Try out an 'idea of the week' with your team.

Summary

Making learning for all central to your team vision is essential. Being committed to supporting your colleagues to be the best they can be and achieve their career goals is good for them and good for their students. Even reluctant learners and teachers 'stuck in a rut' can move forward if handled well. Work hard at creating a learning culture in your team even if this is not the prevailing ethos in school. Focus as much time as possible on talking about teaching and learning, agreeing what good practice looks like and experimenting with new ideas. Use students' feedback as a rationale for changing practice. Make full use of experienced and capable colleagues in your team by using them as coaches. Show that you value less secure members of staff and encourage reflective practice and self-evaluation. Bring focus and rigour to improving pedagogy through development linked to appraisal targets.

10

Improving the quality of teaching and learning

Case study by Kathryn Stephenson

Introduction

Teaching and learning is the core business of all schools. Where high quality teaching and learning takes place, students will be engaged, enthused and inspired and, consequently, make measurable progress. Get the teaching and learning right and everything else falls into place. That's the challenge for middle leaders working within the whole school framework. You have an exciting opportunity to ensure that the development of your subject ensures that students see the value of it, engage with it, ask questions about it and take it beyond the four walls of the classroom!

As explored in earlier chapters, it is vital to have a shared departmental vision. Ask the following questions: What will students gain by studying your subject? What skills, knowledge and understanding will they develop in your subject that they can't get anywhere else in school? How will their lives be shaped by the things that they study in your classrooms? Decide on this, then return to it. Keep it central. When making decisions about what to change and how to develop, discuss how it will help to reinforce the vision and improve the quality of teaching of learning. If it doesn't, then don't do it!

Think also about the time that you spend as a middle leader discussing teaching and learning. In a typical week, what priority do you give to ensuring that high quality teaching and learning takes place? How often do you have a conversation with members of your department that is specifically about teaching and learning? How often do you create time for meaningful pedagogical discussion? How often do you ask students what they think about lessons in your department and how they can be improved? How often do students have the opportunity to co-construct the learning?

So how do we continuously improve the quality of teaching and learning? This chapter will focus on three key questions:

- What are the key features of high quality learning to secure progress for students in your subject?
- How do you create a culture in which to improve the quality of teaching and learning?
- What strategies can you use to drive improvement?

The strategies shared in this chapter have been used, developed and modified by departments in my school, an 11–18 comprehensive school, where our school aim is 'Arete', to be the best we can be. Some of the strategies will be appropriate for your context, others not! Select and adapt only the things that will have an impact on your faculty or department.

What are the key features of high quality learning to secure progress for students in your subject?

Three things can be considered here: what happens in lessons, what can we do to make homework an integral part of learning and how can written feedback be used to ensure that students make progress?

Taking into consideration your vision, identify as a team the key features of high quality learning in your subject. Rank them and discuss what progress in each of them looks like so that you have a shared team understanding. To delve deeper, subject associations are good places to seek guidance along with using Ofsted subject specific criteria to identify which areas are currently being closely examined in your subject. For example, currently outstanding teaching in Geography must include fieldwork opportunities for students whereas in Design & Technology there is a focus on students 'designing' rather than just making.

Homework is a great opportunity for students to develop their independence and extend their thinking. If homework is not an integral part of learning and seems irrelevant to students then it can not only prevent students from making as much progress as is possible but can also reduce their interest in the subject. This was highlighted by the Sutton Trust (2013) in their toolkit, which states that,

> Evidence also suggests that how homework relates to learning during normal school time is important. In the most effective examples homework was an integral part of learning, rather than an add-on. To maximize impact, it also appears to be important that students are provided with high quality feedback on their work.

While it is likely that you will have whole school guidance on when home-work should be set and the frequency of it, the content and approach is most commonly up to you. Discuss the following key questions. Is it important for students to have homework with a different topic every week or is it possible to give students the opportunity to take on a longer project where deeper thinking will be required? For example, in Modern Foreign Lan-guages, weekly learning of vocabulary is crucial for acquisition of language whereas in Humanities and Performing Arts, where students are taught less frequently, a longer-term project can ensure that students arrive at lessons armed with a range of questions based on their homework. It also requires students to organize their time encouraging greater independence. Is it some-times better to set homework as preparation for a lesson rather than follow up to a lesson? Follow up work often requires students to evaluate and syn-thesize (higher order skills) rather than simply show knowledge. Are these higher order skills better applied in class rather than at home where there is no teacher support? For example, in History it makes a lot of sense for pupils to gather key facts and events before a lesson (as a homework task) so that in the lesson there is time to create arguments, discuss cause and effect, motiva-tion, reliability of sources etc.

Our student feedback shows that homework is most valued when it is rele-vant to the learning, has clear success criteria, gives students the opportunity to make some choices in what they do and how they do it, has a deadline that all students are required to meet and which will be given written feedback upon completion. Find out what your students think and incorporate their views into your practice.

What constitutes high quality written feedback often causes discussion and occasionally disagreement. Written feedback has a very clear purpose to enable students to make progress. However, how frequently should writ-ten feedback be given? What does high quality written feedback look like? How can a meaningful dialogue that ensures each student can address their areas for improvement and make progress be created? Use your whole school policy then agree on some department principles i.e. written feed-back should be clear, concise, accessible to the student and focus on the subject success criteria. It should enable students to take the next steps in their learning. However, written feedback is limited in its impact unless the feedback loop is complete with students responding. Make sure that stu-dents are working as hard as teachers! Therefore giving students the oppor-tunity to demonstrate that they have made progress is crucial. In Maths, for example, in their written feedback students are given a further equation or problem to solve to either demonstrate that they have addressed a miscon-ception or developed further by completing a more challenging question. In English, feedback on structure on a piece of extended writing can be used to help a student to identify an area to improve and, when they've done so, they can apply their newly developed skills to their next piece of written work and demonstrate the progress that they've made. Don't overlook the opportunity to use homework time for students to respond to their personalized feedback.

How do you create a culture that will improve the quality of teaching and learning?

Be positive and inspire

As a middle leader, you have the role to 'set the standard'! Inspiration comes as much from daily interaction as from departmental speeches! Just as when you deal with students, if you stay positive and encouraging with your team, you are more likely to get the same in return.

Create as much time as possible to discuss teaching and learning

Use e-mail or a weekly newsletter to share information that does not require discussion, such as deadlines and forthcoming events. This will create the time in meetings to discuss the things that are going to have the greatest impact on teaching and learning and therefore student progress. To maintain focus have a regular template for meeting agendas with three key areas: student progress, teaching and learning and development plan priorities. See Figure 10.1 for an example.

Use the department meeting time, which you could call a department development meeting, to carry out shared planning, discuss teaching strategies, use exercise books to evaluate written feedback and increase consistency by moderating levels and grades awarded to students. Get the agenda out early and ask others to lead teaching and learning items, bringing their own ideas, so that everyone comes to the meeting prepared to contribute and good practice can be shared effectively. By approaching meetings in this way, it will set the tone that professional development is the responsibility of every teacher and that we have a professional responsibility to help develop those around us.

Ensure that high quality teaching and learning are supported by thoughtful schemes of learning

These should include clear progression of knowledge and skills based on pedagogical understanding of the subject. Remember, while it is your responsibility as the subject leader to ensure that the schemes of learning are of a high quality, it is not your responsibility to write them all and indeed the discussions that take place when having more than one member of the team working on a scheme of learning usually increases the quality. It can also be very rewarding

Department meeting				
Present:				
Agenda	Led by	Outcomes/Actions	By whom?	Deadline
Student progress - - -				
Teaching and learning - - -				
Development plan priorities - - -				

FIGURE 10.1 Framework for departmental development meetings.

for a team member to see their scheme of learning being used by the rest of the department to plan high quality lessons. While Key Stages 4 and 5 will generally have topic titles determined by exam board specifications, at KS3 it is possible to use topic titles that will engage students as well as the teachers. For example, in Science, students start with a topic entitled 'Being a Scientist', which looks at how scientists do things before moving on to areas such as 'Doctor Doctor' where students investigate the part that science has to play in diagnosing medical problems.

Work with a monitor, evaluation and review cycle

This should feed into a shared self-evaluation process and development plan. While as a subject leader you may need to evaluate your departmental evidence as part of your self evaluation process, the sharing of priorities will give members of the team clarity and ownership of what needs to be done to achieve overall success. When there is such clarity, it is also easier to maintain accountability. There are numerous ways of structuring departmental self-evaluation and it's likely that your school will have an outline, however if not, the headings provided by Ofsted are a good starting point. At the time of writing these are:

- Students' achievement
- The quality of teaching
- Behaviour and safety
- Leadership and management
- Overall effectiveness, including the promotion of the pupils' spiritual, moral, social and cultural development.

Discuss your self-evaluation and development plan with the member of SLT who line manages your work so that they can aid you in identifying how your department fits into the wider priorities of the school.

Be strategic in the way in which you embrace school and national initiatives

Do this by identifying how they can enhance the quality of learning in your subject area. Recently, AfL has been used as a powerful tool to engage students in their own learning by creating opportunities for students to reflect on their own learning, and that of their peers, in order to identify the next steps in their learning. Where this is effective, and based upon clear success criteria linked to the learning activity, it can really deepen the learning and increase student engagement. For example, peer assessment in Years 10 or 11 using GCSE mark schemes as a tool can enable students to gain a deeper understanding of the requirements of a good answer which they can use to develop their own writing as well as giving informative feedback to their peer. Therefore, always make sure that subject development, not the use of the strategy, is the focus. As schools develop their Reading, Writing, Communication and Mathematics strategies it will be similarly crucial to ensure that they are used to deepen the subject learning. For example, a student who develops the skills required for discursive writing, who can then apply them to Humanities subjects to discuss complex issues, is clearly going to reach a much higher level.

Encourage your team to get involved in teaching and learning activities beyond the department

This can have a number of positive impacts. Teachers can get a broader understanding of the school experience of students and can share strategies that are proven to work with students that they teach. This also gives people the opportunity to hear about and develop strategies that they can then share with their teams during department development time. At my school, we have an optional Deep Learning team who meet three times every term, the agenda for which is set by members of the team who either have a good idea that they want to share or ask for the focus of the meeting to be an area on which they'd like further information. Areas that we've looked at have ranged from using online tools to get student feedback, differentiation and growth mindsets.

What strategies can be used to drive forward teaching and learning?

This section will focus on strategies within a department, which, if effectively led, can be used to establish the current quality of teaching and learning, identify the next steps then monitor their impact as part of an improvement agenda.

In order to evaluate the quality of teaching and learning, three key areas of evidence need to be triangulated; progress data, lesson observations and student work. Combining these three areas means that crucial questions can be asked about the typical quality of lessons being taught and how they are enabling all groups of students to make sustained progress.

Progress data

This includes departmental data that is generated at common assessment points. This may feed into a whole school system and be supplemented with data from Raise Online and the Fischer Family Trust (FFT). Use the data to identify departmental trends and areas of relative strength along with areas for improvement, before delving deeper into individual teacher performance across the classes that they teach. A word of caution, however; make sure that teachers have the opportunity to moderate and standardize the assessments that they are using to assess students' progress to ensure that you as a department leader have an accurate evidence base.

Link the progress data to lessons observed

Lesson observations can be used in a number of ways; to assess the quality of learning, to identify strengths of the team and individuals and to give feedback to improve performance. Have a conversation with the teacher before the observation so that the purpose of the observation is clear. Use your whole school lesson observation outline but modify it so that it's really relevant to your subject using the discussions you've had when establishing the characteristics of high quality learning in your subject. The three areas which we assess across the school are progress, teaching and learning and behaviour for learning along with recording the development of the spiritual, moral, social and cultural (SMSC) dimension.

Alongside more formal observations, encourage team members to observe each other to share good practice or get informed, constructive feedback. The most successful departments have teachers observing all or parts of each other's lessons when teachers are trialling a new strategy, dealing with a challenging class or teaching an area of the subject that they may feel less confident with. Recording lessons is also a really powerful tool for people to reflect on their own performance and assess the impact on the students that they're teaching.

For more of a snapshot on the quality of learning that is taking place within your department, and to assess typicality, a *focused learning walk* can yield important information. For example, if three Year 7 lessons are taking place simultaneously and you observe each for twenty minutes, you will be able to check consistency in level of challenge, differentiation and approach.

Students' progress

Students' progress over time can be evaluated by looking at their work. It is best to do this with them present so that you can talk to them using the discussions that you've had as a team about quality written feedback and identifying what progress looks like. By carrying out a work scrutiny with the students and their work, you can ask appropriate questions to get to the heart of the learning that has taken place and to see if students are both demonstrating progress over time and can talk about the progress that they have made, before identifying areas for improvement. Looking at books without the narrative of the student can be misleading.

Student feedback

This has a valuable place in evaluating the quality of teaching and learning. To gain a general overview, a good place to start is with the Ofsted student questions. Make sure, however, that you add to and modify them in order to reflect your department priorities and get the specific information that you need. An example of how the Ofsted questions can be modified for a department, along with those added to investigate departmental priorities, is shown in Figure 10.2 *(in italics)*.

While this is a good starting point, in order to gain qualitative responses, which are often much more helpful in effecting improvement, take a smaller group of students and discuss their responses. The second question that you ask often yields more that the first. For example, you may ask students if they think that they learn a lot in lessons with an initial response of 'most of the time'. Follow this up by asking, 'How do you know?' and students are likely to give you information about a number of areas such as feedback in

(please tick)	All of the time	Most of the time	Sometimes	Never
1	I am happy to come to * lessons.				
2	I learn a lot in * lessons.				
3	*I feel challenged in * lessons.*				
4	The department helps me to do as well as I can.				
5	I know how well I am doing in *.				
6	Adults in * explain to me how to improve my work.				
7	*Written feedback helps me to make progress.*				
8	*I have the opportunity to respond to written feedback.*				
9	Teaching in * is good.				
10	Teaching in * helps me develop skills in communication, reading, writing and mathematics.				
11	Behaviour is good in * lessons.				
12	The * department deals with all types of bullying very well.				
13	I feel safe when I am in * lessons.				
14	* teachers are interested in my views.				

*insert subject area

FIGURE 10.2 Student questionnaire.

lessons, written feedback, self assessment, ability to tackle homework independently and so on. Getting a colleague from a different subject area or your line manager to carry out the student discussions, particularly if this approach is new, will often ensure more accurate responses. At first, students often just want to please their teacher! Don't underestimate the power of student views; few teachers can resist honest feedback from informed, reflective students.

In order to create a meaningful, longer term dialogue, having a subject 'learning group' can add an extra dimension. When given a clear remit to focus on teaching and learning, students will share honest ideas and opinions about areas that they think are good, and useful in helping them to make progress, whilst also identifying areas for improvement. For example, if a project-based homework idea is introduced and trialled, students can then give feedback, which can be used to modify the project for those students or influence thinking for the next year. The ideal with a student group is to get to the point where both teachers and students raise items for the agenda so that true consultation takes place and opportunities to co-construct the learning are possible.

Performance management (appraisal)

Appraisal should be used to drive forward improvements in teaching and learning. Using the methods outlined above, you'll have an in-depth understanding of the strengths and weaknesses of each member of your team, which you can relate to the Teachers' Standards. Use this to set focused, challenging targets and identify clear key performance indicators expected at different stages throughout the year. These should link to the development plan of the department as well as linking directly to the whole school priorities. Identify the support that your team will need to reach their targets and make sure you provide the opportunities to support them in achieving them. By viewing performance management (appraisal) as a process rather than an event, you can have regular conversations focusing on these objectives so that progress towards them can be recognized before embarking on the next phase of development.

Summary

As a subject leader have a clear vision for teaching and learning and make sure that everything you do focuses on this. Create opportunities for your team to develop and contribute to the improvement and make them accountable in doing so. By working with an improvement agenda you are focusing on securing consistently high quality learning experiences for your students. This will not only enable them to make progress, succeed and move forward confidently to the next phase with relevant skills, but will ignite in them a passion for your subject and, more importantly, help them to develop a lifelong joy for learning.

However, remember that the most valuable resource you have, to drive forward improvements in teaching and learning, is you! Make sure that you invest time in yourself and in your own professional development so that you can lead by committed enthusiastic example, inspiring those around you to do the same.

11

Monitoring and developing the performance of your team

Introduction

When it comes to formally evaluating the performance of colleagues many middle leaders get cold feet. This is despite making informal judgements about members of their team day in and day out. Evaluating and developing the performance of self and others is, in fact, a key aspect of middle leadership. The most successful individuals, teams and schools are those who are the most effective learners. In a supportive culture individuals should be able to see that, ultimately, the students gain from the evaluation of teachers, because the purpose of the exercise is to improve teaching and thus outcomes for students. With appraisal now formally linking performance to pay for all teachers it is essential that middle leaders have the right skills and outlook to be effective with both monitoring and developing their team.

Much has already been made in this book of the importance of getting the ethos right. In promoting high expectations through a collaborative team culture you will be helping to create the conditions for improvement and fostering commitment to continuous learning and development. These are essential preconditions for monitoring and evaluation to be unthreatening. However, there are occasions when even the most inclusive and positive leaders have to deal with underperformance and not shying away from tackling this is an important ethical dimension of authentic leadership. Treating people well while being consistent in your expectations and fair and transparent in the judgements you make will bring you the respect of your colleagues. In the end, a team can only be strong and successful if all members are performing well.

Setting high expectations

Much has already been said about setting high expectations through developing a 'can do' culture, modelling your expectations, engaging in honest self-evaluation based on valid data and having robust and well-focused development plan targets. In the excellent guide for middle leaders called *The Heart of the Matter* (2003) NCSL listed the following ways in which middle leaders can set high expectations:

- Articulate and exemplify what high expectations mean in the team, in each year, at each level.
- Use data with students and staff to raise expectations, to challenge preconceptions and stereotypes. Develop dialogue within the team that progressively moves from an expectation for a whole group to focus on the attainment of individual pupils. Train staff to understand and interpret the internal and external data they are being given.
- Recognize that teachers in local partner primary schools also know a great deal about what we should expect from children in our school. Find ways of building dialogue, for example in looking at samples of Year 5, 6, 7 and 8 work in your area, or reviewing schemes of work together.
- Invite an expert from another school to give subject advice and conduct observations or inter-school subject-based review of pupils' work. (At the time of writing this book Specialist Leaders in Education, available through Teaching Schools, would fit this bill.)
- Share the team's short- and medium-term vision and revisit it regularly. Make it real by relating this, in practical terms, to what is and could be happening in classrooms. Ask: how does this look and feel today? How will it look and feel when it is put into practice for pupils, staff, parents and the wider community? What do we need to do next to get there?
- Don't be afraid to change working partnerships, to move staff and responsibilities around to improve results and raise expectations.

There are many ways in which high expectations are institutionalized and supported through policy and practice in successful schools. Figure 11.1, familiar to North Yorkshire schools, provides examples.

Reflection point

Go through Figure 11.1 and consider how many of these elements are in place in your school. If any of them are missing don't despair. Ask yourself how you can raise expectations in your own team by making better use of the elements identified in the diagram. For example: Do you induct new colleagues thoroughly? Is tracking data used regularly with individuals in your team as part of monitoring performance? Is personalized support being provided to individuals to assist with developing pedagogy?

Monitoring

Monitoring, evaluation and review are separate processes, though they are usually linked. Monitoring is concerned with the systematic collection of data to establish how well, say, a subject team is performing. Monitoring

Conveying expectations	Understanding expectations	Effective CPD in school and beyond	Improving performance across school	Polices and guidance
School vision and aims are clearly communicated and regularly reviewed	The staffing structure identifies clear lines of accountability at all levels	A culture of trust, collaboration and professional learning is embedded	Clear lines of accountability are in place	School Vision or Mission Safeguarding Codes of Conduct Staffing Structure
School Development Plan with clear priorities is owned by all staff and governors	Robust appraisal objectives are informed by relevant professional standards and SDP priorities. These contribute to improving the educational provision and outcomes of pupils	The CPD plan is transparent and addresses both current SDP priorities and future needs. Induction, statutory requirements, role specific and individual needs are all included	Appraisal linked to school priorities is used to improve practice. Objectives are re-set mid-cycle when appropriate	School Development Plan School CPD Policy School Appraisal and Pay Policies Professional Standards
Active involvement of all staff in the school self evaluation process	Tracking and regular review of pupil data is shared with staff to monitor progress and identify appropriate strategies	Appraisal is used to identify a range of effective development strategies appropriate to need, and to support career development	Personalized professional support is provided to meet identified learning needs	Lesson observation Guidelines to Support Appraisal Document Ofsted framework
Clear expectations and outcomes of monitoring and development activities, team meetings and line management meetings	Regular feedback: planning, lesson observation, learning walks, work scrutiny, student and parent feedback	Evidence from lesson observations, learning walks, work scrutiny and peer assessment informs personalized professional learning	Early identification of development needs leads to appropriate interventions, aimed at avoiding progression to capability procedures	Appraisal, Pay and Capability Policies
Effective induction for all staff, generic and personalized	Individuals reflect on their own performance to build upon strengths and identify development opportunities, to keep up to date with professional knowledge and skills	Mentors support key role transitions, e.g. NQTs, new heads of department. Evaluation of induction, transition support, training and development interventions informs future provision	Unresolved patterns of under-performance are clearly evidenced and so are addressed through capability procedures	School's Induction Policy Statutory NQT Induction Guidance
Job descriptions for all staff	Teachers set targets that stretch and challenge pupils	Role specific training, e.g. appraisal and target setting for appraisers, is routinely offered		Job descriptions
Staff understand which professional standards apply for the purposes of appraisal review				School Appraisal and Pay Policies

FIGURE 11.1 Developing and reinforcing high expectations in school.

provides the evidence for evaluation, which is concerned with issues of quality; it involves considering whether or not performance or service could be improved. The review process is concerned with using the outcomes from monitoring and evaluation to develop strategies for improving performance or service. Many teachers associate monitoring and evaluation with accountability but a more powerful reason for engaging in monitoring and evaluation is that it helps a team or school to consider how things might be done better in the future. In other words, the process can benefit students. In effective schools, monitoring, evaluation and review are integral elements of the school development planning process (discussed in chapter 8).

The prospect of monitoring provision and standards may seem overwhelming to a newly appointed middle leader. It is important, therefore, to break the task down into manageable parts. There are several important sources of evidence that can be used: documents relating to curriculum planning; qualitative feedback on the experienced curriculum; observation of teaching; work sampling, learning walks and quantitative statistical data relating to student performance.

An audit of planning undertaken collectively can be a good starting point. It can provide an effective opportunity for colleagues to identify areas for departmental development and improvement. A collaborative approach to auditing curriculum plans can be an effective staff development exercise. The implication that colleagues are being monitored can be avoided in favour of sharing good practice and agreeing goals and classroom strategies. Asking teachers to submit their weekly lesson plans for 'inspection' is much less common in secondary schools than primary and it would be counter-productive for a head of department to try and introduce such a system for all without good reason. However, if a team leader had clear evidence that a colleague was underperforming then looking at their lesson planning may be an important aspect of the support needed to bring about improvement. Likewise, NQTs are entitled to support from their team leader, who will probably be their designated induction tutor. One way in which this can be done is through regular discussions that focus on lesson plans.

Evidence for monitoring the experienced curriculum can come from colleagues, students and parents. Discussions with team members can yield useful information about students' responses to particular approaches, activities and resources and students can certainly provide useful feedback through course review questionnaires (see chapter 9). In some schools students have become involved in curriculum design, identifying at the outset of planning areas that might be of particular interest. Parents will often comment at consultation evenings on whether or not their child has enjoyed a particular subject. Of course, team leaders must use evidence gained from all sources with caution: a small number of dissatisfied students does not mean a course has been badly taught, for example. More systematic monitoring and evaluation can be achieved through moderation exercises. The benefits of discussing individual pieces of work are considerable. It is likely that at GCSE level moderation will be an exam board requirement, but it is also good practice to develop this in years 7–9 with pieces of work for portfolios used to assist in assessing pupils in relation to national expectations. Try and develop a culture in which colleagues in your team are used to looking together at work produced by students they teach. Collecting and analysing such samples can assist in focusing discussion on expectations and standards. *Learning schools* are not frightened of discovering what has worked well and what not so well. Armed with this information they can plan for improvement.

Middle leaders should be involved in monitoring teachers through class-room observation, both as part of appraisal procedures and as a means of knowing their department thoroughly. The emphasis must be on observation as a means of supporting improvement in performance rather than as a process for making negative judgements about colleagues. Observations alone don't improve pedagogy. As is sometimes noted, you can weigh a pig as much as you like but it won't get fatter without the right diet. Observations, therefore, are best when they are an integral part of well thought out staff development programmes and especially when linked to coaching. Certainly, there is much to be gained from teachers watching excellent practitioners at work, so long as the observation is done with a clear focus in mind.

Most schools have developed their own schedules and forms for use when lessons are observed. The criteria used by Ofsted inspectors for judging the quality of teaching and learning usually informs school observation schedules. The important thing to remember is that a tick list approach is likely to be counter-productive with teachers, especially those who are very experienced. Looking for things teachers do or don't do in a lesson is not the way Ofsted inspectors operate. They are only interested in what teachers do in so far as it impacts on students' learning. According to the 2013 Inspection Handbook inspectors will judge the extent to which:

- Teaching engages and includes all pupils, with work that is challenging enough and that meets their individual needs, including for the most able pupils
- Pupils' responses demonstrate sufficient gains in their knowledge, skills and understanding, including of literacy and mathematics
- Teachers monitor pupils' progress in lessons and use the information well to adapt their teaching
- Teachers use questioning and discussion to assess the effectiveness of their teaching and promote pupils' learning
- Assessment is frequent and accurate and used to set relevant work
- Pupils understand well how to improve their work
- All pupils are taught well so that they are properly prepared for the next stage in their learning

Seeing lesson observation as part of an on-going strategy for raising standards will only be possible if a school has developed an ethos in which colleagues are committed to continuous improvement through collaboration. Team leaders must be willing to be observed by colleagues, both to demonstrate good practice and gain feedback concerning specific aspects of their own practice, as well as being observers.

Using student performance data

There is a considerable amount of quantitative data available to assist the head of department in evaluating the performance of their team. Y6 SAT scores as a guide to likely future performance, internally devised tests and assessments for tracking purposes, GCSE results and 'A' level results as output measures are all useful. However, the important thing is to avoid making comparisons between colleagues on raw data alone or on very limited samples. For example, a number of tests may be used by a department with all Year 7 pupils. Comparing the results in these tests of one teacher's class with another will only be a meaningful measure of teachers' relative impact if you are certain that all groups contain pupils of similar ability and that these pupils all began Year 7 with a similar level of knowledge and understanding. Even in mixed ability groups it does not follow that all groups really do contain a normal distribution of all abilities, therefore making judgements based on raw test scores is usually inappropriate. Progress made is a better measure of teacher effectiveness.

For this reason a reliable baseline test is required. Year 7 pupils have a baseline score from their Y6 SAT scores and 'A' level students have a baseline score from GCSE results, for example. With a baseline score it is possible to compare subsequent test scores with pupils who had the same baseline test scores. In this way a 'value added' or progress figure can be arrived at. This is a better way of comparing the performance of one teacher's students with another, though it is still very dangerous to jump to conclusions on the basis of small numbers of students. The use of such data to identify particular students who appear to be underperforming in order to target them for support is, of course, good practice. *Learning schools* ensure that teams analyse progress data together in order to look for trends and evidence of good practice boosting results. If one teacher, for example, seemed to be successful in helping the very able to make exceptional progress then their methods would be worth sharing with other colleagues.

This approach still has its limitations. Even when there is clear evidence of value added it is not clear whether you are adding greater value than other schools dealing with similar students and whether your aspirations are high enough. This is where more sophisticated evidence is required. All schools now will use 'Raise on Line' and Fischer Family Trust (FFT) data to inform their self-evaluation and to set challenging targets for student progress. If you are new to your role, it is a very good idea to meet with your school's data manager and work through what the data is saying about your area.

In addition to Raise and FFT around a quarter of secondary schools use Durham University's value-added information systems ALIS ('A' level information system) and YELLIS (Year 11 information system) in order to establish how well students in their school are performing compared with *similar students* nationally.

In the case of YELLIS all students complete two tests (mathematics and vocabulary) and a questionnaire on their 'cultural capital' in Year 10. The results are processed to place students into one of four bands A to D. 'Chances graphs' are provided to give indicators of potential student performance within these bands in a wide range of GCSE subjects. These are derived from a large-scale sample of past performance. After a school's GCSE results have been analysed, the school receives feedback on the performance of each department within the school measured against each other, to give a positive or negative 'residual'. The GCSE performance of students by subject is also compared with similar students in other schools to produce residuals for each department. This can be seen as the 'value added' measure of each department in the school. By looking at the results for each student, it is possible to see how students taught by member of staff X have performed compared with students taught by member of staff Y.

The important difference between this data and raw performance data is that it comes much closer to comparing like with like and is therefore fairer. With this information it is not possible for a colleague to explain away poor student performance with excuses like 'my group was weaker', 'children always do less well in this particular subject because it is harder' or 'the results are good for the children in our school'. Clearly, small numbers of students will still limit the validity of conclusions reached from the data but there is no doubt that the ALIS/YELLIS information helps a head of department to ask the right questions about the achievement of students taught by teachers in their team. Used well, the data can help colleagues in a team become more reflective and analytical and can help to pinpoint areas of excellent performance as well as areas of concern. Where excellent value added is in evidence praising the teacher concerned and sharing the good practice that produced the results are essential.

As a middle leader it is very easy to feel overwhelmed by attainment data as there is so much of it. You need to tease out the key headlines and trends from everything you have. If the data you have access to doesn't paint a good picture, rather than trying to report the data in a way that shows your team in a better light, it makes sense to work out why the figures are not good and then act to address the issues that will make the biggest difference to students' learning.

Appraisal

Appraisal for teachers is based on legislation and is a legal requirement. Appraisal for support staff is not required by law but should still be seen as an entitlement, as many benefits follow from effective appraisal. These include greater clarity about expectations, clear links between development priorities and agreed objectives, acknowledgement of hard work and achievements and access to appropriate training. Of course, appraisal discussions need to be honest and objectives set need to be challenging. In the case of areas of concern,

TABLE 11.1 Appraisal questions

Current role	**Possible questions**
Confirm the job description reflects the key responsibilities of the reviewee and is still relevant.	• Have your responsibilities changed in the last year? • Have you taken on new roles and responsibilities that are not covered in your current job description? • Which aspects of your work do you enjoy?
Review and evaluation of the past year Review overall performance against job description and Standards for Teachers Review and evaluation of outcomes, successes and achievements of the last review period Review: • Whether objectives have been achieved and the impact this has had on student progress. • Whether support/learning and development have been effective and the impact this has had on practice. • Recommendation on pay to eligible teachers.	• What have you achieved over the last year that you are particularly proud of? • To what extent have your objectives been achieved? • What skills, knowledge, strengths have helped you achieve your objectives? • How do you think this has benefited the students and the school? • What evidence is there to support these judgements? • Are there ways in which you could be using your skills and knowledge more effectively? • Has anything been difficult or disappointing for you this year? What caused these difficulties/disappointments? • How helpful was the support and professional learning you received?
Planning for the year ahead Discuss possible areas for improvement and set objectives.	• What do you want to achieve in the next year? • Are there any aspects of your work you would like to improve or develop?
Support and development Agree a development plan including relevant development activities.	• What knowledge and skills do you need to gain? • How will this be useful to you in your work? • What support / professional learning would help you achieve your objectives?

these should be addressed as they arise, not saved up until the once-a-year formal appraisal meeting.

If appraisal meetings are to be productive it is important to prepare for them thoroughly. Both the reviewer and the reviewee should come prepared to discuss the areas mentioned in Table 11.1.

In using appraisal to help staff improve their work and thus improve provision and outcomes for students, effective target setting will be necessary. A target is a particular aspect of work agreed by appraiser and teacher to be raised to a high priority for achievement within a set timescale. In most schools teachers are given three targets or objectives. Typically, one related to student performance, one related to a development plan priority and one more openly negotiated. As targets for teachers should be informed by the Teachers Standards (2013) it is likely that improving aspects of pedagogy relate closely to one or more of the targets. For example, a teacher might be tasked with improving differentiation or assessment feedback in order to achieve an agreed numerical performance score. Detailed guidance on how to word targets effectively is provided later in this chapter.

In a well-managed appraisal interview it is quite likely that the teacher will propose targets for improvement. In a few cases it may be necessary for the appraiser to impose targets. Good team relationships and a vision of continuous improvement will, of course, help to make target setting both natural and uncontroversial. Table 11.2 is an appraisal conversation that goes well because the appraisee is well prepared and committed to improving.

TABLE 11.2 Appraisal conversation

What would you like to be better at?	Challenging more able students.
Why? What's the current picture? What's the evidence?	School tracking, GCSE results, work samples and my gut feeling is that last year average students and those with special needs made at least expected progress but my more able students' results were disappointing; they could have done better. Their parents were not as pleased as parents of average and SEN students. Some of the very able students messed around too much, claiming they were bored.
How does this fit in with the school development plan?	The school priority is to raise the achievement and rates of progress of all students.
How does this fit in with your career plan and Teachers' Standards?	It will help me be a better teacher, and help me gain evidence for moving to the upper pay scale.
How will you know that things have improved?	Higher attainers will be engaged in lessons, will produce good work and will make progress at least in line with expectation based on FFT data. As a consequence of their achievement the rest of the class may also improve.
What do you need to do to meet this objective?	Use FFT predictions to identify students expected to attain A/A* grades. Plan more challenging work, with extension activities. Raise expectations of what they can achieve. Develop my questioning skills so that I can really get them thinking. Give clearer feedback on how to improve further. Use older, successful 'A' level students as role models.
What support from the school, including professional development, will help you?	Time to discuss strategies and resources with the gifted and talented coordinator, including how to use *Bloom's taxonomy for questioning*. Find ideas from websites. Observe a teacher from a higher achieving school with a reputation for challenging more able students, and discuss strategies with them.
How should your progress and its impact be monitored?	Keep track and ensure that activities occur by the dates agreed. In the third week of March, the reviewer should observe a lesson and look at the work of my more able students to monitor impact. Discuss tracking data with me as it is gathered.

Responding to underperformance

Subject leaders and pastoral team leaders are accountable for the performance of colleagues in their team. With the current emphasis on target setting and the wealth of statistical information now available on student achievement clear evidence of teachers' impact on learning exists, though clearly there are other important measures of a teacher's performance. Middle leaders with underperforming team members must establish the nature of the underperformance and devise strategies to raise standards and develop the skills of underperforming team members not only for the benefit of the students but for their own credibility as leaders.

When judging a teacher's competence it is important not to act purely on first impressions, anecdotes or information provided by others. There are many different styles of teaching and you should not jump to conclusions about a teacher's skill level simply because their style of teaching is idiosyncratic. If there is clear evidence of underperformance based on a significant amount of student achievement data or if repeated negative comments about a teacher are being made then you need to investigate. Evidence needs to be gathered from a variety of sources, including observation of lessons, students' work, lesson plans, students' course evaluations and student performance data. In well led teams these forms of evidence will be being regularly discussed and any under achievement is likely to be out in the open anyway.

If you approach leadership positively, set high expectations for all and provide opportunities for your team to learn from each other the chance of anyone in your team coasting is minimized. However, if you have evidence of underperformance specific to any individual then the colleague concerned must be informed of your concerns. Sometimes new middle leaders find they have a team member who is ineffective but the previous middle leader has not tackled the issue and has chosen instead to work round the underperforming colleague. This approach shows weak leadership, unfair to both the colleague concerned and to the students.

The initial meeting about performance should provide opportunities for the underperformer to respond and provide an explanation or express a viewpoint. Targets should be set, with a time limit for their achievement and a date for review. These should be realistic and challenging and the timescale manageable, generally within a term. These should be set down in writing. The section below on challenging conversations provides further guidance.

Part of being able to improve someone's performance comes from understanding what is causing the underperformance. It is rare for teachers to be below par in all aspects of their work and context can be very important. Teachers sometimes cope well with some groups but not others; successful teachers in some schools may flounder when they move to a school with a very different intake of students. Assistance must be offered to enable under-performers to improve. Training, guidance or development may be necessary and this is often best provided by an appropriate colleague acting as a mentor. In some circumstances, underperformance may be caused by factors outside school such as marital problems or family illness. Such situations are often temporary and effective leaders try and support colleagues through a bad patch in their lives. However, it is important to put the needs of the students first. Personal problems may be a reason for short-term dips in performance but not a justification for continuous underperformance. Sympathy and practical support are vital but if you and senior colleagues allow very poor performance to continue for several terms or even years you are failing in your duty as leaders. Under the current Ofsted framework, leadership will be judged critically where underperformance exists but leaders have taken no effective action to address it.

Senior leaders must be kept informed of the support you have given and the targets you have agreed for any teacher you are concerned about. If these targets are not met a review meeting must move matters forward. Discuss the implications of the meeting with the appropriate senior member of staff. If you have supported and provided practical help while at the same time being clear about the areas that need to be improved you have acted reasonably. Some teachers can improve their performance rapidly once they have been challenged about it but for others there is no 'quick fix' and if progress is not made it is likely that capability procedures have to be initiated. Capability procedures (which can lead to dismissal if progress is not made) will be the responsibility of senior members of staff. It is important that you have done all you can to help your colleague improve before this point; your strategy to date will inform future targets and support under capability arrangements. If capability proceedings are started you will probably be involved in monitoring progress and/or providing support. You will need to keep records of all meetings and targets. Capability proceedings can be stressful both for the colleague concerned and their team leader, but there is moral justification in this course of action when students are being seriously let down by inadequate teaching.

Always remember that being an effective leader who challenges underper-formance is a very different thing to being a bully. The TUC (2013) defines workplace bullying as 'offensive, intimidating, malicious, insulting or humili-ating behaviour, abuse of power or authority that attempts to undermine an individual'. Bullying behaviour can include constant criticism, public humilia-tion, shouting and even more subtle tactics such as ignoring, failing to include in decision making and aggression and sarcasm in one-to-one situations. There should be no place for these behaviours in school. It is entirely possible for lead-ers to be humane, respectful and positive while still holding others to account. No one is helped to improve by having their dignity removed; teachers know this to be true for students and should apply the same reasoning when working with adults.

Challenging conversations

No one relishes having a challenging conversation, but as a middle leader you need to consider the consequences of avoiding such conversations and of not addressing poor performance. Not only are the students being sold short but so is the underperforming colleague. Once you have clear evidence there is a problem, by not tackling it you are misleading the colleague concerned by giving the impression that all is well, denying them the opportunity to put things right, and possibly lowering the morale of other team members who see a colleague who is underperforming not being challenged.

Talking face to face with a colleague about unacceptable behaviour or underperformance takes most middle leaders out of their comfort zone the first time they do it. This is usually because they worry about how the individual will react and the impact the discussion might have on their relationship with the teacher concerned. This sense of anxiety is very normal; most effective middle leaders are cheerful and upbeat in their dealings with people and so to undertake a challenging conversation that will be more formal can seem out of character. As discussed in chapter 4, this is why the ability to use a leadership style that is 'fit for purpose' from a range of possible styles is so important.

As with most things the '5 P rule' (proper planning prevents poor performance) applies to challenging conversations. You need to have your evidence relating to the issue you want to discuss and you need to meet in a suitable place and at a suitable time so the meeting will be private and not rushed. It is a very good idea to write prompts of the things you want to cover and say so that you don't forget things and don't lose focus.

While listening is very important, middle leaders must avoid getting bogged down in too much detail, dwelling on the past or allowing the underperformer to put up barriers or make excuses. It is always better if the individual is able to see the problem for themselves and suggest ways forward, but if they can't the leader needs to have thought through the words they will use and the strategies they will advocate to improve things. Being able to state the issues clearly and simply is important but using open and probing questions is also essential to ensure the underperformer engages with the discussion and enables you to understand their position. The types of questions that can be used are explained in Table 11.3.

Using active listening is important. During a challenging conversation the middle leader needs to be aware of the words, tone and facial expressions being used by the other person. The listener needs to use supportive gestures such as nods. Eye contact is important, though intense staring should be avoided.

The key to managing difficult conversations is control. You need to control the meeting and how it progresses. This means you decide if and when you take a break and when and if you need to change your approach. For example, you may have started out being quite friendly but realize that a firmer style is needed to bring the meeting to a conclusion and agree a way forward. Although

TABLE 11.3 Types of questions

Type of question	Example	Benefits	Drawbacks
Open	Why did you...? To what extent would you say? How do you feel about? Open questions normally start with who, where, what, why, when or how.	These encourage the other person to talk freely, with little or no restrictions placed on their answer. They enable people to 'open up' on any topic, opinions and feelings.	The person may talk too much, drift away from the subject you have in mind and start to control the interview. To avoid this use a qualifier. For example, 'Very briefly, tell me how you...' or 'In a few words...'.
Closed	What time was it? Which student left first? How long did it take? Did you speak first? When did you last mark Y9 books?	These questions can be effective in verifying specific information, refocusing on the subject in hand or emphasizing a vital point.	They can be very unhelpful when dealing with feelings. For example, 'Did that make you feel bad?' may not illicit the depth of response you were hoping for.
Probing/ reflective	What was behind you saying that? What, in particular, made you feel like that? How exactly did the class react?	Useful in seeking depth and detail.	The employee may feel threatened, especially with 'why?' questions. Attention must be given to anticipating and monitoring the effect of your probing questions.
Leading	You're not suggesting that ...? You must admit that ...?	These questions should be avoided.	You run the risk of putting words in someone's mouth and leading them towards your own conclusions. The tone of these questions is often bullying.
Multiple	Can you tell me what happened, how you felt and what you did about it?	These questions should be avoided.	The person is unsure what part of the question to answer first and confusion can arise.

it is natural to want to be liked and to maintain a close friendship with the underperformer, most conversations will work best if you adopt a professional manner. Set out from the beginning how the meeting will run, the issues you wish to discuss and what you want to achieve before the close of the meeting. It can be difficult to control your emotions if the colleague concerned becomes confrontational or makes an accusation about you. They may seek to get behind your defences by appealing to you personally and hoping you will identify with their point of view or concerns. Remember to focus on the issue or behaviour and not the person and to remain objective and professional. Being in control is not about finding winners and losers. It is about bringing the meeting to a productive conclusion whereby the problem has been acknowledged and a way forward has been agreed. A framework to follow is provided in Table 11.4,

TABLE 11.4 How to structure a challenging conversation

Introduction – set the right tone	• Begin the conversation by explaining the purpose of the meeting • Set out the structure of the meeting • Agree standards of behaviour required during the meeting • Adopt a calm and professional manner • Reassure them about confidentiality – both prior to and after the meeting
CHECK	• Don't be afraid of referring to your pre-prepared script, it will help you stay in control • Remember to focus on the issue and not the person
State what the issues are and give evidence	• Tell them what the problem is using your knowledge of the situation • Give specific examples and refer to data, dates, observations, documents, complaints or specific interactions as appropriate • Explain the impact the problem is having on the students, the team and the organization • Be clear about the gap between current performance and what is acceptable • Use school or departmental policies to support what you are asking for
CHECK	• If possible, you should have already spoken to the employee informally about the problem – surprises can be very hard to handle! • If you have been monitoring their behaviour or conduct, this should have been agreed with them earlier • If the meeting is just aimed at giving them a reminder about behaviour or conduct then stick to that – be clear about what you are doing
Ask for an explanation; explore understanding	• Listen to what they have to say – they may need to let off steam • Keep an open mind and don't jump to conclusions • Acknowledge their position and any mitigating circumstances • Introduce your questions and explore the issues together • Don't assume even experienced teachers have a clear understanding of concepts such as AfL and differentiation – check for understanding
CHECK	• Remember that you are in control • Use your questioning techniques to avoid diversions or too much repetition • You may have to be firm and keep restating your position • Stay clear of emotive language and don't respond to manipulative behaviour
Agree a way forward	• Ask the employee for suggestions for the way forward and what success will look like • In the case of underperformance discuss the options for support • MAKE A DECISION – you are in charge! • Arrange a follow up meeting, especially if a support plan has to be written • Monitor and give feedback on progress and continue to provide support where agreed

CHECK	• Document what has been agreed and give a copy to the individual concerned. This should set out:
	  – agreed outcomes with dates and standards required
	  – any support or training to be provided by the leader or other colleagues
	  – consequences if what has been agreed isn't achieved

based on ACAS guidance (2012). This framework is geared towards a formal meeting but the same structure could be used for conducting a less formal challenging conversation. For example, in a less formal situation a middle leader might well commence with some open questions rather than explaining procedural matters that would be needed in a formal meeting.

The importance of setting effective targets

The vast majority of people want to do a good job. One of the key functions of leaders and managers is to ensure individuals in their team are clear about what is required of them; what their contribution to the success of the team is. Using targets is one way of ensuring individuals are clear about what is expected of them and understand what success will look like. The use of clear targets to achieve organizational goals, sometimes called 'management by objectives', was first popularized by Peter Drucker in the 1950s.

Targets can be used in many different situations. Highly motivated individuals may set their own targets, sometimes influenced by career goals, regardless of whether or not these are required by managers. In schools targets feature in development plans and action plans and targets will certainly be used when writing support plans for individuals performing below expectation. The most common use of targets, however, is in appraisal.

The benefits of using targets

Effective schools think and act *strategically*. They routinely and systematically evaluate their performance and plan for further success. Target setting linked to appraisal is used to develop individuals and move strategic priorities forward.

With performance related pay for teachers now in place it is especially important that targets are both fair and clear. When the target setting process is managed effectively, there are other benefits also:

- Individuals' targets are linked directly to achieving a team's aims, which increases the likelihood of organizational success
- Individuals are clear about what is required of them and so are likely to make every effort to achieve what is expected
- Individuals are motivated by targets they understand and have agreed to through discussion
- Monitoring and reviewing performance is easier and fairer when clear targets are in place
- Individuals develop and their professional and/or personal effectiveness improves when their targets are challenging but achievable

Getting the language right

In schools the terms goals, aims, objectives and targets are not always used precisely and this can cause confusion.

Goals are usually aspirational and express what is ultimately to be achieved (e.g. to become an outstanding school or department).

Aims express elements that must be achieved if the overall goal is to be attained (e.g. improve teaching and learning so that all students across Key Stage 3 and Key Stage 4 make at least expected progress and 30 per cent make above expected progress).

Targets or objectives are more focused and express what individuals must do as their contribution to ensuring aims are met (e.g. improve challenge for the most able students in your Y11 Maths class so that all gain their predicted A-A* grades).

Objectives or targets usually involve the achieving of a number of *milestones*, which are very specific actions or steps that contribute to the achieving of an objective (e.g. your first milestone in improving Y11 Maths results is to write an action plan by _____ showing how you will improve challenge for your most able pupils).

SMARTER targets

The acronym SMARTER is used to help remember how to write effective targets. To be effective targets must be SMARTER.

Specific – Measurable – Achievable – Relevant – Time limited – Extending – Rewarding

---

If they are not, then there is a strong possibility that they will not have the desired impact. The leader or manager who wrote the target must then accept at least some of the blame for this.

What exactly are **SMARTER** targets or objectives?

Specific

This means the target or objective must be focused and succinct. It must express clearly what has to be done. SMARTER objectives typically contain an action verb such as to report, to organize, to implement, to coordinate, to review, to plan etc.

Measurable

Objectives should contain a standard of achievement. If they don't this can lead to misunderstanding about what is expected and uncertainty about whether or not an objective has been achieved. For example, an objective such as 'to improve achievement in Maths' is not clear with regard to measurement. Add more detail – 'to improve the performance of five identified underachieving students (names) so that they gain at least a grade C in Maths GCSE next summer' and the objective becomes measurable.

Achievable

All leaders and managers should have high aspirations and high expectations. However, overly ambitious objectives and *unreasonable* high standards lead to failure and demotivation. Objectives should be achievable with effort, not easy or simple to achieve, but they should not be unrealistic.

Relevant

When setting objectives it is important that the individual understands why the objective is important and how it fits into the overall aims of the team or goals of the organization. This makes it relevant and relevance increases motivation. The objective must also, of course, involve something within the control of the individual.

Time limited

Individuals must be given a reasonable time frame in which to achieve any objectives set. Usually, objectives run over a year but it is reasonable that some objectives will be completed within a shorter and very specific time-frame, for example the completion of a report for publication by a certain date. The important thing is that the time allowed for completion is realistic and reasonable. Similarly, some ambitious objectives might run over two years, but with very clear milestones to enable monitoring of progress towards the objective.

Extending

There is no point setting objectives that are easily achieved or that require the completion of tasks that should be being routinely done anyway. Objectives are more motivational if they require the individual to develop new skills or reach a higher level of performance. People feel very proud when they have achieved objectives that stretched them. The skill of the manager is to think about what is just outside a person's 'comfort zone'. Too much outside can result in failure, stress and demotivation whereas just outside (coupled with encouragement and support) can be morale boosting and confidence building.

Rewarding

If objectives bring some reward to the individual, they are more likely to be motivational. Rewards might be financial (e.g. objectives allowing a person to gain pay progression) but they do not have to be. For example, a teacher with an objective to improve behaviour management will be rewarded with less stressful working days, an objective to undertake a curriculum review might improve career prospects.

Reflection point

In schools, what sort of things might make sensible objectives but might be difficult to measure precisely? What sort of evidence might show success in such cases?

Although there is a wealth of numerical data relating to student performance there are many areas of school life (and student development) where numerical scores cannot easily be given. For example, developing pupils' skills in working in groups is desirable but measuring it is hard. If this was to be a target, therefore, clear monitoring arrangements, which shed light on progress made with group work, would be required. Also, clear criteria regarding what constitutes effective group work would be needed to support the process. Once the criteria are agreed, observations of pupils working in groups at different points in the year would help a reviewer assess the skills they were developing. Discussions with pupils about their understanding of effective group work skills could also provide valuable information. Such data is known as qualitative (as opposed to quantitative – numerical – data) and is perfectly acceptable to use for gathering evidence of success with some objectives. In this example it is likely that the improved group work would result in improved outcomes for pupils in drama, debate or even written work (where group discussion is an important element of preparing for a piece of writing) but it would be impossible to prove that numerical scores in writing were the result of improved group work alone.

Thinking about objectives and success criteria

When writing objectives it is important to think about whether or not you are setting someone up to fail. Any school should have aspirational goals, but an aspiration and an objective/target are not the same thing. For example, a school may have the aspiration that no incidents of bullying occur, but might decide not to make this a target. If it is a target and one incident of bullying is reported, they have failed. Here it is helpful to draw a distinction between the aspiration and the standard against which they will be judged. Similarly, teachers should have aspirational targets relating to pupil progress and/or outcomes, but if a target is phrased as '90 per cent of your GCSE class will attain A*–C grades' and 86 per cent gained these levels, the teacher has failed. If the target of 90 per cent was aspirational (i.e. possible but unlikely given students' prior attainment) then a result of 86 per cent is, in fact, a very good outcome. It is important not to word objectives in such a way that they become demotivating.

Another point to consider is that objectives should focus on what really needs to change. For example, if a school wants to improve attainment in GCSE History simply setting a numerical target might not achieve this. What is required is that the teacher of GCSE History improves the quality of teaching and learning so that pupils better understand the subject and perform better in the GCSE exams as a result. So, what is needed is to identify aspects of pedagogy that need to improve (e.g. differentiation, challenge for the most able, assessment and feedback, planning for skills development) and then set an objective to improve the identified aspect(s) of practice, with a numerical GCSE score or student progress data being one of the success criteria (an outcome).

When setting an objective it should be clear why the objective is needed, where performance or practice is now and where it needs to get to, how progress will be monitored and what success will look like. This is often captured in a simple grid like Table 11.5:

TABLE 11.5 Format for appraisal objectives

Why needed	Objective and timescale	Success criteria	Monitoring arrangements	Agreed support

Words, words, words

The correct wording of objectives is critical. It is unfair to the person being given a target to work on if there is uncertainty about what is required or how success will be measured.

Reflection point

The words below are often seen in objectives. What would need to be added to them to avoid confusion and uncertainty?

Improve – Successfully – Regularly – Effectively – Efficiently – Appropriate

Let's consider just a few of these words in order to see if your thinking was along the right lines.

| **Why needed** |
| Lesson observations show that your use of questioning in class is not sufficiently challenging and this limits students' understanding of some concepts. |

| **Objective and timescale** |
| Consistently to use questioning based on Bloom's taxonomy (initially in Y10 History lessons during the autumn term, across all lessons by the summer term) |

| **Success criteria** |
| 1 Lesson planning includes key questions linked to Bloom's taxonomy (History in autumn term; all by summer) |
| 2 Questioning based on Bloom is embedded across all lessons by summer term |
| 3 Students' written work shows clear analysis and debate which can be linked to planning and higher order questioning |

| **Monitoring arrangements** |
| 1 Weekly Y10 History planning to be seen by PF (autumn term) |
| 2 Two agreed 20-minute observations of Y10 History lessons by PF (autumn term) |
| 3 Two random drop-in observations by PF (summer term) |
| 4 Monitoring of students' written work following observations |

| **Agreed support** |
| 1 Meeting with AS to jointly plan some Y10 questions |
| 2 Observation of one of AS's lessons in which questioning technique will be modelled |
| 3 One lesson team taught with AS who will coach in questioning technique |

FIGURE 11.2 A clearly worded objective.

- *Successfully – the standard or level required to do something 'successfully' is a matter of opinion unless it is specified.*
- *Regularly – is once a year often enough? Be specific.*
- *Improve – by how much? Unless you specify this or clarify what improvement will look like, it is just a matter of opinion and a potential source of disagreement.*

This is why having clear success criteria is so important.

Figure 11.2 provides an example of what this might mean in practice.

Summary

Effective middle leaders evaluate the performance of individual colleagues as well as their team overall. They work hard to create the kind of open and supportive culture which makes self-evaluation a natural and unthreatening feature of their team's work. They see learning together, spreading good practice and enabling colleagues to improve aspects of their work as necessary if pupil performance is to be improved. They use appraisal objectives to reinforce high aspirations and are not reluctant to tackle underperforming individuals. There is now a wealth of data available relating to the performance of pupils. The use of this data is important for evaluating a department's performance, development planning and setting future targets. It is also very helpful in appraising individual teachers.

While there are very few incompetent teachers if a middle leader has evidence that a colleague is seriously underperforming then it is important to grasp the nettle by putting in place a programme of support and targets to help the member of staff to improve. In extreme circumstances it may be necessary to consider capability procedures. This will be a matter for senior leaders to handle but it is vital that you work closely with them, adhere to procedures and keep accurate records of all meetings with the colleague concerned. In conducting challenging conversations middle leaders should be certain they have clear evidence relating to underperformance or unacceptable behaviour and should follow a clear framework designed to ensure the issue is 'owned' by the individual concerned and a clear plan for improvement has been agreed.

12

Looking after yourself
Time and stress management

Introduction

It is important in a book on middle leadership to consider the management of stress as the pressures and demands on middle leaders are such that some potential for stress is almost inevitable. Of course, school middle leaders, and indeed teachers, are not the only people who have to deal with stress; many would argue that stress is endemic to modern working life and that understanding the causes of stress and strategies for dealing with it are therefore essential life-skills. Leaders certainly have a responsibility to be aware of when they are stressed themselves and of when those they manage are stressed. Their 'duty of care' means that in their approach to team relationships middle leaders should aim to reduce the stress felt by their colleagues. They should avoid passing their stress and anxiety on to others. By managing their own stress appropriately middle leaders can make themselves more efficient, effective and self-fulfilled.

Many people feel that lack of time to do jobs properly is a major cause of stress and because of the perceived link between time and stress time management is also considered in this chapter. Being able to organize time effectively is essential for all leaders; those who are unable to do this will find that work encroaches further and further into their evenings, weekends and holidays and, except in the case of workaholics, this in itself will become a major source of stress. The good news is that there are some surprisingly simple techniques for improving time management and, while some people seem to be *naturally* better at managing time than others, everyone can improve their time management if they are determined to do so. Effective middle leaders are usually effective managers of time and as such act as role models in attaining an acceptable work-life balance.

Some thoughts on stress

Although the expectations of teachers and leaders in school have increased in recent years, teachers feeling stressed is nothing new. According to the

Education Service Advisory Committee (1992: 13) stress at work is 'a process that can occur when there is a mismatch between the perceived pressures of the work situation and the individual's ability to cope with it'. Notice here the use of the word 'perceived' as different people will have different perceptions of pressure. The Health and Safety Executive (HSE) (2013) defines work related stress as 'the adverse reaction people have to excessive pressure or other types of demand placed on them at work'. Note here the use of the term 'excessive pressure' as what one person regards as excessive another person may consider reasonable. David Fontana (1989: 21) defined stress as 'a demand made upon the adaptive capacities of the mind and body. If these capacities can handle the demand and enjoy the stimulation involved, then stress is welcome and helpful. If they can't and find the demand debilitating, then stress is unwelcome and unhelpful.' This definition is useful for several reasons. Firstly, it reminds us that stress can be both good and bad. Secondly, it isn't so much pressure that determines whether or not we're stressed, it is our reactions to it. Thirdly, if our body's capacities are good enough, we respond well to stress, if they aren't we give way. Typically, too little pressure results in boredom and frustration, a moderate level of pressure is stimulating and actually improves performance, whereas too much pressure becomes debilitating and reduces performance (Figure 12.1).

Each individual, of course, has a different capacity for dealing with pressure and so a task that causes little anxiety for one person may cause considerable anxiety for another. Much depends on the individual's personality, experience and motivation, as well as support received from colleagues, leaders

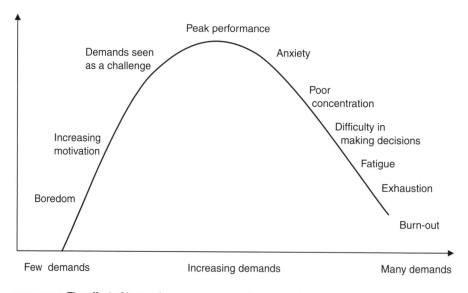

FIGURE 12.1 The effect of increasing pressure on performance at work.

and line managers, as to how they will react to a potentially stressful situation. In addition, people's experiences outside the workplace are important. A stressful domestic situation coupled with pressure in the workplace could produce an intolerable level of stress for some people. It is very important, therefore, that middle leaders encourage a culture in which colleagues are willing to talk about stressful situations they face and in which people support each other. Similarly, middle leaders should be approachable and sensitive to the different pressures their colleagues are under. A newly qualified teacher may be finding the behaviour of a particular class stressful whereas an experienced colleague may be undergoing the stress of marital separation, which is having an impact on their working life. Clearly, there are ways in which an effective leader could provide support in order to help both colleagues. This would be likely to generate respect and appreciation and to be repaid with goodwill in the future (the 'emotional piggy bank'). In supporting colleagues in the short term the hope is that they are soon able to perform to an acceptable standard. If, longer term, they are not then clearly a different approach is needed (see chapter 11).

Causes of stress

It is generally acknowledged that death of a spouse, divorce, marital separation, death of a close family member and pregnancy are all causes of stress. These events are clearly outside the control of middle leaders, though being aware of them happening in the lives of team members and responding with sensitivity is important. Across a wide range of jobs the following are regularly mentioned as causes of stress: poor relationships with managers, leaders and colleagues, bullying managers, leaders and colleagues, relationships with peers, working conditions, salary, status, and job insecurity. Some of these are outside the control of middle leaders in schools but some can be very much affected by them. Relationships feature very strongly as causes of stress. This underlines the importance of creating the positive relationships and empowering culture through authentic leadership.

I sometimes discuss the causes of stress in schools with teachers in my leadership and management training sessions. It is interesting that the same causes are always listed. These include:

- Heavy workload
- The term time treadmill
- Constant change
- Not enough time to do things thoroughly
- Ofsted
- Being unable to satisfy the (sometimes conflicting) demands of parents, students and SLT
- Negative media coverage of education

- Lack of recognition for skills
- Increasing accountability
- Worrying about colleagues' perceptions of them as teachers
- Not feeling valued for all the time devoted to the job
- Difficult or underperforming team members
- Bullying line managers and leaders
- Mismatch between personal educational values and target culture that exists in schools

The last bullet point seems more fundamental than some of the other things listed. According to Gold and Evans (1998: 50) 'an unresolved mismatch between a personal philosophy of education and the organization's educational philosophy is a potential source of stress'. It is a seemingly relentless focus on data and targets which some teachers and some middle leaders find alienating, but this accountability is unlikely to change given the close political scrutiny schools are under. Even so, middle leaders can still have a massive influence on the values, culture and practice within their teams. Exciting, engaging and adventurous pedagogy shouldn't be at odds with reaching attainment targets. A clear vision can ensure that the values a middle leader holds dear are not lost and productive relationships and a collaborative team culture can minimize stress for everyone. Recognizing and celebrating people's skills, increasing autonomy, involvement in decision making, providing effective and support-ive feedback on performance and acknowledging commitment are all things that have been encouraged in this book and which help to keep morale up and stress down.

It is often claimed that Ofsted inspection causes stress. One possible explanation for this, provided by Day et al. (2006), is that teachers are unable to separate work and personal identity. Teaching is so personal that when Ofsted comes into a school they feel *they* are being assessed not their teaching. If they are criticized they can begin to feel worthless as *individuals.* Likewise, if they are praised their self-esteem is boosted and they feel good about *themselves*, not just their teaching. Margaret Scanlon (2001) found that even good or better teachers experienced a loss of confidence in their profes-sional ability when their school was placed in 'special measures', causing them considerable stress. With the current (2012) Ofsted framework using 'requires improvement' rather than 'satisfactory' as a category debates rage about the stress being caused to teachers and school leaders as a result of inspection.

Good middle leaders help to minimize the stress of an inspection by ensur-ing their house is in order and there is therefore nothing to be anxious about. Good teams have a positive ethos, clear goals, well-designed schemes of work and good monitoring procedures. They are secure in their pedagogy and regularly discuss teaching and learning in meetings. Data is used well to inform planning and in lessons and over time all students make good progress. When teachers are confident in what they are doing they feel more relaxed with inspectors. Well led departments with effective teachers have little to fear from inspection. Confident middle leaders are proud of their team's achievements and will want to help inspectors to see their area at its best by being proactive from the start. If middle leaders have confidence in their team and are relaxed about inspection because they know all is well they will be helping team members to feel confident and in control. Of course, if a department is not effective, if confidence is unjustified because all is not well or if there is a panic leading up to inspection to put things right it will not be easy for team members to feel in control and confident. In these circumstances stress is much more likely and the ineffective middle leader must accept a major part of the responsibility for this. Unavoidably, some middle leaders face Ofsted shortly after being appointed. In these circumstances, and especially if student outcomes are poor, it is important to be certain about what needs to be done to improve practice and to have clear and credible plan of action for improvement to share with inspectors.

Identifying stress

Stress can affect people emotionally and mentally resulting in changes in behaviour and physical health. Someone suffering stress may exhibit some or all of the following symptoms:

- A general deterioration in performance at work
- An increase in sickness absence, which may fall into a particular pattern of frequent short periods of absence, possibly due to stress symptoms such as headaches, difficulty breathing, poor sleep patterns, indigestion and palpitations
- Emotional outbursts
- An increase in irritability resulting in conflict and tension with other colleagues and deterioration in relationships
- Loss of motivation and job satisfaction
- Confusion and indecision
- Less contact with people outside work
- In some cases, over eating and/or an increase in alcohol consumption

Middle leaders are not doctors and cannot diagnose stress. However, they should look out for the signs of stress. If there are a number of signs and these continue over time they should talk to their colleague about their concerns and encourage them to visit their GP. If stress is not tackled it can result in high blood pressure, heart disease, anxiety, depression, ulcers and thyroid disorders.

Controlling the stress of team members

The responsibility for the creation of a safe place of work lies with the employer but it is down to senior and middle leaders to enact this responsibility. Sound leadership and management can prevent teachers and other employees becoming over stressed in several ways.

- The school and team culture should ensure that stress is not seen as a weakness in the individual and that employees suffering stress will receive support without being made to feel guilty.
- The job itself must be manageable and the person's abilities, skills and experience must match the requirements for the job.
- Stress often occurs during periods of change. Team involvement in planning and managing change will go a long way towards reducing its negative impacts.
- Training and development should be provided to assist teachers and support staff in meeting the demands of change.
- Effective communication must exist so teachers have an accurate perception of the role they have to perform and what is expected of them.

Of course, the above points need to be considered against an understanding that teachers must be able to demonstrate consistent achievement of the Teachers' Standards (2013). It is not unreasonable for middle leaders to expect these Standards to be met and meeting them should not be a cause of stress or undue pressure to most teachers.

Controlling your own stress

Psychologists identify some individuals as being more stress prone than others. They are usually people who have high expectations of themselves, are very task and result orientated, tend to work very quickly and find inefficiency in others very frustrating. It is, of course, much harder for such people to control stress than other personality types, but not impossible. Recognizing your potential for stress and being proactive in controlling stress are both very important. If stress really is endemic to modern working environments then it is important to anticipate it and develop strategies that will prevent you becoming stressed rather than waiting until you feel stressed and then considering what you ought to do about it. Here are a few pointers on reducing stress:

- Get your time management right (see below). This will make you much more effective in all aspects of your job.
- Maintain a sense of humour. Take what you do seriously but don't take yourself too seriously. It is important in teaching to be able to laugh at

yourself and if you cultivate humour as part of the team culture this will be a real antidote to the pressure of the job.

- Remain optimistic. If you focus on the negative you will soon get yourself on a downward spiral. It is very important to have a positive mindset and recognize the progress made rather than dwelling on the distance still to go. Hackneyed as the phrase may be it really is important to see your glass as half full rather than half empty.

- Have a life beyond work. It is essential that you engage in activities away from school. A successful family life and satisfying social life make you a more interesting and rounded person. Too many late nights on the lap top or too many working weekends build tension and resentment. It is in everybody's best interests that you remain healthy and positive and knowing when to 'draw the line' with work is important. Of course, there will be some evenings and weekends when it is simply impossible to avoid school work but an effective leader does not need to be on the job twenty-four hours a day.

- Some leaders arrive at school an hour or more before the school day begins and work on until 5.00 or 5.30 p.m. and then take no work home. While this wouldn't suit everybody (flexibility over working time can help greatly with childminding arrangements, for example), it is one way of clearly demarcating working life and home life, which really can help you to 'switch off' once you leave the school buildings.

- Learn not to take things personally. Leaders must be able to cope with healthy debate and argument and not be distressed if things do not always go according to plan. A good team is one that allows discussion and diversity of views and leaders need not feel threatened by this.

- Exercise. Obviously, your age will determine the kind of exercise that you can perform but it is important to engage in some form of regular exercise as a means of reducing stress through the release of endorphins.

- Taking up a new post can be stressful but it is also true that for some people staying in one job for too long can become a cause of stress through frustration. With a new job there is much excitement and challenge; you are trying to prove yourself and often don't notice or resent the hours you are putting in due to the satisfaction derived from the impact you are making. Once you have been in post a few years devoting long hours to what have become routine tasks rather than challenges can become a source of irritation. If this is the way you feel then it might be time to think about a job move; motivating others becomes very difficult if you are no longer motivated yourself.

Some thoughts on time management

The principles and skills of time management are just as relevant to teachers and leaders in education as they are to managers in other walks of life. In an ever more demanding and stressful profession effective time management is vital for survival. Far too many middle leaders find themselves *living to work* rather than *working to live*; a situation that is simply not sustainable in the long run and that can cause burn-out and serious health problems. Many teachers devote very long hours to their work out of genuine commitment and a desire to do the best for the children they teach. While this is admirable in one sense *expecting* teachers to devote every evening and weekend to their jobs in order to maintain the nation's education system is simply not acceptable and is actually a recipe for stress-related illnesses and marriage breakdowns amongst teachers.

However, it is important to understand that people are differentially effective. You will be aware of some middle leaders (and some teachers) who are simply more efficient at getting things done than others. Effective teachers and leaders learn to use time productively. It is very revealing to discover that those complaining the most in staff rooms about lack of time are often very inefficient in their use of time. Likewise, teachers who are actively involved in extracurricular activities and award bearing part-time study are often also the very members of staff who can be relied upon to get a job done efficiently. Indeed, it is very likely that they also have fulfilling family lives and an active social life. Some people seem to be *naturally* good time managers and this is reflected in all areas of their lives. Even so, there are strategies that everybody can use to become better time managers.

How is effective time-management achieved?

There is a difference between doing a job effectively and doing a job efficiently. Effectiveness means doing a job to the required standard whereas efficiency involves doing it in the right way and at the right time. Good time management helps people to increase their efficiency and maintain or improve their effectiveness. In recent years teachers have had to cope with increases in workload and the only certainty about the future is that change in education will continue as more and more is expected of schools. Being effective and efficient in such a climate is essential. Working smarter not harder is the way to survive and this requires a systematic approach to work and to life in general.

According to Iain D. Wood (1991) there are three characteristics of effective time managers which he calls the 'three Ts':

- **Thought.** They achieve their goals by thinking about what they have to do, questioning its value and prioritizing. This includes thinking about yourself and your family – not just work.
- **Technique.** They plan when and how they will undertake each task so as to optimize their use of time. This means working smarter not harder; choosing the right tasks for the time available and working at the times of day they know they are most productive.

- **Temperament.** They try not to panic when new tasks come along because they realize that worrying wastes time and solves nothing. Likewise, when things go wrong they do not spend hours thinking 'if only I had...' Instead, they analyse why things went wrong and plan to ensure that the same mistakes are not made in the future.

Planning, prioritizing and deadlines

There is a cliché that suggests that if we fail to plan then we plan to fail. All effective middle leaders need to plan so that they can spread their workload and prioritize. Making effective use of a planner/diary (paper or e-device) is essential. Covey (1994) suggests a variation on planning by use of a Time Management Matrix (Table 12.1).

All tasks should fit into one of these categories. Obviously, the urgent and important matters require your immediate attention. Effective middle leaders try and deal with as many important things as possible before they become urgent. This reduces stress. Items in the other boxes must be dealt with in order of priority. At the bottom of the scale non-urgent and unimportant tasks should probably be crossed off your list altogether. It is useful to try and predict the amount of time needed for each activity beforehand. Bear in mind, though, that initially it is likely that you will underestimate the time required than over-estimate it. With practice you will become more accurate, and the knowledge gained will prove invaluable for future planning.

Setting deadlines for the activities on your list is a good way of focusing the mind and avoiding 'drift', which results in important but not urgent tasks never being tackled. Deadlines for all tasks must be realistic and you should avoid setting deadlines that result in you putting off tasks until the day before

TABLE 12.1 Covey's time management matrix

	Urgent	Not urgent
Important	• Crises • Pressing problems • Deadline driven projects, meetings	• Preparation • Prevention • Planning • Values clarification • Relationship building • Empowerment
Not important	• Interruptions, some phone calls • Some mail, some reports • Some meetings • Many pressing matters • Many popular activities	• Trivia • Many e-mails • Junk mail • Some phone calls • Time wasters • 'Escape' activities

they have to be completed. 'Working to the wire' is a bad habit and one that you should plan to avoid. It allows no further time to reschedule the work should a crisis arise. Set your own target date for completing each task some time in advance of the school deadline. This provides a safety net should a crisis arise. Encourage this practice in your team by negotiating deadlines for work you need from them, which gives some flexibility in case of illness or absence. Encourage a total quality management (TQM) approach so team members see one another as 'internal clients' and all feel responsible for ensuring their part of any task is completed efficiently. If deadlines are missed then someone is being let down and put under pressure, which is not fair. A supportive and empowering team ethos does not mean being sloppy about deadlines. If these are negotiated then everyone should adhere to them.

Action point

Use a blank Covey matrix to capture your work priorities. See how many key things you can get into the important but not urgent box. Try and have the important and urgent box blank so that only unexpected emergencies have to be dealt with at short notice.

Delegation

If leadership is the art of getting things done through people then delegation is essential to good leadership. Most middle leaders spend time doing things that should or could be done by someone else. Delegation should not be abdication but, used properly, should be a feature of effective team work and staff development. As we saw in chapter 4, delegating needs to be used in conjunction with supporting, coaching and directing in order to get the best out of team members. In chapter 5 we considered an effective team to be one that used the strengths of each team player by delegating tasks appropriately. Where there is a gap between the current ability of a person to carry out a task and their potential ability, it is well worth spending time instructing them. Staff development is a good investment in the future, when team members will be able to complete tasks with decreasing levels of supervision. It can be tempting to try to do everything yourself, because it seems quicker, for fear of being outshone by a colleague or simply because you feel you are paid to do more. However, fair and effective delegation is a must for middle leaders and should be cultivated as a key feature of supportive teamwork and your commitment to develop others as leaders.

Making decisions

Procrastination can be a great time waster. While it is a mistake to make snap decisions before you have all the necessary information, dithering between choice A and choice B will not make the eventual judgement any more correct. Leaders must be able to weigh up the facts and make decisions, even if they don't always get them right! Another form of procrastination is continually putting off jobs you don't like doing. Competent time managers identify the tasks they least like doing and tackle them when they feel fresh to overcome their natural reticence to do them. Other strategies include:

- Setting deadlines for completion of unpopular tasks
- Breaking tasks down into manageable stages
- Rewarding themselves for finishing a task
- Getting a colleague to check that they have done the work

When it comes to routine administration procrastination must be avoided. There are three options with any e-mails or pieces of paper: deal with it straight away; deal with it later; bin it. It is essential that junk mail and unsolicited e-mails are put straight in the bin or deleted. Correspondence and messages that can be dealt with quickly should be attended to on the day they arrive in your pigeon-hole or in-box. Paperwork that will require more serious attention should be listed in your planner as a job to be dealt with. Try not to let paper pile up on your desk or e-mails overwhelm your in-box. Use a filing system to save you time. Ensure class lists, letters to parents, exam papers, schemes of work, worksheets etc. are saved electronically (using a logical system so they can be retrieved easily) so that they can be modified rather than completely rewritten. Always remember, though, that modifying anything requires careful proofreading to avoid mistakes being made. You don't want letters home to parents with incorrect dates or reports on pupils containing the wrong name in the text!

Being assertive

Assertiveness is another essential ingredient in good time management. There are occasions when even the most caring leader needs to complete an urgent and important task and so does not want interrupting. If you are respected by colleagues and provide support and encouragement setting aside some time when you don't want interrupting should not be seen as unreasonable. Likewise, if one of your team is in the middle of an urgent task then you should not expect them to drop everything in order to discuss some less important matter with you.

Sometimes middle leaders feel under pressure because of tasks with unrealistic deadlines set by senior colleagues. It is very important for middle leaders *as a group* to be strong if they are presented with unreasonable requests from senior leaders. When asked individually to undertake a task it is difficult to say 'no' because you don't want to offend senior colleagues or appear uncooperative or lazy. However, by taking on too many new tasks aspects of your existing work might begin to suffer and so it is important to learn how to say 'no' without offending. The art of saying 'no' diplomatically lies not so much in what you say but in the way you say it. Speak with confidence, be honest and say what you feel in a controlled way. Try not to allow your emotions to be demonstrated. Do not be sarcastic or aggressive. Don't apologize profusely or put yourself down. Sometimes a compromise rather than a refusal is possible.

Some suggestions of how to say 'no' tactfully include:

- I feel honoured that you have asked me but...
- Yes, but it will have to wait until after...
- Yes, but I couldn't finish it by... because I have...to do
- I would be happy to do that but which would you like me to do first as I already have...to do
- It would be possible but if I devote time to...I won't be able to do...so which would you prefer?

Effective time management does not mean saying 'no' to everything, it is just one of many strategies not a quick-fix solution to your workload. Indeed, if used to excess there is a danger that others will see you as uncooperative. A 'can do' culture cannot be created by people who say 'no' to everything but, equally, hard-working and competent leaders and teachers should not feel guilty if they sometimes say 'no', especially to requests likely to impact negatively on existing areas of their work.

Holding others to account for their work

We have already discussed how delegation can be used to help others grow professionally. This positive approach will work with many but with some colleagues it can be a challenge getting them even to accomplish what are perfectly reasonable aspects of their role effectively. Some middle leaders, in an effort to be supportive or simply to get things done, allow themselves to get into the habit of taking work and responsibilities from teachers that are rightly theirs. There may be occasions when this is helpful, but done frequently it will simply add to the workload and stress levels of the middle leader. If a teacher complains they haven't had time to finish the scheme of work they promised to do it is unwise, except in exceptional circumstances, to complete the work for them. If a teacher asks a middle leader regularly to take a pupil into their class because they are finding that pupil disruptive, it is not sensible to oblige. In both cases the teacher needs to be assisted in finding solutions to *their* problem rather than being allowed to pass *their* problem on to the middle leader. Giving an inefficient teacher a way out will not make them more efficient; regularly removing a difficult pupil from a teacher does not make them better with behaviour management. Creating a 'dependency culture' by behaving like a superhero must be avoided. Middle leaders need to encourage teachers to take responsibility for their work. The mantra 'bring me a solution not a problem' is a very useful one for middle leaders to establish with their team. It makes clear that people are expected to be problem solvers but at the same time indicates that the leader is there to listen and advice on what is suggested. This can be very empowering. 'The best way to develop responsibility in people is to give them responsibility' (Blanchard 2004: 73).

If a colleague comes to discuss a problem, use the steps below to ensure the issue is dealt with by the right person:

- *Step 1* Ensure you both fully understand the nature of the problem and you are in agreement about what should happen next to begin to address the problem.
- *Step 2* Ensure you have clearly defined the most appropriate person for dealing with the problem. This might be the teacher who brought the problem, it might be you or it might be another colleague with relevant defined responsibilities.
- *Step 3* Make sure that before the person with the problem leaves, they understand what *their* next steps are.
- *Step 4* Make a note of what you have agreed. Ask for feedback within an agreed period about progress made.

Reflection

Are you a stress-prone person?

Below are a series of questions to help you identify how stress-prone you or your colleagues are. They are based on a questionnaire provided by Cooper and Sutherland (1997). Give yourself or your colleague a score on a 1–11 scale for the bi-polar statements provided. The first one has the scale included so you can see where low and high scores fall.

Casual about appointments 1 2 3 4 5 6 7 8 9 10 11 Never late

Not competitive	Very competitive
Good listener	Anticipates what others are going to say (attempts to finish for them)
Never feels rushed, even when under pressure	Always rushed
Can wait patiently	Impatient while waiting
Takes things one at a time	Tries to do many things at once
Slow, deliberate talker	Fast and forceful speaker

Cares about satisfying him/herself no matter what others may think	Wants a good job recognized by others
Slow doing things	Fast – eating, walking, etc.
Easy-going	Hard-driving, pushing yourself and others
Expresses feelings	Hides feelings
Many outside interests	Few interests outside work/home
Unambitious	Ambitious
Casual	Eager to get things done

Analysis of scores

The higher the score received on this questionnaire, the more firmly an individual can be classed as stress-prone. People who are highly stress-prone are, in fact, often blind to their own behaviour. If you are scoring this questionnaire to assess your own personality and suspect that you are stress-prone it is likely that you will find it hard to be completely honest in your self-assessment. To get a more accurate assessment it is useful to ask someone else who knows you well to complete the questionnaire based on their perceptions of your workplace behaviour.

Psychologists use the term 'Type A personality' for those who exhibit strong stress-prone tendencies. Such people can actually be very difficult to work with. They display the following characteristics:

- Devotion to work, working long hours, feeling guilty when not working
- A chronic sense of time urgency
- Attempting to schedule more and more into less and less time
- Often attempting to do two or more things at the same time
- Hate being kept waiting, especially in queues
- Find it difficult to talk about anything other than work
- A strong need to be in control
- A very competitive outlook

The reason why Type A people can be difficult to work with is because of their constant need to compete. They tend not to be good listeners and like to keep strict control over what is going on. They often do jobs themselves rather than taking the time to show someone else what to do, so they fail to develop their staff and rarely delegate. They often expect everyone around them to work to their demanding pace and schedule, including long hours of working and skipping lunch breaks in order to meet unrealistic goals and deadlines. Ironically,

Type A people are often rewarded with promotion because, in the short term at least, they manage to move things forward. In the longer term, however, Type A behaviour can become dysfunctional for an organization.

It is important that leaders who recognize Type A behaviour in themselves consider what effect they might have on others in their team. Arguably, it is impossible to change personality but it is possible to modify some behaviour associated with personality. Reflective leaders with Type A tendencies, therefore, must be aware of the potential dysfunctional effects of their competitiveness and drive and must acknowledge that their desire to control will not help to produce an effective and empowered team. Through knowledge comes strength and with greater self-awareness Type A middle leaders can adapt their behaviour so that they maintain their sense of drive but use leadership techniques that are likely to produce effective and focused teams. The techniques required for this have been stressed throughout this book.

Summary

Too little pressure can result in boredom, a moderate level of pressure is stimulating but too much pressure causes stress and thus reduces performance. An effective middle leader should know his or her team well and be able to judge the level of pressure needed to get the best performance out of each team member. While maintaining high expectations they will protect their team from unnecessary stress by encouraging a supportive and open culture and manage their own stress by cultivating a positive outlook and ensuring that they have a fulfilling life beyond school.

Stress management and time management are linked. By using time efficiently middle leaders can increase their effectiveness and reduce stress. Considering what constitutes inefficient use of time and the thinking that goes with it can help to clarify the strategies that can be used to improve time management. Consider the following and then do the opposite:

- Don't invest in a planning device and never have your diary to hand – you have a good memory and that should be enough
- Don't bother with deadlines – team members might feel too pressured
- Never prioritize the tasks you have to do – you work more efficiently when you suddenly realize the deadline is tomorrow
- Don't make a daily and weekly list of things to do – if a task is really necessary someone will remind you it needs doing
- Never delegate – you're paid to do more and team members have enough on with teaching
- Always bail out your colleagues when they fail to complete tasks – they need to know they can rely on you

- Never say 'no' however unreasonable the request – senior leaders might think you lack commitment
- Never reply to e-mails immediately – decisions are always better for being given plenty of thought
- Allow people to interrupt you at all times – it shows you are a caring leader
- Never throw junk mail straight in the bin – you need to consider whether it might come in handy one day
- Each day and at weekends take as much paperwork home as you can manage to transfer from your desk to your briefcase – the more you have with you the more you are likely to do
- Don't efficiently save class lists, letters to parents, schemes of work, handbooks, worksheets, exam papers etc. electronically – you rewrite them every year anyway so what's the point?

Finally, remember your priorities. Work is important and you want to be a good leader but your family and loved ones are important too and you have a right to a life beyond school. If you neglect your family or fail to recharge your batteries you will feel resentment and burn out. Make sure you plan into your week time for your family and your interests as top priorities, and fit your school commitments around them. You will be a better person and a more interesting and rounded leader for doing so.

Subject leaders' self-review and individual professional development plan

This self-review is based on the National Standards for Subject Leaders (Teacher Training Agency 1998). It supports subject leaders in examining their current role and the contribution this makes to promoting the quality of education provided by the school and the standards being achieved by the pupils.

The self-review is in two parts:

1 The self-review
2 The Individual Professional Development Plan

1 The self-review

When completing this section, you should indicate your response to each statement by ticking one of the following:

a I am confident that I do this well
b I can do this well and would like to help others
c I do this satisfactorily but there are aspects I must improve
d I need to be able to do this better
e I can't do this or haven't yet had the opportunity

2 The Individual Professional Development Plan

Subject leaders are encouraged to use the outcomes of the self review to complete an Individual Development Plan as the basis of a discussion with their line manager

Subject leader's self-review – National Standards For Subject Leaders

TABLE A1 Subject leader's self-review – National Standards for Subject Leaders

SKILLS AND ATTRIBUTES						
A	**Leadership skills, attributes and professional competence – the ability to lead and manage people to work towards common goals.**	a	b	c	d	e
	I feel confident I can secure commitment to a clear aim and direction for the subject.					
	I feel confident I can prioritize, plan and organize for my subject area.					
	I can work as part of a team.					
	I feel confident that I deal sensitively with people, recognize individual needs and take account of these in securing a consistent team approach to raising achievement in the subject.					
	I feel I acknowledge and utilize the experience, expertise and contribution of others.					
	I feel I set high standards and provide a role model for pupils and other staff in the teaching and learning of the subject.					
	I devolve responsibilities and delegate tasks as appropriate.					
	I seek advice and support when necessary.					
	I feel I have credibility with my colleagues.					
	I feel I make informed use of research and inspection findings.					
	I feel I apply good practice to and from other subjects and areas.					

SKILLS AND ATTRIBUTES						
B	**Decision-making skills – The ability to solve problems and make decisions**	a	b	c	d	e
	I feel confident I can judge when to make decisions, when to consult with others, and when to defer to the head teacher or senior managers.					
	I feel I can think creatively and imaginatively to anticipate and solve problems and identify opportunities.					

C	Communication skills – the ability to make points clearly and understand the views of others.	a	b	c	d	e
	I feel I can communicate effectively, orally and in writing, with the head teacher, other staff, pupils, parents, governors, external agencies and the wider community, including business and industry.					
	I feel I can negotiate and consult effectively.					
	I feel I ensure good communication with, and between, staff who teach and support the subject.					
	I feel I can chair meetings effectively.					
D	Self management – the ability to plan time effectively and to organize oneself well					
	I can prioritize and manage my own time effectively. Particularly in relation to balancing the demands made by teaching, subject management and involvement in school development.					
	I achieve challenging professional goals.					
	I take responsibility for my own professional development.					

KEY AREAS OF SUBJECT LEADERSHIP						
A	Strategic direction and development of the subject	a	b	c	d	e
	Policies and practices for the subject reflect the school's commitment to high achievement, effective teaching and learning.					
	The climate enables other staff to develop and maintain positive attitudes towards the subject and confidence in teaching it.					
	We have clear, shared understanding of the importance and role of the subject in contributing to pupils' spiritual, moral, cultural, mental and physical development, and in preparing pupils for the opportunities, responsibilities and experiences of adult life.					
	I feel confident I can use data effectively to identify pupils who are underachieving in the subject and, where necessary, create and implement effective plans of action to support those pupils.					
	I feel I can analyse and interpret relevant national, local and school data, plus research and inspection evidence, to inform policies, practices, expectations, targets and teaching methods.					
	I feel I have established with the involvement of relevant staff, short, medium and long-term plans for the development and resourcing of the subject, which: ■ contribute to whole-school aims, policies and practices, including those in relation to behaviour, discipline, bullying and racial harassment; ■ are based on a range of comparative information and evidence, including in relation to the attainment of pupils;					

	a	b	c	d	e
■ identify realistic and challenging targets for improvement in the subject; ■ are understood by all those involved in putting the plans into practice; ■ are clear about action to be taken, timescales and criteria for success.					
I feel I monitor the progress made in achieving subject plans and targets, evaluate the effects on teaching and learning, and use this analysis to guide further improvement.					

KEY AREAS OF SUBJECT LEADERSHIP					
B **Teaching and learning**	**a**	**b**	**c**	**d**	**e**
Through my own teaching:					
I ensure curriculum coverage, continuity and progression in the subject for all pupils, including those of high ability and those with special educational or linguistic needs.					
I ensure that teachers are clear about the teaching objectives in lessons, understand the sequence of teaching and learning in the subject, and communicate such information to pupils.					
I provide guidance on the choice of appropriate teaching and learning methods to meet the needs of the subject and of different pupils.					
I ensure effective development of pupils' literacy, numeracy and information technology skills through the subject.					
We have established and implemented clear policies and practices for assessing, recording and reporting on pupil achievement, and for using this information to recognize achievement and to assist pupils in setting targets for further improvement.					
We ensure that information about pupils' achievements in previous classes and schools is used effectively to secure good progress in the subject.					
I set expectations and targets for staff and pupils in relation to standards of pupil achievement and the quality of teaching; establish clear targets for pupil achievement, and evaluate progress and achievement in the subject by all pupils, including those with special educational and linguistic needs.					
I evaluate the teaching of the subject in the school, use this analysis to identify effective practice and areas for improvement, and take action to improve further the quality of teaching.					
I ensure effective development of pupils' individual and collaborative study skills necessary for them to become increasingly independent in their work and to complete tasks independently when out of school.					

		a	b	c	d	e
	I ensure that teachers of the subject are aware of its contribution to pupils' understanding of the duties, opportunities, responsibilities and rights of citizens.					
	I ensure that teachers of the subject know how to recognize and deal with racial stereotyping.					
	We establish a partnership with parents to involve them in their child's learning of the subject, as well as providing information about curriculum, attainment, progress and targets.					
	We develop effective links with the local community, including business and industry, in order to extend the subject curriculum, enhance teaching and to develop pupils' wider understanding.					
C	**Leading and managing staff**	a	b	c	d	e
	I feel I help staff to achieve constructive working relationships with pupils.					
	I feel I establish clear expectations and constructive working relationships among staff involved with the subject, including through team working and mutual support; devolving responsibilities and delegating tasks, as appropriate; evaluating practice; and developing an acceptance of accountability.					
	I feel I sustain my own motivation and, where possible, that of other staff involved in the subject.					
	I appraise staff as required by the school policy and use the process to develop the personal and professional effectiveness of the appraisee(s).					
	I audit training needs of subject staff.					
	I lead professional development of subject staff through example and support, and coordinate the provision of high quality professional development by methods such as coaching, drawing on other sources of expertise as necessary, for example, higher education, LAs, subject associations.					
	I ensure that trainee and newly qualified teachers are appropriately trained, monitored, supported and assessed in relation to the Teachers' Standards.					
	I enable teachers to achieve expertise in their subject teaching.					
	I work with the SENCO and any other staff with special educational needs expertise, to ensure that individual education plans are used to set subject-specific targets and match work well to pupils' needs.					
	I ensure that the head teacher, senior managers and governors are well informed about subject policies, plans and priorities, the success in meeting objectives and targets, and subject-related professional development plans.					

D	Efficient and effective deployment of staff and resources	a	b	c	d	e
	I establish staff and resource needs for the subject and advise the head teacher and senior managers of likely priorities for expenditure, and allocate available subject resources with maximum efficiency to meet the objectives of the school and subject plans and to achieve value for money.					
	I deploy, or advise the head teacher on the deployment of staff involved in the subject to ensure the best use of subject, technical and other expertise.					
	I ensure the effective and efficient management and organization of learning resources, including information and communications technology.					
	I maintain existing resources and explore opportunities to develop or incorporate new resources from a wide range of sources inside and outside the school.					
	I use accommodation to create an effective and stimulating environment for the teaching and learning of the subject.					
	I ensure that there is a safe working and learning environment in which risks are properly assessed.					

Individual Professional Development Plan

TABLE A2 Skills and attributes for subject leaders

Area	Your development needs/desires	Suggested solution	Timescale Priority ⟨ I = Immediate / M = One year / L = Three year
a) Leadership skills			
b) Decision making skills			
c) Communication skills			
d) Self-management skills			

TABLE A3 Key areas of subject leadership			
Area	**Your development needs/desires**	**Suggested solution**	**Timescale** — I = Immediate · Priority — M = One year · L = Three year
a) Strategic direction			
b) Teaching and learning			
c) Leading and managing staff			
d) Efficient and effective deployment of staff and resources			

B

The subject leader's file
Suggested contents – this is not a prescriptive list, nor is it exhaustive!

1 **Vision and aims**
   - Key sections from the School Development Plan, the school's vision, ethos and aims
   - A statement about how the department's aims and values fit with the school's aims and values
   - The vision for the subject

2 **School policy documents – Guidance on how to apply in your subject**
   - Teaching and learning
   - Assessment, recording and reporting
   - Marking and assessment for learning
   - Differentiation
   - Equal opportunities
   - Literacy across the curriculum
   - SEN
   - Closing the gap

3 **Subject review**
   - Annual review identifying strengths and areas of development
   - Analysis of previous three years' results
   - Outcomes from team discussions
   - Relevant sections of last Ofsted report
   - List of priorities for development
   - Action plan for the current year (or maintenance plan)
   - Attainment and progress targets
   - Curriculum targets

4 **Monitoring and evaluation processes**
   - Agreed criteria and forms for monitoring and evaluating
   - Timetable of monitoring activities

- Monitoring and evaluation records/reports based on:
  - i   Analysis of performance data
  - ii   Analysis of planning
  - iii Lesson observations
  - iv   Analysis of students' work
  - v   Assessment data
  - vi   Discussions with students
  - vii Results from questionnaires
  - viii Feedback from stakeholders
  - ix   Summary of any LA monitoring reports
  - x   Reports to governors
- Evidence of action taken against recommendations
- Evidence to indicate measures taken to support school improvement

5   Staff development
- Record of training and development
- Evidence of dissemination to others
- Performance management objectives where relevant

6   Resources
- List of resources within the department (and location)
- Special instructions/care details
- Useful references e.g. websites, museums, visiting artists

7   Financial information
- Details of budget/bids/orders
- Resource audit
- Planned replacement (e.g. ICT equipment)
- Shopping list/wish list

8   Documentation
- Long-term plan
- Medium-term plans / scheme of work
- Job description (including teaching standards)
- Assessment materials
- List of G&T/SEN/vulnerable/pupil-premium pupils
- Health and Safety Risk Assessments

9   Tracking Data (possibly kept in a separate file)
- Tracking for all students in all year groups
- Categories of students clearly identified (e.g. SEN, pupil-premium)
- Intervention strategies for students identified as under-achieving

C

Effective departmental self-evaluation

TABLE C1 Effective departmental self-evaluation

PRINCIPLES	Yes	No
Has the purpose been clearly communicated to those involved?		
Do you know how you will communicate your findings to the intended audience?		
Does it tell the department's story (its own thinking and priorities)?		
Does the department understand that this is an on-going process of development rather than a single event?		
Will those involved find the activity meaningful and motivating?		
Are you achieving the balance of bottom-up development with top-down support?		
Are you willing to question your existing practice honestly and openly, whilst retaining your self-confidence?		
Will you involve an 'external eye' as a way of affirming and challenging your current thinking and practice?		
PROCESS	**Yes**	**No**
Do you involve staff, pupils, parents and governors at all levels?		
Are you asking the most important questions about students' achievements, learning and development?		
Do you use a range of telling evidence to answer these questions?		
Do you review and evaluate the work of the department against your aims and targets?		
Are your self-evaluation processes integral to your processes for developing, monitoring and evaluating learning and teaching?		
Do the conclusions from your self-evaluation processes feed into development planning?		
Do you benchmark your department's performance against the best comparable departments?		

PRODUCT	Yes	No
Have you identified the key priorities?		
Have you identified trends and set challenging targets?		
Do teachers have specific targets for improvement, linked to the progress made by students during the year?		
Do teachers have a clear understanding of what needs to be done to achieve those targets?		
Do your improvement plans describe the intended impact on learning in a way that can routinely be measured?		
Do your plans lead to positive changes and strategies to manage these changes?		

Subject leader self-evaluation of roles and responsibilities

Use these review sheets to identify priorities for development and existing areas of good practice in key areas of the subject leader's responsibilities. Once areas for development have been identified, decide in what order you will address your priorities.

TABLE D1 Core task 1: Judging standards

Core task 1: Judging standards	Fully in place	Partly in place	Not in place
A: Analyse and interpret data on pupils' attainment in the subject. 1 Compare pupil performance in tests / annual assessments with: prior attainment information; other subjects; previous cohorts. 2 Make judgements for year groups / classes / individuals in relation to: school, local and national expectations, based on value-added and expected progress data. 3 Use the outcomes of annual analysis to: set curricular targets; prompt further investigation; initiate staff training and resource development. 4 Use data to inform areas for development.			
B: Review with teachers their assessments of progress for classes, identified groups and individuals. 1 Review regularly with colleagues progress related to key curricular targets, underperforming groups and individuals. 2 Use the outcomes of the reviews to: share effective practice, design support, and agree ways of tackling pupil under-performance. 3 Monitor any intervention strategies agreed.			
C: Sample pupils' work. 1 Agree with colleagues the sample and how the outcomes will be used. 2 Arrange for a suitable sample of pupils' work to be available, ensuring a range across ability and year groups.			

3 Make judgements of standards in relation to objectives and rates of progress. 4 Use the outcomes to discuss with colleagues areas of effective practice, development issues and groups of pupils for intervention.			
D: Discuss work, progress and attitudes with sample groups of pupils. 1 Agree with colleagues the sample and how the outcomes will be used. 2 Arrange meetings with a sample of pupils, taking into account the ability range and year groups. 3 Make judgements about pupils' attitudes, engagement and confidence in their learning. 4 Use the outcomes of the sample to discuss with colleagues areas of effective practice, development issues and groups of pupils for intervention.			
E: Construct and monitor strategies to gather the views of stakeholders 1 Conduct regular discussions with pupils about how they like to learn, what obstacles they face and what they enjoy about the subject. 2 Involve pupils in evaluating the impact of any changes in teaching and learning approaches and in reviewing schemes of work. 3 Engage parents in dialogue about how they can specifically support their child's learning in your subject. 4 Use findings to inform departmental discussions of teaching and learning.			

DEVELOPMENT POINTS AND PRIORITIES		
Area to develop (e.g. A1)	**What do you need to do differently? What priority has this got?**	**Who could help you with this?**
Source: Modified from materials produced by NYCC Quality & Improvement Service		

TABLE D2 Core task 2: Evaluating teaching and learning			
Core task 2: Evaluating teaching and learning	**Fully in place**	**Partly in place**	**Not in place**
A: Evaluate the schemes of work to ensure that they focus on consistent and effective teaching and learning. 1 Ensure the schemes of work focus on teaching objectives – what teachers intend that pupils should learn, include cross-curricular themes, and promote a range of appropriate teaching and learning styles. 2 Confirm full understanding and active use of the agreed scheme of work by all teachers of the subject. 3 Ensure that assessment opportunities built into the scheme of work support improved learning and progress.			
B: Observe teaching and feed back to colleagues. 1 Implement a regular system of lesson observation and feedback to teachers. 2 Discuss themes from the observations with the department. Share effective practice and devise strategies for action when learning and progress do not meet planned objectives. 3 Discuss the key points arising from the observations and subsequent discussions with the line manager. 4 Discuss any concerns with any individuals.			
C: Review teachers' planning. 1 Hold regular meetings with colleagues to review medium- and short-term teaching plans, especially with temporary, inexperienced and non-specialist teachers. 2 Ensure that medium- and long-term planning supports pupils' progression. 3 Encourage joint planning, especially of lesson starters and plenaries. 4 Evaluate the effectiveness of the continuing professional development programme in improving teaching and learning. 5 Ensure there is regular debate and discussion about the quality of teaching and learning, and expectations for pupils' achievement.			
D: Provide evidence of subject contributions to learners' personal development. 1 Evaluate how the subject promotes independent learning. 2 Use pupil interviews and focus groups. 3 Develop pupil peer and self-assessment and pupils' awareness of learning objectives and success criteria. 4 Where possible, make links with other subjects and with the world of work.			

DEVELOPMENT POINTS AND PRIORITIES		
Area to develop (e.g. A1)	What do you need to do differently? What priority has this got?	Who could help you with this?

Source: Modified from materials produced by NYCC Quality & Improvement Service

TABLE D3 Core task 3: Leading sustainable improvement			
Core task 2: Leading sustainable improvement	**Fully in place**	**Partly in place**	**Not in place**
A: Lead the department in discussion about priorities for the subject in all Key Stages. 1 Allocate regular department meeting / training time to discussion of teaching and learning. 2 Embed agreed values and approaches in department handbook and the schemes of work for each Key Stage. 3 Make explicit links between national, school and departmental strategies for raising standards at each Key Stage and embed these within the action plan.			
B: Agree targets for raising pupils' attainment within the context of whole-school targets. 1 Establish targets for improvement for cohorts, groups of pupils and individual pupils, using the outcomes of review and monitoring. 2 Link targets for pupils' attainment to targets for pupils' learning. 3 Cross-refer targets for each year group with the scheme of work and teaching plans.			
C: Develop a strategy to lead improvement in teaching. 1 Use self-evaluation processes to establish your capacity for improvement and to identify curricular / staff / resource implications. 2 Establish curricular targets and staff development priorities with clear success criteria linked to raised pupil attainment and clear monitoring and evaluation procedures. 3 Allocate time, resources, status and responsibilities, and relate precisely to time, finance and personnel available.			
D: Lead the improvement of teaching quality. 1 Identify and provide for staff training and development needs. 2 Share, extend and improve effective teaching. 3 Challenge and support the improvement of ineffective teaching. 4 Use appraisal to improve pedagogy.			
E: Lead the review, construction and resourcing of the curriculum. 1 Take action as required following the regular review of the scheme of work, ensuring suitable differentiation and progression for pupils. 2 Build commitment to a set of agreed standards across the subject.			

F: Liaise with other school leaders and keep them informed. 1 Liaise with other middle leaders and their teams to share and collaborate in approaches that will support success for pupils in your own area. 2 Liaise with and keep informed senior leadership through regular progress meetings with your line manager.			

DEVELOPMENT POINTS AND PRIORITIES		
Area to develop	**What do you need to do differently?** **What priority has this got?**	**Who could help you with this?**

Source: Modified from materials produced by NYCC Quality & Improvement Service

TABLE D4 Core task 4: Manage and maintain the area of learning

Core Task 4: Manage and maintain the area of learning	Fully in place	Partly in place	Not in place
A: Manage the department's human resources. 1 Oversee the induction of new teachers / TAs / NQTs / trainees within the Department. 2 Monitor staff absence within the Department; act on concerns. 3 Check that an absent departmental colleague has set work for pupils to complete when he/she is absent. 4 Direct, monitor and develop departmental support staff 5 Use appraisal processes to develop individuals and raise standards. 6 Play a leading role in ensuring that behaviour is effectively and consistently managed within the department, providing guidance, support and advice to colleagues when necessary.			
B: Manage the department's involvement in whole school issues. 1 Work collaboratively with the SLT in contributing to whole school developments and initiatives. 2 Attend relevant meetings and ensure that the views of the department are represented. 3 Ensure your team understands how your department contributes to the school vision and development priorities.			
C: Carry out required administrative tasks. 1 Oversee examination entries and ensure that they are at an appropriate level. 2 Ensure the school's reporting, assessment and student tracking procedures are followed. 3 Produce and regularly review a Department Handbook. 4 Ensure your part of the school website is up to date. 5 Monitor the implementation of school policies. 6 Maintain, and regularly update, an inventory of risk assessments for activities undertaken within the department.			
D: Manage the department's learning resources. 1 Review, maintain and replace resources. 2 Liaise with the learning resource manager/Librarian to ensure that the subject area is adequately catered for. 3 Manage the department's contribution to on-line learning.			

DEVELOPMENT POINTS AND PRIORITIES		
Area to develop (e.g. A1)	**What do you need to do differently? What priority has this got?**	**Who could help you with this?**
Source: Modified from materials produced by NYCC Quality & Improvement Service		

CPD audit

On a scale of 0–4 with 0 being low and 4 being high, how true are the following statements?

TABLE E1 CPD audit	0	1	2	3	4
1	I am encouraged to identify my training and development needs					
2	The development I receive usually helps me perform my role more effectively					
3	I am provided with opportunities for development towards a career goal					
4	I can usually see how the development I receive is linked to the school's development priorities					
5	I agree CPD with my team leader/reviewer as part of my performance management interview					
6	I feel this school is committed to training and developing all employees					
7	I have access to a wide range of development opportunities					
8	Staff who join the school or who take on new duties are given an effective induction programme					
9	I have engaged in a wide range of types of CPD other than training during the last three years					
10	After training or development activities, my team leader/reviewer discusses with me how what I have learned can be used and what will be the benefits to my work in school					

Comments

General pupil questionnaire

1 Where would you put .... in a list of favourite subjects?
2 Do you think you are doing well in ....? Why (not)?
3 Think back to your last lesson. Were you clear what you were supposed to **learn** from it?
4 Did you succeed? What was it you learned?
5 What is the best thing you have achieved in your .... so far?
6 What do you need in order to learn ....? E.g. you may need a good memory. What other skills do you need?
7 What sort of problems do you come across when you are trying to learn?
8 When you get a problem, do you usually get enough help of the sort you need?
9 Where do you get help?
10 Do you use a textbook in lessons? Is it helpful? How?
11 Do you have your own textbook?
12 How does you teacher help you to raise the standard of your work?
13 Do you think it's important to learn ....?
14 What do your parents think about your learning ....?
15 How did you feel about your first ever .... lesson?
16 Have your feelings changed? If yes, in what way and why?

G
Student interviews

Example 1: General views

- What do you enjoy most about English/mathematics/science?
- What do you like least?
- In general, do you find your EN/MA/SC work too easy, too hard or just right?
- How are lessons in Year 10 (or 11) different from those in Years 7, 8 and 9?
- What grade(s) are you aiming to get at GCSE? Have you been told?
- How do you know how well you are doing?
- How does your teacher help you improve your work?
- What do you do when you receive work back from your teachers?
- What helps you learn best in your GCSE course?
- How do your parents know how well you are doing?
- How do your parents help you with your school work?
- What's the best thing about this school?
- What could be done to improve the school?

Example 2: Basic questions for an interview

- What do you enjoy most about.....?
- What do you like least?
- How does/did your teacher help you prepare for tests/exams/SATS?
- To prepare for the exams, your teacher helped you with various approaches. How did you find them?
- How do your parents know how well you are doing?
- Would you recommend .... to someone you know who is just starting at ....?

Example 3: Questions for an interview about KS4 uptake

- What did you most enjoy about .... in Y9?
- What did you least enjoy?
- What influenced you to drop .... at the end of Y9?

- What might have made you change your mind about the importance of studying … at KS4?
- Was your decision anything to do with the way the option choices were organized?

Example 4: What helps you learn?

- What makes a good teacher?
- What do teachers do that you don't like?
- What's important in a classroom environment?
- Why do you like having your work displayed?
- What advice would you give to a new teacher?
- What lessons do you like and why?
- How is Y10 different?
- What advice would you give to a teacher taking a Year 10 class?
- What makes a good lesson?
- What type of feedback helps most?
- Tell us about the workload (in Year 10).
- What can teachers do to help you revise?
- Tell us about boys and learning.
- What can teachers do to help pupils who find it difficult to learn?

Student feedback

The double checklist[1]

Tick the box in each line that best explains what **you** think.

TABLE H1 Student feedback: The double checklist

This happens					It helps me			
Very often	Quite often	Only sometimes	Rarely or never		Learn a lot	Learn quite a lot	Learn a little	Learn nothing
☐	☐	☐	☐	My teacher explains the purpose of the lesson	☐	☐	☐	☐
☐	☐	☐	☐	My teacher explains how work will be assessed	☐	☐	☐	☐
☐	☐	☐	☐	I am expected to respond to marked work	☐	☐	☐	☐
☐	☐	☐	☐	My teacher makes constructive suggestions	☐	☐	☐	☐
☐	☐	☐	☐	I understand what my marks/grades mean	☐	☐	☐	☐
☐	☐	☐	☐	My learning targets are clear	☐	☐	☐	☐
☐	☐	☐	☐	My learning targets increase my motivation	☐	☐	☐	☐
☐	☐	☐	☐	Feedback gives me a sense of ownership	☐	☐	☐	☐
☐	☐	☐	☐	Feedback helps me improve my work	☐	☐	☐	☐
☐	☐	☐	☐	I assess other students' work	☐	☐	☐	☐
☐	☐	☐	☐	I assess my own work	☐	☐	☐	☐
☐	☐	☐	☐	My teacher is available to help me	☐	☐	☐	☐

1 One way to analyse this is to assign a value of 3 to very often/learn a lot, 2 to quite often/learn quite a lot, 1 to only sometimes/learn a little, and 0 to rarely or never/learn nothing.

Developmental lesson observation

Focus – improving questioning

TABLE I1 Developmental lesson observation: Focus – improving questioning			
Questioning activity	Number of occurrences in 10-minute session (first sample)	Number of occurrences in 10-minute session (second sample)	Number of occurrences in 10-minute session (third sample)
Closed – factual information and comprehension			
Open – prompting more than one answer			
Time for reflection before answer required			
Further prompts to elicit extended answer			
Opportunities for pupils to explain why they have offered that response			
Opportunities for pupils to confer before answering			
Teacher initiates, pupils respond, teacher provides feedback			
Pupils initiate their own questions			

Bibliography

ACAS (2012) *Challenging Conversations and How to Manage Them* Available: http://www.acas. org.uk/media/pdf/9/1/Challenging_conversations_and_how_to_manage_them_ APRIL-2012.pdf (accessed 15 May 2013).

Adair, J. (1997) *Leadership Skills*, London: IPD.

Ainscow, M. (1994) *Creating the Conditions for School Improvement*, London: Fulton.

Barber, M. and Brighouse, T. (1992) *Enhancing the Teaching Profession*, London: IPPR.

Bird, J., Wang, C., Watson, J. and Murray, L. (2009) 'Relationships among principal authentic leadership, teacher trust and engagement levels.' *Journal of School Leadership*, 19(2): 153–171.

Branson, C. (2007) 'Effects of structured self-reflection on the development of authentic leadership practices.' *Educational Management, Administration and Leadership*, 35(2): 225–246, London: Sage.

Belbin, R.M. (1981) *Management Teams: Why They Succeed or Fail*, London: Heinemann.

Belbin, R.M. (1993) *Team Roles at Work*, Oxford: Butterworth-Heinemann.

Blanchard, K. (1994) *Leadership and the One Minute Manager*, London: HarperCollins.

Blanchard, K. (2004) *The One Minute Manager Meets the Monkey*, London: Harper Collins.

Bush, T. (1994) 'Theory and Practice in Educational Management' in Bush, T. and West-Burnham, J. (eds.), *The Principles of Educational Management*, Harlow: Longman, pp. 33–54.

Cibulka, J., Coursey, S., Nakayama, M., Price, J. and Stewart, S. (2000) *Schools as Learning Organisations: A review of the literature*, Nottingham: NCSL.

Clarke, P. (1998) *Back from the Brink: Transforming the Ridings School – and Our Children's Education*, London: Metro Books.

Cooper, C. and Sutherland, V. (1997) *30 Minutes to Deal with Difficult People*, London: Kogan Page.

Cooper, M. (1998) 'The right time to sack a poor performer', Times Educational Supplement, 9 October 1998.

Covey, S. (1994) *First Things First: Coping with the Ever Increasing Demands of the Workplace*, London: Simon and Schuster.

Davies, B. and West-Burnham, J. (1997) *Reengineering and Total Quality in Schools*, London: Pitman.

Day, C., Kington, A., Stobart, G. and Sammons, P. (2006) 'The personal and professional selves of teachers: Stable and unstable identities', *British Educational Research Journal*, Vol. 32, No. 4 (Aug., 2006), 601–616, Taylor & Francis.

DfE (1992) *Effective Management in Schools: A Report for the Department for Education via the School Management Task force Professional Working Party*, London: HMSO.

DfE (2012) *Teachers' Standards*, London: Crown Copyright.

DfEE (1998) *Teachers: Meeting the challenge of change*, London: DfE.

Drucker, P. F. (1954) *The Practice of Management*, New York: Harper Row.

Earley, P. and Weindling, D. (2004) *Understanding School Leadership*, London: Sage/Paul Chapman Publishing.

Education Service Advisory Committee (1992) *Managing Occupational Stress: A Guide for Managers and Teachers in the School Sector*, London: HMSO.

Fontana, D. (1989) *Managing Stress*, London: Routledge.

Fullan, M. (2008) *The Six Secrets of Change: What the Best Leaders do to Help their Organisations Survive and Thrive*, San Fransisco: Jossey-Bass.

Fullan, M. and Hargreaves, A. (1992) *What's Worth Fighting for in Your School?* Milton Keynes: OU Press.

George, J.M. (2008). *Emotions and Leadership: The role of emotional intelligence*, CA: Sage Publications.

Giles, C. (1997) *School Development Planning: A Practical Guide to the Strategic Management Process*, London: Northcote House.

Gold, A. and Evans, J. (1998) *Reflecting on School Management*, London: Falmer Press.

Goleman, D. (1995) *Emotional intelligence*, NY: Bantam Books.

Hammersley-Fletcher, L. and Brundrett, M. (2008) 'Collaboration, collegiality and leadership from the head: the complexities of shared leadership' in *Management in Education*, 22(2): 11–16, Sage.

Handy, C. and Aitken, R. (1986) *Understanding Schools as Organisations*, Harmondsworth: Penguin.

Hardingham, A. (1985) *Working in Teams*, London: IPD.

Hargreaves, D. and Hopkins, D. (1991) *The Empowered School: The Management and Practice of Development Planning*, London: Cassell.

Harris, A. and Spillane, J. (2008) 'Distributed leadership through the looking glass' in *Management in Education*, 22(1): 31–34.

Hay McBer (2000) *Research into Teacher Effectiveness*, London: DfES.

Health & Safety Executive (2013) *What is Stress?* Online. Available: www.hse.gov.uk/stress/furtheradvice/whatisstress.htm (accessed 21 May 2013).

Holly, P. and Southworth, G. (1989) *The Developing School*, London: Falmer.

Hopkins, D. (2001) *School Improvement for Real*, London: RoutledgeFalmer.

Hopkins, D. and MacGilchrist, B. (1998) 'Development planning for pupil achievement' in *School Leadership and Management*, Vol. 18, No. 3: 409–424.

Jarvis, A. (2012) 'The necessity for collegiality: Power, authority and influence in the middle' in *Educational Management, Administration & Leadership*, Vol. 40, No. 4: 490–512.

Lewis, P. (1975) *Organisational Communications*, Colombus, Ohio: Grid.

Maddux, R.B. (1986) *Team Building*, London: Kogan Page.

Marris, P. (1975) *Loss and Change*, London: Anchor Press.

Marsh, J. (1992) *The Quality Tool Kit: An A-Z of Tools and Techniques*, New York: IFS International.

Martin, J. and Holt, A. (2002) *Joined Up Governance*, Ely: Adamson Books.

Maslow, A.H. (1943) 'A theory of human motivation', *Psychological Review*, 50(4), 370–96. Available: http://psychclassics.yorku.ca/Maslow/motivation.htm (accessed 25 March 2013).

Mayer, J.D. and Salovney, P. (1997) 'What is emotional intelligence: Implications for educators' in Salovney, P. and Sluyter, D. (eds.), *Emotional Development, Emotional Literacy, and Emotional Intelligence*, NY: Basic Books.

McGregor, D. (1960) *The Human Side of Enterprise*, Maidenhead: McGraw-Hill.

National College for School Leadership (2003) *The Heart of the Matter: A Practical Guide to What Middle Leaders can do to Improve Learning in Secondary Schools*, Nottingham: NCSL.

National College for School Leadership (2012) *Nine Quick and Easy Things to do to Promote a Professional Learning Culture*. Available: http://www.nationalcollege.org.uk/index/interactiveinfo.htm?id=186183 (accessed 10 June 2013).

Ofsted (2010) *Workforce Reform in Schools: Has it Made a Difference?* Available: http://www.ofsted.gov.uk/node/2409 (accessed 4 April 2013).

Ofsted (2013) *School Inspection Handbook.* Available: http://www.ofsted.gov.uk/resources/school-inspection-handbook (accessed 20 July 2013).

Pacific Institute (1997) *Investment in Excellence: Personal Resource Manual,* Seattle: Pacific Institute.

Plant, R. (1987) *Managing Change and Making it Stick,* London: Fontana.

Portman, J. (2012) *Why Are Middle Leaders so Important in Schools?* Online posting. Available: www.jamieportman.com/blog/leadership (accessed 18 February 2013).

Ravasi, D. and Schultz, M. (2006) 'Responding to organisational identity threats: Exploring the role of organizational culture' in *Academy of Management Journal,* Vol. 49 No. 3: 433–458.

Reynolds, D. (1998) 'Schooling for Literacy: A review of research on teacher effectiveness and school effectiveness and its implications for contemporary education policies' in *Educational Review,* Vol 50(2), 147–162.

Riches, C. and Morgan, C. (1989) *Human Resource Management in Education,* Milton Keynes: OU Press.

Sale, J. (1998) 'Keeping the dynamism: Some basic tactics for avoiding stale meetings' in *Managing Schools Today,* September 1998, Birmingham: Questions Publishing.

Sallis, J. (1997) 'Studies on change' in *Managing Schools Today,* September 1997, Birmingham: Questions Publishing.

Sammons, P., Hillman, J. and Mortimore, P. (1995) *Key Characteristics of Effective Schools,* London: Institute of Education.

Sammons, P., Thomas, S. and Mortimore, P. (1997) *Forging Links: Effective Schools and Effective Departments,* London: Paul Chapman.

Scanlon, M. (2001) *The Impact of Ofsted Inspections: The Experience of Special Measures Schools* Available: http://www.nfer.org.uk/nfer/PRE_PDF_files/01_25_06.pdf. (accessed 28 May 2013).

Smith, P. (1996) 'Tools for measuring quality improvement' in *Management in Education,* 10(2): 5–7.

Sutton Trust EEF (2013) 'Teaching and learning toolkit'. Available: http://educationendowmentfoundation.org.uk/toolkit/approaches (accessed 15 June 2013).

Teacher Training Agency (1998) *National Standards for Subject Leaders,* London: TTA.

Teachers' Standards (2013) DfE, Crown copyright.

Thomson, R. (1998) *People Management,* London: Orion.

TUC (2013) Hazards at Work. Available: http://www.tuc.org.uk/workplace-issues-7 (accessed 17 February 2014).

West, N. (1997) 'A framework for curriculum development, policy implementation and monitoring quality' in Preedy, M., Glatter, R. and Levocic, R. (eds.) *Educational Management,* Philadelphia: Open University Press, pp. 42–57.

Walumbwa, F., Avolio, B., Gardner, W., Wernsing, T. and Peterson, S. (2008) 'Authentic leadership: Development and validation of a theory based measure,' *Journal of Management* 34(1): 89–126.

Whitmore, J. (2013) *Coaching for Performance: growing human potential and purpose,* London: Nicholas Brearley.

Wood, I. (1991) *Time Management in Teaching,* London: NEP.

Index